HAIL,
COLUMBIA

HAIL, COLUMBIA

by
Rochelle Larkin

ARLINGTON HOUSE·PUBLISHERS
NEW ROCHELLE, NEW YORK

Manufactured in the United States of America

Library of Congress Cataloging in Publication Data

Larkin, Rochelle.
  Hail, Columbia.

  Bibliography: p.
  Includes index.
  1. Columbia Pictures Industries.   I. Title.
PN1999.C57L37   791.43'0973   75-5781
ISBN 0-87000-239-2

To Julie, Kim, and Teddy—three young kids who love old movies

Contents

Acknowledgments

I want to thank the following for their invaluable assistance in providing books, films, files, photographs, and other research materials for the compilation of this book: Sey Roman, Richard Kahn, Edward L. Justin, Myrna Masour, and Francine Lehrman.

My thanks, too, to Kathy Dobkin for her professionalism in editing the final manuscript.

And special thanks to Martin Gross, at Arlington House, for his encouragement and support—the marks of a gifted editor.

The internationally known symbol that the company calls its Proud Lady

1 | The Beginnings

THREE MEN STARTED IT AND THEY NAMED IT AFTER themselves: C.B.C. Film Sales Company, for Jack Cohn, Joe Brandt, and Jack's younger brother, Harry Cohn. But the wise-acres in the fledgling film industry called it Corned Beef and Cabbage, a name that was to stick for a while, just as the term Poverty Row became the designation for the patch of California geography where the company set itself up in business.

It was a magic time in a magic world, Hollywood in the 20s. Movies were no longer a nickelodeon novelty, but a big industry, making and spending millions of dollars annually, changing the entertainment ideas of the whole world.

Even by 1920 the industry had a well-established pecking order. The major studios were already growing rapidly, sprawling over acres, pushing past Hollywood itself and extending into such outlying areas as Burbank and Culver City. But when Harry Cohn arrived to set up the West Coast operations of the new company, he was master of no such domain. Gower Street was Poverty Row, all right, and it was on Sunset Boulevard between Gower and Beachwood that Harry Cohn set up his first studio as an independent producer.

The men who make movies have been aptly tagged the dream merchants, but no dream that Cohn produced for his prospective audiences was sweeter or grander than the one he dreamed for himself.

The movie business was divided into two unequal parts: The best film properties went to the major studios, the rest to the novices and dreamers of Poverty Row.

Harry Cohn was going to bridge that gap.

No one had ever done it before. The rich got richer and the poor scrambled for every inch of celluloid that could be converted from reel to revenue. The major studios were building and buying nationwide networks of movie palaces in which to display their product, while the schemers and dreamers of Gower had to settle for whatever playing time they could scrounge in between. They borrowed money, they borrowed stars, they borrowed sets. Every so often, someone would make a quick killing, and then just as quickly fade. No one from Poverty Row had ever been able to put together a string of profitable hits that could provide the financial base to make the transition to the big time—to major studio status.

Along came Harry Cohn to change all that. As history would have it, he was a man uniquely qualified—for good reasons and bad—to make such a change and to have his dream. Cohn came up with a concept, stunning in its simplicity, that seemed never to have occurred to any of his Poverty Row precursors or contemporaries: to make a lot of money by making good movies. Very good movies. And this, in the final analysis, is what made Columbia a major studio, after very minor beginnings.

True, Cohn had more than his fair share of nerve, guts, and chutzpah. So did every other Hollywood producer, successful or otherwise. That was the nature of the business. But it was Cohn's rather lofty concept of quality that kept him from being just another otherwise.

Not that the idea was that loftily arrived at. Rather, it was born of a lowdown need, but it was shrewdly birthed and delivered by Cohn. And it didn't happen overnight, either. It took closer to nine years than nine months for this baby to come full term.

What Cohn gauged better than anybody else was that exhibition time in the theaters was the greatest factor in a film's commercial success. Since the major studios were operating their houses in order to showcase primarily their own films, they had to have damned good reason to sandwich in someone else's stuff. Harry Cohn would give them reason enough in his films.

That was the way to the dream, but like most dreams, it had to be deferred for a while, pushed to the background by the more insistent needs of just staying alive in the day-to-day business of making movies. It was a hand-to-mouth existence, the income from one film providing seed money for the next. C.B.C. was producing two-reelers and having particular success with two of its series—Cohn's original independent venture, *Screen Snapshots*, a sort of cinemated fan magazine devoted to the new idols of the marquee; and a comedy based on what had been both a vaudeville routine and a comic strip, *Hall Room Boys*.

Grinding these and other shorts out was a tough road to travel —not the straight route to the fortune and status that Harry Cohn craved. He wanted to make full-length features, but his partners were happy with the steadily increasing success of the operation as it was. A split was in the making that would be as wide as the continent separating Harry Cohn's Hollywood operation from the New York office of Jack Cohn and Joe Brandt. It was a schism that would affect every aspect of the company and haunt it in years to come.

In that giddy time, however, the separation of Columbia's powers wasn't all that grim. It had its compensatory factors. Bills received by the New York office would be paid by checks from Hollywood, and vice versa; the slowness of the mails worked for the young company in the constant fund-shuffling necessary to keep them afloat. It also afforded the opportunity for the respective partners to pepper their conversation with such tasty phrases as, "My New York office says . . ." and, "I'll discuss it with the Coast," camouflaging their meager resources with the panache of a multinational.

On a more realistic level, it might have required the three thousand miles between them to keep the Cohns from each other's throats. Both brothers possessed highly volatile personalities, deadly competitiveness, and diametrically opposed viewpoints on moviemaking. Jack was much more the businessman, with both eyes in the ledgers and the other (the one in the back of his head) firmly focused on his younger brother in California. Harry, on the other hand, was a moviemaker, pure and simple. Well, perhaps not so pure and surely not simple, but a man who put everything he had and all he was into the making of his films and the running of his studio. His method was a single-minded and simultaneous attack and embrace that left no doubt as to what he wanted. It also made Harry Cohn one of the most respected, feared, and hated men in all the long annals of Hollywood. But all that was still far in the future as C.B.C. struggled through the 20s.

Much as the mails and the long distance lines were splattered with their constant bickering, the Cohn brothers agreed on one point, and it was one vital to the growth of the company: The big money was in feature films—not in the shorts they were pushing out, but the big films Harry was so eager to make.

In 1922 they took the plunge. Five new partners and their money were brought into the company. Harry took the money and spent it all in one place—on a film called *More to be Pitied than Scorned*. The $20,000 investment brought back $130,000, but something in the way C.B.C. did business frightened off the new backers, who took their profits and ran. Harry was back to shoestringing it on his next production.

But unlike so many small-time operators who never make the adjustment to large-scale schemes, Harry Cohn did exactly what he had set out to. Moreover, he did it not by eschewing all he had learned as a Poverty Row entrepreneur, but by incorporating all those time- and money-saving techniques by which the low budgeted films managed to get made. Every operating economy, every cost-cutting trick was employed, and that practice was to carry over even to Columbia's expansive, money-making golden era. Even lavish production numbers in the musicals to come would be mounted on sound stages a fraction of the size used by the major studios. All the skills that go into making a movie were finely honed to super-technique by the people who wanted to remain on the Cohn payroll. The result was a finished product, polished by crack professionals in every area, that stood up to anything produced by the majors, whom Cohn so much wanted to impress.

It worked. The seams didn't show. If they had, the boss would have it ripped up and started over again.

Of course, that was something that Cohn didn't relish doing. So distasteful was the idea of any waste to him that directors soon learned to make the first take the final one. There were very few directors who could get away with more than that.

Some actors needed a great deal of rehearsing to get into their parts; others gave it all away with the first rehearsal. The director on Cohn's lot had to learn his performers' idiosyncrasies early on. Film was almost measured by the inch.

Usually, scenery was painted on one side, used and discarded.

14

Cohn decreed that both sides of the boards be utilized, and cut down half of Columbia's lumber costs.

Cohn's tight-fisted economics tried and frustrated his creative people at first, but the best of them rose to the challenges. Not only directors, but cinematographers, set designers, art directors, and prop men developed new approaches that helped create the quality feeling of a Columbia picture.

By 1924 the company had become Columbia Pictures. Their primary productions were features now, and the old Corned Beef and Cabbage sobriquet didn't fit the new image. The studio saw itself consuming more and more footage on Poverty Row, incorporating a jumble of property that was eventually to encompass the entire block. Harry Cohn never moved from Poverty Row; he just swallowed it, piece at a time, until it disappeared. If his own office grew to be large and lavish, it was the only one on Gower Street that did. Any money that the company had to spend was put directly into the production of films, not frittered away on nonsense like better working conditions for the employees. His guiding business philosophy seemed to fall somewhere between Machiavelli's and Mussolini's (whose decorating ideas he incorporated in his own office).

Harry Cohn, the prime force at Columbia during the early and middle years. Official studio portrait

There was only one Harry Cohn and he was one of the most feared yet respected of the great Hollywood moguls

Jack Cohn, who ran the New York end of the company

16

Jack Cohn and some of the Columbia stars in 1942: Jinx Falkenburg, Cohn, a blond Ann Miller, William Holden (in uniform) and Evelyn Keyes

As much as he ran the studio as if it were his personal property, Harry wasn't the only Cohn at Columbia. There was Jack, who was usually in New York. And there was Joe Brandt, who held the title of president, to answer to. The films were booked from New York, and the financial records were kept there, too. So money flowed from east coast to west, and when New York asked questions, Hollywood had to have the answers. That's why Harry Cohn counted every coin the studio spent. As long as his films could continue turning a profit, he could keep New York on the defensive. If he were to come a cropper, they could have his head. And like everything else he owned, Harry Cohn was most possessive about his head. He was going to keep it; where else would he be able to place the crown he was fashioning for himself!

His moviemaking policy was also well formed by this time, and it worked. Just as the studio expanded by footage, not acreage, staying out of the real-estate business and keeping money available for production, so did Cohn keep down payroll costs by avoiding the popular practice of maintaining a huge stable of stars. This policy also afforded an aesthetic flexibility that was to serve the company well. There was no pressure to buy story properties for idle and expensive stars or to thrust them into unsuitable vehicles, as the top-heavy majors so often did. Stars were always available on loan from the big studios, and there was a free-floating pool of unemployed personalities looking for either the big break or the big comeback.

Not all the ideas that gave Columbia its artistic and economic edge came from Cohn. It was Joe Brandt, back in New York, who decreed that the company build no theaters, but confine itself to the production of motion pictures. This policy, formulated in the early 20s, had two great and favorable consequences. First, it forced the company to produce something better than run-of-the-mill features that were poor carbons of what the majors were hacking out and force-feeding into their burgeoning strings of bijoux. Columbia *had* to make movies that those theaters *had* to show. This was very much in line with Cohn's thinking; he wanted to produce pictures that would attract the respect and attention of both the film industry and the paying public.

And it wouldn't be too long before those Paradises and Palaces became like albatrosses around the necks of the major movie companies—both during the Depression and then again in the 40s, when the government insisted that the movie companies sever their production and exhibition divisions totally.

But that was in the future. In the early and mid-20s, the time of Columbia's first expansionist maneuvers, the lack of controlled playhouses was a real problem that was only partly offset by superior offerings in the marketplace. The terms under which the independents' features were distributed generally called for sale on a flat-fee basis, in a specified area of the country. Thus, a big hit might not bring the producer any more income than something that just did so-so at the box office.

Joe Brandt's name and reputation had been whittled down to virtual shavings by the pushy activities of the frères Cohn, but the man was something of a genius in the marketing of movies. Under his direction, Columbia established its own sales offices in a rapidly expanding national network that serviced theaters directly and at much greater profit than the hold-over methods from the earliest days of filmmaking ever could have realized. All the other studios would follow suit, and the new pattern and selling techniques which Brandt pioneered still prevail today.

Columbia's need for more space had forced it to build its own studio, rather than rent from others. Perhaps the entire Columbia Studio could fit into one mammoth MGM sound stage, but Harry Cohn had his own fief at last. It has been likened to Bedlam

Abe Schneider succeeded Harry Cohn as president of the greatly expanded company

Leo Jaffe was the fourth president of Columbia

Manor by those accustomed to toiling in the more serene vine-yards of the majors, but its wines were becoming headier and headier. Columbia would soon produce its vintage year, an accomplishment heretofore unknown on Poverty Row.

Cohn himself was just as much a phenomenal happening as his pictures were to be. Big talk and boundless dreams, coin of the realm in the small time, weren't news. But a man whose braggadocio turned true was something else. When Harry first hit Hollywood, he boasted that he would live the life of the movie mogul, with the houses, cars, yachts, and women that that style symbolized. The ex-song-plugger, out of Tin Pan Alley by way of the tough east side, may have been boasting, but it wasn't idle chatter.

Harry Cohn had quit school while in his early teens. The first job he had picked up was as a singer in a choir. Then he teamed up with a piano player whose talent was more apparent than his own, and for a while the two earned a living working in a New York nickelodeon. Harry Ruby, later a successful composer, accompanied the flicks and his partner Harry joined him with a few vocals while the projectionist changed reels.

They tried working night clubs, but were never successful and soon went their separate ways. Harry put in a stint as a trolley car conductor, but even then, nickels and dimes were not his forte. Although the general public had not been seduced into giving up their own hard-earned coin to hear him sing, Harry knew that his voice could bring him a livelihood—if utilized in conjunction with a far better developed attribute of his salesmanship.

He became a song plugger, a highly specialized occupation peculiar to the music publishing trade, largely centered, then as now, in a few grimy loft buildings in the Broadway area. It was the job of the song plugger to push a publisher's material primarily in retail outlets. Harry would demonstrate the new tune, extoll its soon-to-be massive public demand, and get the store to stock the sheet music.

Remembering the warm audience reaction to his between-reel stints at the nickelodeon, he got the idea of producing short films for new songs as a means of introduction to the public. He set himself up in an office to produce just such films.

The reaction was good, and soon Harry was producing short films for several music publishers, including his ex-employer.

By now his older brother Jack was working for Carl Laemmle in the movie company that was to become Universal Studios.

20

Alan J. Hirschfield is the current
president and chief executive of
Columbia Pictures Industries, Inc.

David Begelman is the president of
Columbia Pictures division

A later portrait of Harry Cohn

Harry produced several song shorts featuring Laemmle's top attractions. Laemmle was impressed with Harry's hustle, and soon another Cohn was on his payroll.

Harry was made Laemmle's West Coast secretary and was soon off to Hollywood. The dream of every success-driven young man of those times seemed to come to life in the still-forming movie capital. And Harry Cohn did his dreaming with his eyes wide open.

He was a man of strong physical presence, gruffly masculine, attractive to women. The ambition instilled in him by his mother from early on never left him. He was raised on her version of the American dream and now he could see all its possibilities unreeling like a strip of film from the can.

He worked for that dream. Cohn scrutinized film and time as if they were money, which of course they were. Egged on by his New York partners, whom he characterized as bookkeepers, he shouted down the costs of production in every imaginable way.

He was not the easiest person in the world to work for. He possessed none of that *noblesse-oblige* that permits a duke to act like a stable boy and treat a stable boy like a duke. Actually, he had no *noblesse* of any kind, and thus unhindered, he treated everybody like a stable boy.

The stories about Cohn and his treatment of people are legion and legendary in the annals of Hollywood. But despite it all, Harry Cohn commanded a fantastic loyalty from the people who worked for him. Some may have hated him, but they all respected him. And most importantly, no matter how mean or crude the tools he used, he got the best from some of the best talents that ever made films. Actors and directors might have gone on to greater rewards in terms of fame and fortune after their Columbia stints, but many of the biggest never achieved any finer performances than they did under Harry Cohn's less than benevolent dictatorship.

The little studio with the big boss was now well on its way. In 1928, a Columbia film, *The Blood Ship*, was selected to premiere at the Roxy Theater in New York, then the largest and most prestigious motion picture showcase in the country. Unquestionably, it was the happiest thing to happen to Harry Cohn since the company had taken the plunge into full-length features. At about the same time, a new director came to work at the studio. There was no blare of trumpets or any other fanfare to announce the new arrival, but its consequences both for Columbia and for moviemaking would last long after both *Blood Ship* and, indeed, the Roxy itself were gone.

His name was Frank Capra.

Building new sound stages, *c.*1929, as the company expands.

The old studio office

The cutting room at the old studio

An early scene in the print department

Where some of the magic came from—the old prop department

The carpentry shop, called the mill at movie studios, where all wood products are turned out

The original studio laboratory

An aerial view of the burgeoning Gower Street lot

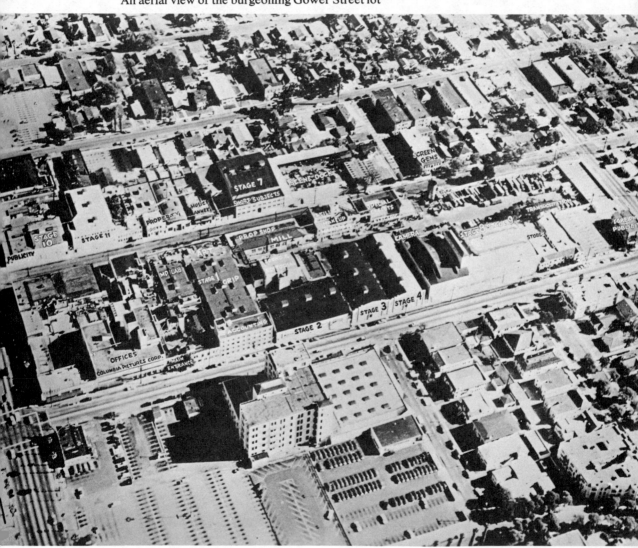

A nighttime shooting scene

A street within the studio complex. Note the plus fours on the man going upstairs

A new sound stage

The new front door. But the address is still Gower Street

Columbia's back lot was not part of the complex, as at other studios, but 10 miles away in Burbank! Typical western "towns" built at the company's ranch

City sets even include an elevated subway line. Note klieg lights atop buildings.

34

A picturesque set near completion

Set for an oriental movie. Calligraphy is faintly visible on door and walls

MORE TO BE PITIED THAN SCORNED

(Box Office)*
(1922)

Director: Edward J. Le Saint
From the play by Charles E. Blaney
6 reels

Players:
J. Frank Glendon
Rose Mary Theby
Philo McCullogh
Gordon Griffith
Alice Lake
Josephine Adaire

LAMP IN THE DESERT

(Special)*

PASSIONATE FRIENDS

(Special)

ONLY A SHOP GIRL

(Box Office)
(1922)

Director: Edward J. Le Saint
From the play by Charles E. Blaney
Footage: 6400 feet

Players:
Josephine Adaire
William Scott
Mae Busch
Estelle Taylor
Willard Louis

Claire Du Brey
James Morrison
Wallace Beery
Tully Marshall

MYSTERIOUS WITNESS

(Special)

---

*Box Office and Special indicate films made by Harry Cohn before the formation of C.B.C., which Cohn turned over to the new company.

HER ACCIDENTAL HUSBAND

(Special)
(1923)

Director: Dallas M. Fitzgerald
Story: Lois Zellner

6 reels

Players:
Miriam Cooper
Forrest Stanley
Maude Wayne

MARY OF THE MOVIES

(Special)
(1923)

Director: John McDermott
Story: Louis Lewyn
Photography:
  George Meehan
  Vernon Wallace
Title: Jos. M. Farnham
7 reels

Players:

Marion Mack	Alec Francis
Harry Cornelli	Estelle Taylor
John Geough	Tom Moore
Raymond Cannon	Richard Travis
Louise Fazenda	Creighton Hale
Dr. Le Saint	George O'Hara
Rosemary Theby	Johnnie Walker
Bryant Washburn	Barbara LaMarr
J. Warren Kerrington	Craig Biddle
David Butler	Elliott Dexter
Rose Mary Cooper	Gaston Glass
John Bowers	Herbert Rawlinson
Marguerite de la Motte	Miss Du Pont
	Frank Glendon
Stuart Holmes	Francis MacDonald
Zasu Pitts	James Seiler
Anna May Wong	Douglas McLean
Clara Horton	Carmel Myers
Rex Ingram	Malcolm MacGregor

TEMPTATION

(Box Office)
(1923)

Director: Edward J. Le Saint
Story: Lenore Coffee
Photography: King Grey

Footage: 6462 ft.

Players:

Eva Novak	Phillip Smalley
Bryant Washington	Vernon Steele
June Eldridge	

YESTERDAY'S WIFE

(Columbia)
(1924)

Director: Edward J. Le Saint
From a story by Evelyn Campbell,
  published in *Snappy Stories*
Photography: King Grey

Footage: 5915 ft.

Players:

Irene Rich	Lewis Dayton
Josephine Crowell	Eileen Percy
Lottie Williams	Philo McCullough

THE BAREFOOT BOY

(1924)

Director and adaptor:
David Kirkland
Story: Wallace Clifton
Suggested by the poem by
John Greenleaf Whittier
Photography: David Abel

Footage: 5958 ft.

Players:
Frankie Lee
George Periolat
Harry Todd
Tully Marshall
Raymond Hatton
Virginia True Boardman
Brinsley Shaw
Gertrude Messenger

Jean O'Rourke
True Boardman
Lottie Williams
George McDaniels
John Bowers
Otis Harlan
Sylvia Breamer
Marjorie Daw

THE BLOOD SHIP

(Released: August, 1927)

Director: George B. Seitz
Story: Norman Springer
Cameramen:
J. O. Taylor
Harry Davis

Footage: 6843 ft.

Players:
Hobart Bosworth
Jacqueline Logan
Richard Arlen
Walter James
Fred Kohler
James Bradbury, Sr.

Arthur Rankin
Syd Crossley
Frank Hemphill
Chappell Dossett
Blue Washington

Nobody's going their way 'til Claudette shows some leg

2 | The Capra Years

HARRY COHN DIDN'T ATTEND ANY SCHOOL THAT TAUGHT him how to produce movies or run a studio, and the school Frank Capra attended didn't teach film directing. What the California Institute of Technology thought they were turning out was another chemical engineer. This son of Italian immigrants struggled mightily to get his Caltech degree, but when he finally made it, after a series of events that could have filled the screen as dramatically as one of his own later films,* the demand for engineers had tapered off to naught. The poor boy, with the hard-earned but suddenly unmarketable education, packed up his degree and his disillusion and went on the road, to find his opportunities where and when he could.

Thus it was almost by the sheerest chance that Capra stumbled into moviemaking.

And it was even more capricious fate that brought him to

---

*Capra tells his own story much better than anyone else could in his marvelously candid and intriguing autobiography, *The Name Above the Title*.

Columbia. He was doing his second stint at Mack Sennett's studio when his agent told him he was to report to Gower Street for a meeting with Columbia's production head, Sam Briskin. Briskin was acting on orders, of course, from Harry Cohn.

Why had Cohn picked the almost unheard of Capra? Because his was the first name on an alphabetical listing of available directors. (A man who was eventually to direct two Oscar-winning Best Pictures for Columbia, Fred Zinnemann, would never have made it if this system of selectivity had remained in use.)

That's how it happened. Columbia. Cohn. Capra. For a decade, that combination would turn out some of the choicest nuggets of Hollywood's first Golden Age. For a while, though, the workings of the Poverty Row studio would be rather inauspicious.

That was only natural. Capra had directed his first film years before, learning as he shot. At Mack Sennett's, he was a writer and gag man who created great bits of comedy for the silent film clown, Harry Langdon. And although he directed Langdon in some of his best efforts, Capra was still feeling his own way around with the two-reelers Columbia expected from him.

But novice though he was, Frank Capra had a vision about movies that many older, more experienced directors didn't bother themselves with. Capra wanted to know everything. He wanted to do everything. He insisted on having complete control over the making of his films—in the writing and producing as well as the directing. Columbia—and Cohn—gave him his head, letting him conceive his stories and see them through to the final editing, something he could never have done at any of the major, tightly structured studios.

Capra was shrewd enough to see through Cohn's bluster and Cohn was shrewd enough to gamble on Capra, especially after he came up winners with his first film for the studio, *That Certain Thing*. Two more two-reelers quickly followed: *So This is Love* and *Matinee Idol*. All three were lightly romantic comedies, brought in for far less cost then the Mack Sennett comedies Capra had written. Capra was learning moviemaking in the Cohn-Brandt-Cohn mold, but it was grist for his inventive mind. It tightened his mastery of the technical end of the business and led to many directorial innovations. More importantly, it didn't hamper the development of Capra's inner vision, his concept of what movies could and should do. The budgets may have strained and bucked on the floor, but Capra's intellectual approach to what he clearly understood to be an art form—film—soared and expanded as he learned his craft.

Ralph Graves is falling for a piece of exotica. Jack Holt doesn't approve. A scene from *Submarine* (1928)

His next films were larded with heavier situations than he had tackled with the comedies. Capra was learning his own limits, as well as those of the new medium. Soon, he would expand both, stretching to new dimensions scarcely hinted at in his dramas, *Say It with Sables* and *Way of the Strong*, his next Columbia releases.

These early movies were classroom and laboratory for Capra. In making them, he was teaching himself what couldn't be learned in any academic institution at that time. There was no curriculum on cinema, not even in anyone's dreams. But it was with a student's thirst for learning that Capra first tackled movies, and how well he taught himself soon would be universally acknowledged.

But first, the movies had an innovation that would test the mettle of all its performers, producers, and other assorted creators. Sound had arrived, with a bang.*

---

*Years later Columbia would recapture that magic moment in *The Jolson Story*, one of its most successful films.

43

After finding the missing submarine Jack Holt receives congratulations from captain and crew

Capra had proven his ability to handle full-length features when Cohn assigned him to bail out an ailing *A* effort called *Submarine*. This underwater epic had been slated to be Columbia's first plunge into the bigtime, budgeted at $150,000, a previously unheard of sum for Gower Street. The first rushes had Harry Cohn climbing the walls. He yanked the director, sent Capra to the seaside location where filming had been halted. Capra scratched everything that had been shot, laid down his hard and fast rules to an almost mutinous crew, and made *Submarine*.

It was the start of a profitable partnership. The film's two stars, Ralph Graves and Jack Holt, early Columbia stalwarts, were at first wary of Capra, but like all performers before and since, quickly succumbed to the magic of a hit. Capra was to

The usual cast of several anxiously await the return of Ralph Graves on his solo *Flight* (1929)

Flight was a pioneering effort in the use of aerial photography. Ralph Graves, Jack Holt, and everybody else was winging it

Jack Holt and Ralph Graves in a quiet moment from *Dirigible*. Jack's girl is Fay Wray (1931)

direct the two in *Flight* and *Dirigible*, both winners, patterned on the success of *Submarine*.

With that last-named, a new momentum was building on Gower Street. Columbia had proven it could handle *A* pictures. Harry Cohn could run a real studio, almost on par with the big moguls he so admired. And Frank Capra could bring a freshness and inventiveness to the screen that would change the movies forever.

Capra had none of the almost mystical awe many other directors felt regarding sound. It was another technical aspect, albeit the most significant, in his always-expanding tool kit for making movies. He had used it to great effect at the climax of *Submarine*, when a tapping of fingers, audible to the audience, signaled that the crew of the submerged vessel was still alive and that the film would have a happy ending.

But *The Jazz Singer*, released by Warner Brothers in 1927, had electrified audiences, and now the public wanted to hear more than fingernails. Hollywood, as it always did in a crisis—

Barbara Stanwyck as the female evangelist of *Miracle Woman*. With David Manners (1931)

then and now—quavered and procrastinated. Was sound really trumpeting in a new era for motion pictures, or was it just a novelty that would soon go away, leaving its practitioners broke and saddled with its costly apparatus? The movie business, ever playing one of its own favorite roles as the reluctant virgin, dipped its toe in but stopped short of the plunge.

The bastardized result were films that talked—but only part of the time. The Capra-Columbia contribution to this phase of history was *The Younger Generation*, from a play by Fannie Hurst, and starring Jean Hersholt. It talked only during its second half, but that was enough for Capra. He used it to teach himself how to direct actors with speaking parts just as he had taught himself to handle drama while making those old two-reelers.

Now the New York office was yelling for talkies only, and Cohn and Capra were ready. The first Columbia all-talkie was a mystery called *The Donovan Affair*. The cumbersome new sound equipment limited them to shooting indoors, but despite this

Ralph Bellamy with Barbara Stanwyck and a somewhat skeptical Adolph Menjou in *Forbidden* (1932)

limitation, Capra recognized and welcomed sound as progress. To him the advent of talkies was not an adversary, as it was viewed by many in the movies, for whom sound would cut short flourishing careers. The film companies that chose to remain stubbornly silent would crumble and fall or be absorbed by newer, more aggressive outfits.

Again, its economic policies stood Columbia in good stead. There were no squeaky-voiced he-men studio stars or brass-throated ingenues with contracts to be bought out. The waxing coffers had sufficient funds for the good properties that dialogue demanded. Harry Cohn, as always, could find personalities on the conceptual see-saw of talent—on the way up or on the way down. After the *Flight* follow-up to *Submarine*, he found someone on the way up.

The original *Platinum Blonde,* Jean Harlow, loses Bobby Williams to the always proper Loretta Young (1931)

◄ Joe Cook starred in *Rain or Shine,* Capra's first Broadway transplant (1930)

The medium for getting almost all of Harlow's charms across was the massage

She had starred in a couple of Broadway shows and then knocked about in some small movie parts, nothing like her New York notices would have intimated. But Harry Cohn had a hunch about her, and Frank Capra had learned to respect those hunches. When he put her in front of the camera for his next opus, *Ladies of Leisure*, Barbara Stanwyck became a movie star.

The Golden Age of the silver screen had begun. But it didn't always shine so brightly, even for Capra. When he starred Stanwyck in *Miracle Woman*, an early entry in the Elmer Gantry religioso sweepstakes, the magic didn't work. But it was one of the few unhappy items in the steadily growing Capra collection. So was the slightly less unsuccessful *Forbidden*, which he wrote, also for Stanwyck.

Counterbalancing the less successful efforts were some of the early films that were soon to become part of the longest streak of successes that any film director has ever accumulated. Capra's most notable films were not conspicuous solely because of their commercial successes. He was a film talent, and once he found his own approach his films were important, memorable ones that added a new dimension to American entertainment.

Before 1932, though, he was still searching. Once again, Broadway was tapped, not for a star this time, but for a play. It was called *Rain Or Shine*, and while it had played the boards as a musical, Capra was astute enough to see it another way. He played it as a straight comedy, with the Broadway cast intact, but throwing out all the musical numbers. Capra knew his comedy. It worked. It had to. Harry Cohn refused to foot the bills for an expensive musical production, preferring to let the fat cats at MGM and Warners go to the expense of developing the public's taste for this peculiarly American brand of entertainment. (He would patiently wait for the 40s—and color and Rita Hayworth—before cashing in on musicals.)

In 1931, Capra loosed another kind of miracle woman on the screen and into immediate stardom. Jean Harlow had made a brief appearance in *Hell's Angels*, but her Columbia work was in a film whose title would become synonymous with her—*Platinum Blonde*. Although she lost the hero to the always immaculate Loretta Young, the film clearly belonged to Harlow. It was a comedy, Capra's forte, and he proved that a girl could be funny without losing her sex appeal. Harlow zoomed to the top with *Platinum Blonde* and stayed there until her untimely death in 1937.

Hollywood people had lost their investments along with everybody else in the great 1929 stock market debacle, but the industry was one of the last to be affected by the Depression. The movies had indeed become an escape of major magnitude—a safety valve for the millions who were thrown from the hedonism of the 20s into the shock of poverty. By 1932, lines were forming for bread and soup, not for the plush-and-gold picture palaces. The big studios with the real estate were the hardest hit, but picture-making continued. For those who could still afford the price of a ticket, it was the only entertainment available. And when life becomes as dreary as it did in the Depression-ridden 30s, some form of relief becomes an absolute necessity. The emperors of Rome, with their programmed bread and circuses, knew this instinctively; the moguls of Hollywood knew it too.

At first, Capra dealt with the facts of the Depression directly, in a film that mirrored the problems and fears of the everyday audience. Written by Robert Riskin, *American Madness* depicted unemployment, foreclosures, and even a bank run. The cast was headed by Walter Huston and Pat O'Brien, portraying a bank president and an ex-con cashier, respectively. Capra had thought up the story line, and it was the first foreshadowing of what was to become his major theme in almost all his future work: the celebration of the basic goodness and honesty of most men. It was the genius of Capra to deliver this simple homily, not embroidered on a sampler nor hammered home via the cinematic dull-

Capra finally got the crowds he wanted in *American Madness*. Effect was so real viewers started a real run on banks (1932)

ness of message movies, but through characters and situations as delightful, brash, entertaining, and enjoyable as anything ever put on the screen. The theme is large if simplistic, while the characters are "little" though complex, but it is in terms of the total Capra package that the sheer accomplishment takes hold as a lasting contribution.

Before the ideas that were seminal in *American Madness* came once more to the fore, Capra embarked on a film completely outside what was to become the main body of his work. *The Bitter Tea of General Yen* was about the love between an American girl and an oriental warlord. More than a decade passed before its theme would be repeated on film. As taboo as interracial love was as cinematic subject matter, *General Yen* was nevertheless

Nils Asther and Barbara Stanwyck and the insoluble problem of *The Bitter Tea of General Yen* (1933)

May Robson played Apple Annie to the hilt, making *Lady For a Day* believable. Jean Parker and Barry Norton are the lovers (1933)

chosen to be the first feature to play at the then-debuting Show-case of the Nation, New York's Radio City Music Hall.* (Trans-formed by the magic of make-up, Nils Asther went from Scandi-navian to Cantonese in the title role very credibly.) However, it was an uncertain success: Aesthetically, it worked, but it was banned as objectionable for consumption by the colonialist British empire (which was still running in those days), and that put quite a crimp in its earnings.

Perhaps it was the official British reaction to *General Yen* that led Capra to cast about for a property more indigenous to the land of Mom's apple pie and hence more palatable for over-seas consumption as well. In any case, what he landed was a city-style hokey script, as down-home as you could get; it was a gem of a Damon Runyon short story called "Madame La Gimp." It had all the elements that Capra knew and loved to do: loads of

---

*Dirigible had played Hollywood's Grauman's Chinese Theater the year before, also a signal honor for an independent like Columbia. This last of the Ralph Graves/Jack Holt epics featured not-yet famous Boris Karloff in the cast.

down-and-out characters with fine comedic value, a simple but suspenseful plotline, a smattering of light romance.

But what all those ingredients added up to was not all so sure-fire. There was a bit of a teaser in there—the heroine who had to carry the story and hence the film was a seventy-year-old woman. How would the movie-going public, trained to expect youth and beauty on the screen, react to that? The character was no Whistler's Mother type either, no sweet old granny in a wheelchair to tug at the heart strings. No, she was Apple Annie, a Broadway beggar who had sent her only and misbegotten child, a daughter, to Europe secretly, there to be brought up and educated, on Mama's dubiously legitimate funds, and of course never knowing any truth about their origin or Mama's real station in life. Everything is business as usual, until daughter writes home to announce she's intending to marry a Spaniard of high standing and is bringing him home to meet Mother and her supposedly socialite friends. Will she or won't she find out the truth about Apple Annie?

It was Runyon's story, but the plot fell right into Hollywood of the 30s. And what it had to say about the real "little people," the down-and-outers, versus the highborn and fat cats, was pure Capra. He had struck the mother lode.

Robert Riskin, the marvelous writer who was to accompany Capra on his magic journey, had tagged the film *Lady for a Day.* It aptly described Apple Annie's dilemma of having to play the *grande dame*, with all the appurtenances, for the duration of the lovebirds' visit.

A fine actress, May Robson was Annie to perfection. The rest of the cast, shining among the offbeat types who populate all Runyon tales, included Glenda Farrell and Walter Connolly, who had established himself as a top screen performer in *Bitter Tea.*

Lady for a Day played the Music Hall (as all of Capra's pictures eventually would) and it was a smash. Harry Cohn was willing to make book with anyone on the number of Oscars it would garner. In the end, it did receive four Academy Award nominations—including Best Picture and Best Actress (May Robson)—but no wins. The awesome Oscar was still the property of the major studios. At least to the people who ran the movie business, Columbia was still Poverty Row.

Then it all began to change. It happened one year. Or, more precisely, *It Happened One Night.*

No one except Capra and Riskin had any faith in it. Two films with similar themes had just failed at other studios. Capra ran

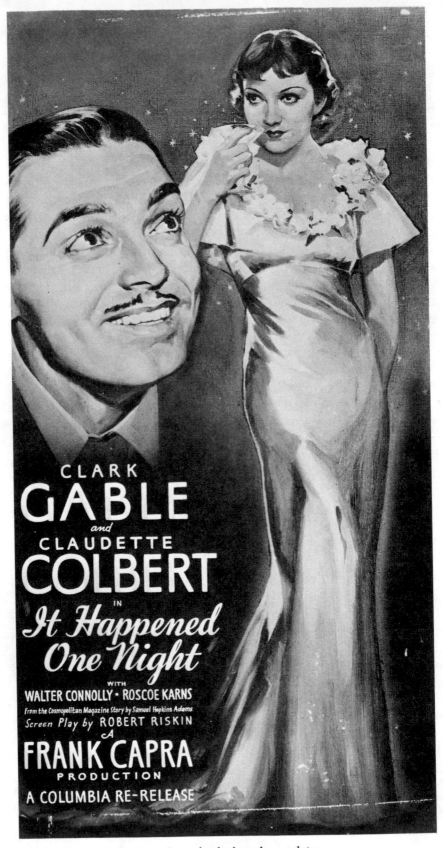

The movie that did it all. A glamorized ad used years later

Roscoe Karns makes a pitch for Colbert, but Gable isn't going for it (*It Happened One Night,* 1934)

The famous "walls of Jericho" scene from *It Happened One Night*

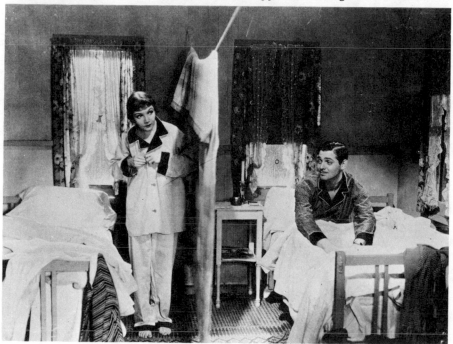

For the elegant heiress, raw carrots for breakfast are unthinkable

into trouble getting both female and male leads. Myrna Loy, Margaret Sullavan, Miriam Hopkins, and Constance Bennett all turned down the female lead flat. Robert Montgomery turned down the male lead. But his boss, Louis Mayer of MGM, had another star in his stable whom the great Louis thought was in need of disciplinary action. One of the usual punishments was exile to Gower Street, or to some other equally ignominious address, as a loan-out to a minor filmmaker.

The bad boy in this case was Clark Gable, the once and future king of films. Mayer owed Cohn the use of a star from a previous deal. And Mayer wanted the king humbled. A bargain was struck.

Because Gable was coming into the film directly from Louis Mayer, Harry Cohn became interested in *It Happened One Night*. He managed to get Claudette Colbert to play the female lead, but only after accepting her condition of a four-week shooting deadline. After all the previous rejections from the other potential female leads, Cohn and Capra were willing to agree to almost any condition. (True to his promise to Claudette Colbert, Capra did wind up the shooting in four weeks!)

The picture was finished, and despite Capra's and Riskin's enthusiasm, despite Cohn's personal interest, despite Gable and Colbert heading the bill, its week-long run at the Music Hall wasn't profitable enough for the big house to hold it over. It was nearly forgotten when it started its dreary route through secondary theaters after its lukewarm reviews.

So, with *Lady for a Day* a smash success, and with *It Happened One Night* nearly forgotten, Capra decided to try his luck with a new film, and to look for his source material in the same place he had found material for *Lady*—the short story market.

This time, he chose a Mark Hellinger story, "Broadway Bill." The setting wasn't Times Square, but the race track. Myrna Loy and Warner Baxter starred, and a young girl making her second film appearance enhanced the production: Lucille Ball. The film had some exciting racing sequences and a cute story line. And it did well.

But by the time the studio could see that *Broadway Bill* was a hit, the returns from the secondary-theater showings of *It Happened One Night* were in. During the first month of its release in the general theaters, something had started to happen. The film-going audience, in its collective wisdom, was discovering the film for itself and apparently ignoring the tepid reception it had received from the critics after its first week at the Music Hall. *It Happened One Night* was being held over for weeks, and in some

Capra returns to the American idiom as Myrna Loy hooks up with Warner Baxter in *Broadway Bill* (1934)

places for months, at a time when a three-week playdate was considered exceptional. People were going back to see it again and again and talking it up among their friends. It was a classic case of "nobody liked it except the public."

But Capra had liked it. He had brought it in on time and under budget, and although even he had never imagined it would do as well as *Lady for a Day*, the audience enthusiasm vindicated his initial belief in the film. And it did more than that; it did something that no other film, before or after, has ever done. *It Happened One Night* won all five major Academy Awards: Best Picture, Best Actor, Best Actress, Best Director, and Best Writer. As of this writing, that is still a record.

The film, with its attendant acclaim, wiped Poverty Row off the map as far as Columbia Pictures was concerned. The jibes and snipes about the studio's meager beginnings were silenced; Harry Cohn had made it in the town where the only thing that counted was the gross on the last release.

The achievement of *It Happened One Night* was justification for enjoying all the flamboyant good living Harry Cohn had yearned for. It meant not only the *means* to the lifestyle of a Hollywood mogul, but the *right* to it. He had earned opulence, if such a thing is possible, and in the Hollywood of the 30s, it probably was.

For Frank Capra, the picture meant official recognition from the highest level—his peers. He had longed to crack the tight-knit fraternity of top directors ever since he had realized how unique his own talents were. Then as now, there was no higher reward than the Oscar. Cohn had given him carte blanche from the moment of his arrival at the studio; the accolades of audiences and the Academy provided the rest of the momentum for a career that remains unsurpassed by any other Hollywood director. Indeed, it would be difficult to find a parallel to Capra's career in any area of entertainment. *Lady for a Day* had been the first, and *It Happened One Night* was the second, in a glorious list of eleven consecutive hits.

The unprecedented popularity of *It Happened* constituted a clarion call from the *vox populi* of America. Moviemakers had responded to an earlier call from their audience and the result had been the star system that was to prevail in Hollywood for decades. When the public began to recognize familiar faces on the screen, they wanted to see them again and again; they wanted to find out all they could of their favorites, and once the studios had caught on to the fact that people were swarming into the theaters that featured certain players over and over, the star system was born. Hitherto unnamed players began getting billings, and the featured stars became almost as important as the whole film.

In *It Happened One Night*, audiences recognized not only the stars, but something of themselves in the fresh, unhackneyed characters. The reaction to beautiful people, credibly behaving (well, almost) gave impetus to a whole new direction that movies were to take. A new genre of film was created with *It Happened*. It was perfect tonic for a Depression-ridden nation, a formula concocted from both realism and fantasy. If the rich heroine was a frothy escape figure, there was always the earthy hero to bring her back down to reality. Somehow, the poor seemed morally better than the rich; deprivation conducted a stricter school than excess. That message was sent out subliminally, though, compared to the carryings-on which joyously and graphically proved that the poor do have much more fun. Even standing in line waiting for the shower in a dank, two-bucks-a-night auto camp has more gaiety than force-fed champagne proceedings in a formal drawing room, or so it would seem. Clark Gable was the ideal image for the poor-boy saviour of the wealthy but unhappy Colbert.

Thus, out of *It Happened One Night*, the screwball comedy was born. And Mr. Capra really went to town on his next one. By this time, the Capra creative team was established: Robert Riskin scripting the Clarence Budington Kelland story, Joe Walker behind the camera, Gene Havlick doing the editing, the last a task whose importance was perhaps better understood by Capra than any of the other early directors. Early on in his film career, he had mastered the craft and throughout its long span he was al-

Gary Cooper is behind the tuba in *Mr. Deeds Goes to Town* (1936)

The only thing about the big town that Longfellow likes is Babe, the inimitable Jean Arthur

At Longfellow's seeming defeat, Babe jumps into the breach to urge him, with her love, to save himself

ways to work very closely with his editor on the final versions of his films. The association with Riskin, Walker, and Havlick was to continue through all of Capra's subsequent Columbia movies.

Mr. Deeds Goes to Town was their next film. The first and inevitable choice for the title role was Gary Cooper. Finding the female lead wasn't as easy. Mr. Deeds' character remains a shining constant throughout his adventures; indeed, that's one of the hallmarks of the story. But Babe Bennett, girl reporter, goes through quite a transformation due to her proximity to the intrepid man. An actress had to be found who could make the changeover believable and touching. Many actresses were eager for the part, a complete turnabout from Capra's experience with *It Happened One Night*, and totally due, of course, to that film's success.

The director found the girl he wanted, already under contract to Columbia, although largely ignored there and at the other studios where she had spent time. She was the woman with the great voice, Jean Arthur, and Capra held up production for six months on *Mr. Deeds Goes to Town* until she was available.

Directing *Mr. Deeds* brought Mr. Capra his second Oscar. The theme of the small-town boy in the big city further defined the major thrust of his work: the poor and real versus the rich and

Margaret Seddon and Margaret McWade are Jane and Amy, the Faulkner sisters, who tell the court that Deeds is "pixilated"

phony, the indestructibility of the honest man, the America that could-be-the-beautiful of people's dreams.

For Capra it had been no dream. America had worked for this immigrant son and the rewards, financial and soulful, had been almost beyond imagining. Now, in his films, Capra wanted to make that dream work for everybody else, too. If his personal brand of patriotism seems too simplistic and naive to us now, it should be remembered that those were ideologically simpler times. Moreover, any comparison of his films with earlier entertainment depictions of love of country—George M. Cohan's for example—shows that Capra was never merely flag-waving. He was dealing with the problems of the times in a way that would drive his points home and at the same time amuse his audience. He never succumbed to the blind jingoism that so many others did. He didn't raise the bloody shirt; rather, he raised questions. It happened to be in his nature and his philosophy, and therefore in his films, that the answers to those questions tended to be positive and optimistic. It would have taken no more mental ability to have been negative and dreary, but that attitude wouldn't have made for nearly such entertaining films.

And entertainment was Capra's first prerogative. He wanted to say something, but he wanted to have fun saying it, and he wanted his audience to have fun hearing it. All through the 30s—the decade of Capra's main work—people deserved at least that much. If, as we're constantly being reminded, we deserve a break *today*, we surely deserved being kept in stitches for a couple of hours at a time during the Depression.

Not all of Frank Capra's films were comedies, though. Being entertained can mean being enthralled as well as being amused. And what could be more enthralling in the bleak world of 1937 than a film of total escape, a leaving of this nasty world for a never-never place of such oriental exotica and tranquility as to make Peter Pan's province—well, somewhat provincial. In Barrie's story, the inhabitants need never grow up, but James Hilton's *Lost Horizon* goes that one better. In Shangri-La, one needn't grow *old*. For the adult audience, that's really much better.

Perhaps that's one reason that *Lost Horizon* became the all-time sentimental favorite film for so many people; the cast that Capra assembled has to be another reason. Ronald Colman, the essential Englishman, surrounded by such superb character actors as Edward Everett Horton, Thomas Mitchell, Sam Jaffe, and H. B. Warner. All the other artifacts of the film far exceeded anything Columbia had ever expended on a single motion picture;

Isobel Jewell, Edward Everett Horton, Ronald Colman, and Thomas Mitchell confront H. B. Warner (Chang) in *Lost Horizon* (1939)

A torchlight procession through Shangri-La

Ronald Colman and Jane Wyatt and the precious serenity of the hidden city

music, make-up (especially making Sam Jaffe 200 years old, and turning a slew of occidentals into orientals), costumes, and above all, the massive sets and special effects needed to create a bona fide Utopia in southern California.

In addition to all the grand actors, there were some very remarkable ladies in Shangri-La too, most notably Jane Wyatt, and a young Mexican woman singularly named (or renamed) Margo, who attracted a lot of attention in this epic but never developed a career as spectacular as her early publicity indicated.

Although it was primarily a romantic film, it was as well-attended by men as by women. The dashing Ronald Colman was a figure of far greater authority than any mere matinee idol would have been, and the added dimension given the film by its mixture of politics and adventure further widened the appeal it held for audiences all over the world. It was one of the earliest of Hollywood films to achieve international prestige.

Again, with fascism on the onslaught and armies on the march everywhere, Capra had made a film of and for its time. Utopia, Erewhon, and especially Shangri-La were eagerly wished for by a Depression-and-war-weary world. The gentle lessons of the High Lama might be drowned out by the thundering goose-steppers, but they remained forever fixed in the hearts of millions in audiences everywhere.

Lost Horizon took in a lot of money, but it had cost more to produce and promote than anything Columbia had ever done before. Harry Cohn's personal lost horizon on this one was the bottom line on the balance sheets. Capra had been producing as well as directing his smash films, and Cohn had been giving him his head. Now, those respective heads clashed. Cohn was having misgivings about how much freedom he had granted Capra, and how much money that freedom was costing *him*. Capra, more than ever, wanted to do his films his way. The success he had brought to the studio had earned him at least that much.

But even that was ambiguous, at least in the mind of Harry Cohn. It was true that Capra's genius had established Columbia, but who had hired Capra in the first place? Harry Cohn. Who had backed all his hunches and given him the leeway to do as he wanted? Harry Cohn. And when costs soared to the skies, who did the New York hierarchy come gunning for? You guessed it.

Another element in Capra's success made the whole thing a sweet and sour pickle for Cohn. He was too much of a showman not to want the spotlight and the credit for himself. At a studio like MGM, the director was just another cog in the apparatus.

He didn't run the whole show on any film. The company was much more structured and the whole civilized world knew who was sitting at the top of the structure. Every time Leo the Lion roared, the sound he made was "Louie, Louie."

And who was calling "Harry, Harry" for all the world to hear? No one. Capra was reaping the acclaim and Cohn wanted to take him down a peg or two. For a year, they fought. Across the ocean, across the continent, and finally, across a courtroom. The court battle involved a Jean Arthur film that was released in England in 1936 and advertised there as a Capra-directed movie. The trouble was, Capra had nothing to do with it—so he sued Columbia. Technically, he was right. But he lost to Cohn, at least in the courts.

All Frank Capra wanted to do was to make movies, and all Cohn really wanted to do was to make money. In the end, that saved the day. After all the shouting, Cohn placated Capra by doubling his salary for his next project. And he bought him the most expensive literary property ever purchased for the movies until that time.

You Can't Take It with You was a fun-drenched Broadway comedy by George S. Kaufman and Moss Hart. It ran and ran and garnered a Pulitzer Prize for itself. The asking price was $200,000. Harry Cohn clinched the deal before Louis B. Mayer could open his checkbook. Capra had his next vehicle.

It was as much in his vein as if he had written it himself. The characters, mostly members of a completely dotty family, were real and new. There was a romance, beautifully, lightly limned by Capra's avowed favorite, Jean Arthur, and a fast-rising young newcomer named James Stewart. But the love interest didn't often hold stage center. There Capra waged his wonderful battle of the titans, the patriarchs of the lovers' respective clans, played by Lionel Barrymore and Edward Arnold.

You Can't Take It with You took it, all right—Best Picture and Best Director—Capra's third Oscar in a five-year span. And at the box office, it took in enough to wipe the frown from Harry Cohn's brow and to give Columbia its heftiest bottom line in several years.

That left Capra with only one more picture owing to the studio under the terms of his contract. Once more, the two combatants were up in arms over what property this last Capra-directed film would be. Capra was ready to throw in the towel when something quite magical happened. An out-of-print, unknown novel had been picked up by one of Capra's associates. As soon as he read

Obviously a banner attraction: a promotional piece designed for a theater *near you*

Ann Miller, James Stewart, and Jean Arthur have somewhat varying reactions to Mischa Auer's point

a short synopsis, Capra knew he had his next film. *The Man from Montana* by Lewis R. Foster became *Mr. Smith Goes to Washington*, and the last bright chapter of Hollywood's CCC—Columbia, Capra and Cohn—was about to be written.

Robert Riskin had left the studio prior to this, and a brilliant new writer was assigned the task of forging a screenplay from the resurrected Foster novel. He was Sidney Buchman, who had already proven himself as a screenwriter at Columbia. He and Capra went to work with relish, Capra especially excited at the prospect of making a film about American democracy in its apotheosis—a test of the political process in the very halls of Congress.

Capra re-paired his screen lovers Jean Arthur and Jimmy Stewart and supported them with an enormous cast: Claude Rains, Edward Arnold, Thomas Mitchell, Guy Kibbee, Beulah Bondi, and other such Hollywood stalwarts. The result was a bouquet of stand-out performances that blended into an integrated, smoothly delivered film, such as only a top director could bring in.

75

A confrontation between giants: Edward Arnold faces Lionel Barrymore as James Stewart listens

Backgrounds were painstakingly researched, and the Senate chambers that were duplicated on the Columbia lot were models of authenticity. The story, in those old pre-Watergate days, was somewhat provocative, dealing as it did with corruption in high places, as high as that Senate chamber itself.

Reaction at the Washington premiere was loud and mixed, depending on which politico was passing judgment. That meant scads of publicity and soon the whole country was flocking to the box offices to decide for themselves whether the republic could withstand Capra's alleged attack on a sacred institution or whether the damn thing should be taken out of circulation. Cooler heads prevailed and the film was shown, and liked, extensively. Had it not been 1939, it would probably have copped an armful of Oscars for its creators. But, alas for CCC, it was the year of *Gone with the Wind* and only Mr. Foster scored, for Best Story.

Finis one of the most productive partnerships in film history.

It is easy, although somewhat lengthy, to recap all of Frank Capra's contributions to movies in general and to this studio in particular. The films themselves will stand by themselves. It is only the revolution in public morality that has occurred during these past two decades that dates the very best of them. The talents he helped to nurture—writers, actors, composers, editors —went on to create more movie magic (and some history) of their own. The genre screwball comedy, which he discovered and developed, has provided some of the grandest entertainment of the century. His conception of the function of the film director still prevails today. Many of his improvised and invented techniques are standard procedure today. Today his films are studied and discussed not only by fans but by the filmmakers of tomorrow. As long as celluloid stays with us, Capra will be remembered.

What is more likely to be forgotten is that during this decade-plus of achievement, Harry Cohn stood behind Capra and said yes. Many times, *any* time, Cohn could have done the reverse. But he put his own prestige, his own money, his very standing as president of the company, on the line. He probably didn't always believe in what Capra was doing, but he always believed in Capra. Both men were hunch players, both came to movies with no preparation, no background at all for it. Each in his own way left indelible marks on what one man considered basically an art, the other basically a business.

A typical day in the madcap household! Spring Byington, Ann Miller, and Mischa Auer entertain; Dub Taylor at the xylophone; Halliwell Hobbes is posing

The U.S. Senate, as recreated for *Mr. Smith Goes to Washington* (1939)

The senior senator, Claude Rains, and the junior, James Stewart, face off on the Senate floor

Stewart during the solo filibuster that climaxes *Mr. Smith*

Capra recently said of Cohn, "He was the toughest man I ever met."

It is not known what Cohn said about Capra. Too bad. But Garson Kanin once said, "I'd rather be Capra than God." To which many other directors might well add, "Amen."

Capra's crowning moment at Columbia—James Stewart and the Capitol dome epitomize the nation's two great strengths, its people and its institutions

THAT CERTAIN THING

(Released: January 1, 1928)

Director: Frank Capra
Story: Elmer Harris
Cameraman: Joe Walker
Film Editor: Arthur Roberts

Footage: 6047 ft.

Cast:
Viola Dana
Ralph Graves
Burr McIntosh

Aggie Herring
Carl Gerard
Sydney Crossley

SO THIS IS LOVE

(Released: February 6, 1928)

Director: Frank Capra
Story: Norman Springer
Adapter: Elmer Harris
Cameraman: Ray June

Footage: 5611 ft.

Cast:
Shirley Mason
William Collier, Jr.
Johnnie Walker
Ernest Adams

Carl Gerard
William H. Strauss
Gene Laverty

THE MATINEE IDOL

(Released: March 14, 1928)

Director: Frank Capra
Story: Robert Lord and
  Ernest Pagano
Continuity: Peter Milne
Adaptation: Elmer Harris
Cameraman: Phillip Tannura
Film editor: Arthur Roberts

Footage: 5923 ft.

Cast:
Bessie Love
Johnnie Walker
Lionel Belmore

Ernest Hilliard
Sidney D'Albrook
David Mir

THE WAY OF THE STRONG

(Released: June 19, 1926)

Director: Frank Capra
Story: William Counselman
Scenario: Peter Milne
Cameraman: Ben Reynolds

Footage: 5752 ft.

Cast:
Mitchell Lewis
Alice Day

Theodor Von Eltz
William Norton Bailey

SAY IT WITH SABLES

(Released: July 13, 1928)

Director: Frank Capra
Story:
  Frank Capra
  Peter Milne
Continuity: Dorothy Howell
Cameraman: Joe Walker, A.S.C.
Film editor: Arthur Roberts

Footage: 6401 ft.

Cast:
Francis X. Bushman
Helene Chadwick
Margaret Livingston
Arthur Rankin

June Nash
Alphonse Ethier
Edna Mae Cooper

SUBMARINE

(Released: August 28, 1928)

Director: Frank Capra
Story: Norman Springer
Continuity: Dorothy Howell
Cameraman: Joe Walker, A.S.C.

Footage: 8374 ft. (Sound)
  8192 ft (Silent)

Cast:
Jack Holt
Dorothy Revier
Ralph Graves

Arthur Rankin
Clarence Burton

THE POWER OF THE PRESS

(Released: October 31, 1928)

Producer: Jack Cohn
Director: Frank Capra
Story: Frederick A. Thompson
Adaptation—Continuity:
  Frederick A. Thompson
  Sonya Levien
Photography: Chet Lyons
  Ted Tetzlaff
Art Director: Harrison Wiley
Film Editor: Frank Atkinson

Assistant Director:
  Buddy Coleman

Footage: 6,465 ft.

Cast:
Douglas Fairbanks, Jr.
Jobyna Ralston
Mildred Harris
Philo McCullough
Wheeler Oakman
Robert Edeson
Edwards Davis
Del Henderson
Charles Clary

YOUNGER GENERATION

(Released: March 11, 1929)

Director: Frank Capra
Story: Fanny Hurst
Adaptation: Sonya Levien
Cameraman: Ted Tetzlaff

Footage: 7866 ft. (Sound)
  7246 ft. (Silent)

Cast:
Jean Hersholt
Lina Basquette
Richard Cortez
Rosa Rosanova
Rex Lease
Martha Franklin

Julanne Johnston
Jack Raymond
Sydney Crossley
Otto Fries
Julia Swayne Gordon
Donald Hall

THE DONOVAN AFFAIR

(Released: April 11, 1929)

Director: Frank Capra
Scenario: Dorothy Howell
From the Play by: Owen Davis
Dialogue: Howard J. Green
Cameraman: Ted Tetzlaff

Footage: 7140 ft. (Sound)
7189 ft. (Silent)

Cast:
Jack Holt
Dorothy Revier
William Collier, Jr.
John Roche
Fred Kelsey
Agnes Ayres
Hank Mann

Wheeler Oakman
Virginia Brown Faire
Alphonse Ethier
Edward Hearn
Ethel Wales
John Wallace

FLIGHT

(Released: November 1, 1929)

Director: Frank Capra
Story: Ralph Graves
Editors:
Ben Pivar
Maurice Wright
Gene Milford
Dialogue: Frank Capra
Sound Engineer: John Livadary

Mixing Engineer:
Harry Blanchard

Footage:
10,670 ft. (Sound)
9,005 ft. (Silent)

Cast:
Jack Holt
Lila Lee
Ralph Graves
Alan Roscoe
Harold Goodwin
Jimmy de la Cruze

LADIES OF LEISURE

(Released: April 5, 1930)

Director: Frank Capra
Ass't. Director: David Selman
Adapted from: The David Belasco
stage play *Ladies of the
Evening* by:
Milton H. Gropper
Editor: Maurice Wright
Adaptation and Dialogue:
Jo Swerling

Sound Engineer:
John Livadary
Mixing Engineer:
Harry Blanchard

Footage: 9277 ft.

Cast:
Barbara Stanwyck
Lowell Sherman
Ralph Graves
Marie Prevost
Nance O'Neil
George Fawcett
Johnnie Walker
Juliette Compton

RAIN OR SHINE

(Released: August 15, 1930)

Director: Frank Capra
Ass't. Director: Sam Nelson
Adaptation:
James Gleason
Maurice Marks
Editor: Maurice Wright
Dialogue and Continuity:
Dorothy Howell
Jo Swerling
Sound Engineer:
John P. Livadary
Mixing Engineer:
E. L. Brends

Cameraman: Joe Wanger

Footage:
8228 ft. (Sound)
8285 ft. (Silent)

Cast:
Joe Cook
Louise Fazenda
William Collier, Jr.
Tom Howard
David Chasen
Allan Roscoe
Adolph Milar
Clarence Muse
Ed Martindale
Nora Lane
Tyroll Davis

DIRIGIBLE

(Released: April 18, 1931)

Director: Frank Capra
Editor: Maurice Wright
Based on a story by:
 Lt. Comm. Frank Wilber Wead
Adaptation and dialogue:
 Jo Swerling
Continuity: Dorothy Howell

Footage: 10 reels

Cast:
Jack Holt
Ralph Graves
Fay Wray
Hobart Bosworth
Roscoe Karns

Harold Goodwin
Clarence Muse
Emmet Corrigan
Al Roscoe
Selmer Jackson

MIRACLE WOMAN

(Released: July 2!, 1931)

Director: Frank Capra
Producer: Harry Cohn
Editor: Maurice Wright
Based on the Play:
 Bless You Sister, **by:**
 John Meehan and Robert Riskin
Dialogue: Jo Swerling
Continuity: Dorothy Howell

Cameraman:
 Joe Walker, A.S.C.

Footage: 8370 ft.

Cast:
Barbara Stanwyck
David Manners
Sam Hardy
Beryl Mercer
Russell Hopton
Charles Middleton
Eddie Boland
Thelma Hill

PLATINUM BLONDE

(Released: October 30, 1931)

Director: Frank Capra
Producer: Harry Cohn
Editor: Gene Milford
Story:
 Harry E. Chandler
 Doug. E. Churchill
Dialogue: Robert Riskin
Adaptation: Jo Swerling
Continuity: Dorothy Howell
Cameraman: Joe Walker, A.S.C.

Footage: 8240 ft.

Cast:
Loretta Young
Robert Williams
Jean Harlow
Halliwell Hobbes
Reginald Owen

Edmund Breese
Donald Dillaway
Walter Catlett
Claude Allister
Louise Closser Hale

FORBIDDEN

(Released: January 15, 1932)

Director: Frank Capra
Producer: Harry Cohn
Editor: Maurice Wright
Story: Frank Capra
Adaptation and Dialogue:
 Jo Swerling
Cameraman: Joe Walker, A.S.C.

Footage: 7938 ft.

Cast:
Barbara Stanwyck
Adolph Menjou
Ralph Bellamy
Dorothy Peterson

Thomas Jefferson
Myrna Fresholt
Charlotte V. Henry
Oliver Eckhardt

AMERICAN MADNESS

(Released: August 15, 1932)

Director: Frank Capra
Producer: Harry Cohn
Editor: Maurice Wright
Story and Dialogue: Robert Riskin
Cameraman: Joe Walker, A.S.C.

Footage: 7093 ft.

Cast:

Walter Huston	Gavin Gordon
Pat O'Brien	Arthur Hoyt
Kay Johnson	Robert E. O'Connor
Constance Cummings	

BITTER TEA OF GENERAL YEN

(Released: January 6, 1933)

Director: Frank Capra
Editor: Edward Curtis
Based on the Story by:
Grace Zaring Stone
Screen Play: Edward Paramore
Musical Score: W. Frank Harling
Cameraman: Joe Walker, A.S.C.

Footage: 8105 ft.

Cast:

Barbara Stanwyck	Lucien Littlefield
Nils Asther	Richard Lee
Toshia Mori	Helen Jerome Eddy
Walter Connolly	Emmett Corrigan

LADY FOR A DAY

(Released: September 13, 1933)

Director: Frank Capra
Editor: Gene Havlick
Based on the Story by:
Damon Runyon
Screen Play and Dialogue:
Robert Riskin
Music Director:
Constantin Bakaleinikoff

Footage: 8928 ft.

Cast:

Warren William	Gene Parker
May Robson	Barry Norton
Guy Kibbee	Halliwell Hobbes
Glenda Farrell	Hobart Bosworth
Ned Sparks	Robert Emmett
Walter Connolly	O'Connor

BROADWAY BILL

(Released: November 21, 1934)

Director: Frank Capra
Editor: Gene Havlick
Based on the Story by:
Mark Hellinger
Screen Play: Robert Riskin
Cameraman: Joe Walker, A.S.C.

Footage: 9407 ft.

Cast:

Warner Baxter	Myrna Loy
Walter Connolly	Helen Vinson
Douglas Dumbrille	Raymond Walburn
Lynne Overman	Clarence Muse
Margaret Hamilton	Frankie Darro
Charles C. Wilson	Harry Todd
Ward Bond	Charles Levison
George Cooper	George Meeker
Jason Robards	Helen Flint
Helen Millard	Ed Tucker
Edmund Breese	Bob Tansill
Clara Blandick	Inez Courtney
Claude Gillingwater	Paul Harvey
James Blakely	Alan Hale

MR. DEEDS GOES TO TOWN

(Released: March 27, 1936)

Director: Frank Capra
Editor: Gene Havlick
Based on the Story by:
  Clarence Budington Kelland
Screen Play: Robert Riskin
Art Director:
  Stephen Goosson
Music Director:
  Howard Jackson
Costumes: Samuel Lange

Special Camera Effects:
  E. Roy Davidson
Cameraman:
  Joe Walker, A.S.C.

Footage: 10,617 ft.

Cast:
Gary Cooper
Jean Arthur
George Bancroft
Lionel Stander
Douglas Dumbrille
Raymond Walburn
H. B. Warner
Ruth Donnolly
Walter Catlett
John Wray

LOST HORIZON

(Released: February 17, 1937)

Director: Frank Capra
Editors:
  Gene Havlick
  Gene Milford
Based on the Novel by:
  James Hilton
Screen Play: Robert Riskin
Musical Score: Dmitri Tiomkin
Art Director: Stephen Goosson
Music Director: Max Steiner
Costumes: Ernst Dryden
Voices: Hall Johnson Choir

Special Camera Effects:
  E. Roy Davidson
  Ganahl Carson
Aerial Photography:
  Elmer Dyer, A.S.C.
Cameraman:
  Joe Walker, A.S.C.
Technical Advisor:
  Harrison Forman

Footage: 12,094 ft.

Cast:
Ronald Colman
Jane Wyatt
Edward Everett
  Horton
John Howard
Thomas Mitchell
Margo
Isabell Jewell
H. B. Warner
Sam Jaffe

YOU CAN'T TAKE IT WITH YOU

(Released: August 23, 1938)

Director: Frank Capra
Editor: Gene Havlick
Based on the Play by:
  George S. Kaufman and
  Moss Hart
Screen Play: Robert Riskin
Musical Score: Dmitri Tiomkin
Art Director: Stephen Goosson
Associate: Lionel Banks
Music Director: Morris Stoloff
Miss Arthur's Gowns:
  Bernard Newman
  Irene
Cameraman: Joe Walker, A.S.C.

Footage: 11,571 ft.

Cast:
Jean Arthur
Lionel Barrymore
James Stewart
Edward Arnold
Misha Auer
Ann Miller
Spring Byington
Samuel S. Binds
Donald Meek
H. B. Warner
Halliwell Hobbes

Dub Taylor
Mary Forbes
Lillian Yarbo
Eddie Anderson
Clarence Wilson
Josef Swickard
Harry Davenport
Ann Doran
Christian Rub
Bodel Rosing
Charles Lane

MR. SMITH GOES TO WASHINGTON

(Released: October 3, 1939)

Director: Frank Capra
Ass't. Director: Arthur S. Black
Editors:
  Gene Havlick
  Al Clark
Based on the Story by:
  Lewis R. Foster
Screen Play: Sidney Buchman
Musical Score: Dmitri Tiomkin
Art Director: Lionel Banks
Music Director: M. W. Stoloff
Montage Effects:
  Slavko Vorkapich
Gowns: Kalloch
Cameraman:
  Joe Walker, A.S.C.

Footage: 11,868 ft.

Cast:

Jean Arthur	Porter Hall
James Stewart	Pierre Watkin
Claude Rains	Charles Lane
Edward Arnold	William Demarest
Guy Kibbee	Dick Elliott
Thomas Mitchell	Billy Watson
Eugene Pallette	Delmar Watson
Beulah Bondi	John Russell
H. B. Warner	Harry Watson
Harry Carey	Gary Watson
Astrid Allwyn	Baby Dumpling
Ruth Donnelly	(Larry Simms)
Grant Mitchell	

Roscoe Karns and Walter Connally won't let Barrymore shoot himself: ''It would make too many people happy''

3 | The Screwball Comedies

COLUMBIA DIDN'T HOLD THE COPYRIGHT ON SCREWBALL comedies. After the enormous success of *It Happened One Night*, smart dialogue between sophisticated sparring partners and great supporting players became standard fare for all the studios who could come up with suitable scripts. But like port from Portugal or sherry from Spain, the product seemed superior when it was bottled (or in the case of films, canned) in the place of origin.

Capra concentrated on one or two films a year at most, and other directors were turned to the task of supplying the increasing public demand for the new genre of films. At about the time that *It Happened One Night* was in front of the cameras, another distinguished director was making one of his few appearances at Columbia: Howard Hawks. He was directing a comedy starring two of the rarest performers ever to face off in front of the lights —the theater's idol, John Barrymore and the movies' goddess, Carole Lombard. The picture was worthy of all three, Ben Hecht and Charles MacArthur's screen version of their smash play, *Twentieth Century*. While not conforming to all of the rules that

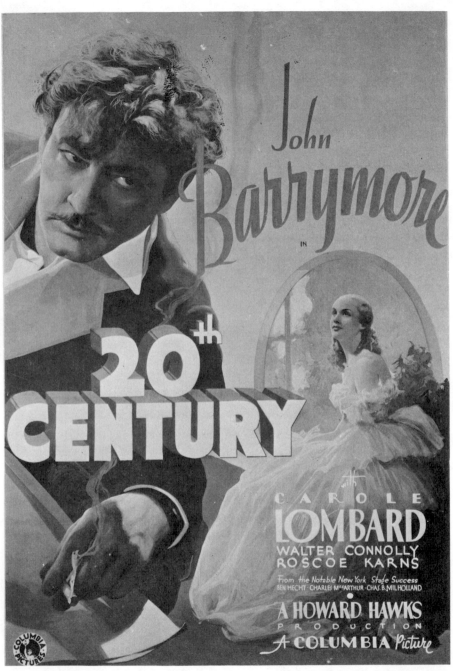

An ad for *Twentieth Century:* it's fabulous art, even if it doesn't tell us much about the movie (1934)

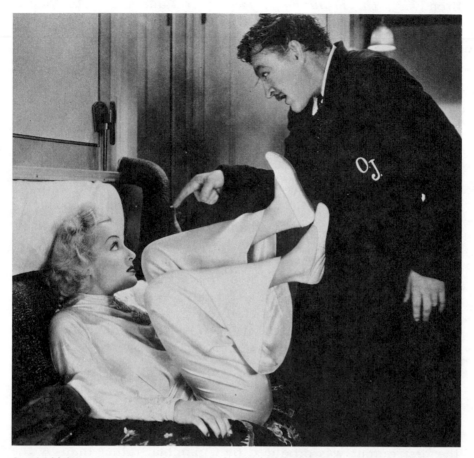

Carole kicks up a storm—and Barrymore in her compartment—on the *Twentieth Century*

define the screwballs, this delicious piece of backstage nonsense certainly belongs in any grouping of sophisticated comedy. Instead of the rich girl/poor boy or poor girl/rich boy leads of so many of the screwballs, it gives us instead the personages of Oscar Jaffe, Broadway impresario, and the star he had created, Lily Garland (neé Mildred Plotker). Barrymore and Lombard are near perfect in their parts, he as the erstwhile director having as many opportunities for histrionics as she does. As this Trilby flees her Svengali to take up a career in Hollywood, he follows her, and the epitome of glamorous travel in those pre-jet days, the Twentieth Century Limited, becomes the setting for their battles and, of course, their eventual reconciliation.

A half dozen or so years later, Hawks was to direct another Hecht-MacArthur opus for the studio. Their newspaper story for

Broadway, *The Front Page*, was cleverly adapted to provide a whopping good role for Rosalind Russell as a newswoman in and out of love with editor Cary Grant. The film was titled *His Girl Friday*, but Hildy Johnson is much more than a quasi-secretary. As snappily portrayed by Rosalind Russell at her best stride, Hildy is a reporter as used to getting her story as she is to getting her man. She and Grant work off each other in exactly the style they are each noted for, the dialogue is delivered at a lightning-quick pace, and the result is pure Hollywood 30s comedy.

That type of film was becoming more and more the directors' medium. There were expert farceurs around: The decade abounds with them, male and female both, stars and secondary players alike. But it took a very sure hand to keep things under control. Some films contained elements of slapstick that added to the effect, others would have been ruined by anything but the most underplayed mood. Thus, many of the directors who were to later make the most important films in Hollywood history polished their craft in the comedies of the 30s.

At Columbia, Capra had led the way. He had demanded and got unprecedented control over his films. Now the studio was able to attract other directors of top calibre like Hawks, and, while he still muttered and fussed over every penny spent, Cohn gave more than lip service to the one-picture, one-director concept that Capra espoused. That, and the less structured atmosphere of the Gower Street operation, often meant that some of the best output was produced by Columbia, rather than by the studios where the directors had much longer lasting affiliations.

Cohn often boasted that he kissed the feet of talent. He didn't add that was equally capable of kicking it in the ass. Thus, the top names came but didn't stay long. Happily, though, the brief tenures were still sufficiently long to produce brilliant results.

John Ford is a case in point. He took the Oscar four times for Best Director (plus twice for documentaries), and his output is unsurpassed. Yet his most notable early film was *The Whole Town's Talking*, made in 1935, and for Columbia. Classified with the screwballs, this off-beat film has moments of heavy drama that make it difficult to categorize. Much of its interest is in the dual performance of the inimitable Edward G. Robinson—who plays both a murderer hunted by the police and the murderer's mousy and meek look-alike, a clerk—and Jean Arthur—the sparkling bright girl who really loves the mouse.

In *The Whole Town's Talking*, Jean Arthur confronts mild-mannered Edward G. Robinson with his look-alike—the killer Mannion (1935)

Robinson meets the press, to his great consternation

Shot in the brooding darks and shadowy grays of 30s pictures, the story moved smoothly from its lighter to its deeper scenes, a chiaroscuro mastered under Capra's tutelage by Robert Riskin and his co-scripter, Jo Swerling. It was of a pattern with *Mr. Smith* and *Mr. Deeds* in that respect—marbling dramatic material with lighter moments for easier audience digestibility.

The rest of the so-called screwballs remain remarkably zany. The light-hearted titles are apt. *She Married Her Boss* connotes no sociological overtones whatever and the film doesn't attempt to deliver any. Claudette Colbert, fresh from *It Happened One Night*, paid Columbia another visit. (It was to be her last.) Admirably directed by Gregory La Cava, who had a sure feel for light comedy, it turned out to be one of the top films of the year. Colbert parried with and got Melvyn Douglas, another stand-by to be depended upon for this kind of action. The theme was the working girl's dream, the not-so-secret fantasy of secretaries, a major key played on in so many minor comedies of the Depression. *She Married Her Boss* said it all in those four little words, and said it better than most of the duplications that predictably followed right on its heels. Unlike Hildy Johnson, the Roz Russell part in *His Girl Friday*, who married and unmarried and remarried her boss, Colbert always put her department store owner before her department store career. Hildy *was* women's lib, but Julia (Colbert) never heard of it. (Come to think of it, except for Russell and maybe Joan Crawford, nobody in the 30s had!)

Another great director, Tay Garnett, was hired the same day as Gregory La Cava. Garnett, later to go on to *The Postman Always Rings Twice* and *Valley of Decision*, directed George Raft and Joan Bennett in a 1935 piece of gossamer called *She Couldn't Take It*. Another favorite Depression theme—the Rich Girl who is taught a lesson—was the basis of this flick.

More directorial greatness landed at Columbia in 1937. No novice at comedy, Leo McCarey had already directed the Marx Brothers and had paired one of the most enduring of all duos, Laurel and Hardy. But the film he produced and directed at Columbia was all slickness and sophistication.

His leading lady was Irene Dunne. Although most of her career up until that point had been spent in weepy women roles, she had made an impression of another sort on Columbia executives. She had starred a little earlier in the studio's decidedly screwball effort, *Theodora Goes Wild*. As the spinster-turned-author in that charming film, she had been a delight. It was almost a double role—the quiet girl from the small New England town who has

In *She Married Her Boss*, Melvyn Douglas' importance is designated by the two phones on his desk; Claudette Colbert's devotion to her career by the severity of her tailored suit (1935)

A novel answer to the parking problem is explored by Joan Bennett and George Raft in *She Couldn't Take It* (1935)

somehow managed to write a racy best seller. Again, Melvyn Douglas turned up to help still another confused young thing find herself. Going from prim Theodora to pseudonymous Caroline wasn't the easiest thing in the world to do. But Dunne did it in style.

A New York Yankee in a Connecticut court: Melvyn Douglas tries to help Irene Dunne in *Theodora Goes Wild* (1936)

Thomas Mitchell, Spring Byington, and the ladies of the town question both sides of Irene's personality

Love at last, the invariable happy ending to any screwball comedy

To play opposite her, McCarey chose another actor more noted for heavier roles, Cary Grant. (*His Girl Friday* was made three years later.) The epitome of male glamour even then, Grant was to add another important facet to one of Hollywood's most enduring careers with this little gem.

It was called *The Awful Truth*, and there was nothing awful about it. It was a sheer delight, the story of a couple, obviously still in love, but through a series of misunderstandings, separated and on the verge of divorce. Grant and Dunne played it to joyous raptures from everyone, even the public which was accustomed to seeing each of them in another kind of role completely. Both stars gave performances that radiated through this pre-conditioning that had typecast so many film personalities into limited careers.

The film made lots of money, and that drew raptures from Harry Cohn. McCarey worked in an extremely unorthodox way,

Cary Grant's the boss, but Rosalind Russell does all the work as *His Girl Friday* (1940)

Crawford and Russell were famous for clothes in the 30s, but Irene Dunne's hats (like Jean Arthur's) are in a class by themselves; with Cary Grant and judge Paul Stanton in *The Awful Truth* (1937)

Cary's hat is pretty *Awful* too, and that's the *Truth!*

but the boss was now willing to overlook that. He offered the director a lucrative, long-term contract.

But McCarey didn't overlook Cohn's own past performance. He fled. In his long, Oscar-studded career, spanning the next three decades, he never worked for Columbia again. It was one way to bat a thousand in Harry Cohn's league—make one hit and never come back.

But a more than one-shot director soon landed on the lot. George Cukor arrived in 1938, a banner year for comedy at Columbia. Capra was shooting the picture that would soon take Best Picture and Director honors, *You Can't Take It with You* at the same time Alexander Hall was putting a stellar cast through its paces. He had Joan Blondell, the ever-present Melvyn Douglas, Mary Astor, and Jerome Cowan in a *Thin Man* shadow called *There's Always a Woman*. And 30s favorite Madeleine Carroll, Francis Lederer, and the irrepressible Mischa Auer were doing *It's All Yours* for Elliot Nugent (director of many film comedies but most remembered for his play co-written with James Thurber, *The Male Animal*).

Lew Ayres plays Kate's brother, and Edward Everett Horton and Jean Dixon are the eccentric puppeteering Potters

100

After the usual complications, Cary Grant and Katharine Hepburn are ready to ▶ embark on their life-long *Holiday* (1938)

Cary Grant and Katharine Hepburn—as polished and handsome a pair of lovers as the screen has seen

Cukor was new on Gower Street, but to him fell the honor of directing the first appearance on the lot of one of the finest actresses and greatest stars of all time, Katharine Hepburn. The film was based on a play by the great American playwright, Philip Barry, both editions called *Holiday*. Barry was one of the period's keenest observers of manners and mores, juicy meats for the famous Hepburn jaw. (He also wrote one of her greatest triumphs both on stage and screen, *The Philadelphia Story*.)

Cary Grant was well at home now in the role of dashing suitor (so well that he was to go to *Philadelphia* with Hepburn later) and the supporting players were super: Lew Ayres, Binnie Barnes, and that mainstay of quiet comedy, Edward Everett Horton.

Cukor was one director with whom Harry Cohn's alleged foot-kissing act went over—he was to return to the studio to make many important and successful films. (Many of Hepburn's finest pictures were his as well.)

In *Holiday*, Grant starts out to win the hand of Hepburn's sister, but damned if as soon as he gets it he doesn't realize that it's the free-spirited Kate he really wants to whirl through life with. The rest of her stodgy family doesn't realize that *Holiday* isn't simply the name of the film; it's Cary's attitude toward life, and who but Hepburn could be expected to understand *that*? Remember, we're still in the midst of the Depression. It's a charming film.

Capra was doing his last Columbia effort, *Mr. Smith Goes To Washington,* as the decade drew to a close. Melvyn Douglas was fooling around with Joan Blondell and Virginia Bruce in *Good Girls Go to Paris* and *There's That Woman Again*, respectively. Both these last were rather minor efforts, and Capra's Jefferson Smith did have a disturbing number of things in common with Longfellow Deeds, if truth be told. (The presence of Jean Arthur was one of them, but that's not a point to quibble with, now or ever. Her quality of constancy is ever-welcome, something like the sunset. It's always there, always composed of the same elements, but somehow, never quite the same.) But Smith has the same reaction as Deeds to the press; for example, he hits reporters in the nose. Deeds hated New York; Smith hates Washington. Deeds wanted to donate land to impoverished farmers, his counterpart of two years later wants to give it to impoverished boys. The formula worked well, with critics and audiences alike, but the art of comedy was not notably advanced.

It was unusual for a studio of Columbia's size to put three top stars in a single film

This is not to suggest that funny films receded completely with the decade and the end of the Depression. Like the rest of the country and the world, things took a different turn. Some of the elements that defined screwball comedy, as well as some of its most accomplished performers, continued to show up on the screen. But screwball worked because it reflected its time and answered a need of that time. Now directors had a new set of facts to work with. The world was becoming embroiled in war, war so vast and on such a scale that few movies could be produced that didn't take some accounting of the global upheaval.

George Stevens came to Columbia at about this time. His first film for the company was *The Talk of the Town* with Cary Grant, Jean Arthur, and Ronald Colman. It didn't deal directly with the war, but it had a great deal to say about freedom versus fascism within the framework of a small American town. It takes the part of the individual and the need for law based on human understanding, principles that the nation would soon go to war to protect. It moves out of the have/have-not framework of the 30s for its moral base.

If the message was deep, the action that enfolded it kept the film from being an exercise in wartime propaganda. The three

The climactic courtroom scene in *Talk of the Town*

leads were deft and warm in very convincing parts and Stevens certainly kept things moving.

So, by the way, did Melvyn Douglas in other post-Depression films. During 1940, *He Stayed for Breakfast* with Loretta Young. He and Fred MacMurray were *Too Many Husbands* for Jean Arthur. The next year Ruth Hussey was *Our Wife* but Rosalind Russell was his own kissless bride in *This Thing Called Love*. The year after *that*, he made *They All Kissed the Bride*, with Joan Crawford. No wonder Douglas enlisted in the army in '42. It was almost in self-defense. (In his military career, this fine actor rose from private to major. When he resumed acting and directing after the war, he went to the top of the profession.)

One of the best of the wartime comedies was Stevens' *The More the Merrier*. Jean Arthur, Joel McCrea, and Charles Coburn tried to make the best of the housing shortage in that beleaguered town of Washington, D.C., to wonderful effect. Mr. Coburn's portrayal of Benjamin Dingle won the venerable gentleman the Oscar for Best Supporting Actor of the year.

As the war wore on, audiences needed some degree of escape

The More the Merrier had Charles Coburn playing Cupid for Jean Arthur and Joel McCrea; Richard Gaines has the upper hand, but not for long (1943)

Jean Arthur, Cary Grant, and Ronald Colman in one of the more serious moments in *The Talk of the Town* (1942)

from its unrelenting grimness. There were all too few subjects that lent themselves to the gentle fun-poking of *The More the Merrier*. Since rich boys and/or girls no longer seemed natural, the screen turned to the supernatural.

Here Comes Mr. Jordan seemed to be taking place in a different time-and-space dimension. Robert Montgomery, less wooden than usual, as he should be in so ethereal a part, is a just-dead prizefighter who is permitted to return to Earth. (Successful premature births had been a fact of life for some time now; *Mr. Jordan* ushered in the era of successful premature deaths, at least for movie folk.) Unable through celestial blundering to return him to his original form, Mr. J. gives the deceased Joe another corpus to inhabit. If this is too confusing, then what follows of the plot will be even more so. Rather than dwell on its intricacies, time and the reader would be better served by a brief discussion of the contribution to this film made by one of the greatest of the character actors, James Gleason. Gleason is privy to the convolutions of the plot that keep bringing the supposedly deceased

Here Comes Mr. Jordan (Claude Rains) to return sax-playing prizefighter Robert Montgomery back to earth to confound manager James Gleason (1941)

108

Montgomery and Rains are joined by Evelyn Keyes, who's for real, and Edward Everett Horton, who isn't

Joe back, and his belief in each reappearance forces the viewer to believe as well, and thus holds the credibility of the film intact. No mean feat, this, and it took an actor like Gleason to fill this key role.

The venerable Edward Everett Horton and the dignified Claude Rains (who played Mr. Jordan) are among the more-or-less-than earthly folk who inhabit this well-received fantasy. It was one of the few films in the supernatural genre to make a lot of money, and imitations as well as self-spawned sequels were not long in coming—in Hollywood they never are. Additionally, the film reaped several Oscar nominations and two wins: Best Original Story, by Harry Segall, and Best Screenplay, by Sidney Buchman and Seton I. Miller.

But Columbia's next important comedy signaled a return to reality. Like *The More the Merrier*, it was concerned with inadequate housing, but of an entirely different nature. This time the apartment was located in a Greenwich Village basement and its tenants were not strangers thrown together by the vagaries of war, but two sisters thrown together by the necessity of seeking careers in the big city.

The film was *My Sister Eileen* in the first of its several translations to the screen. It starred Rosalind Russell and Janet Blair as the two neophytes from Ohio determined to make it big in the big town.

Alexander Hall, who directed *Mr. Jordan* with its other-worldly scenes, is equally at home in the rambunctious basement level apartment that the girls are duped into renting, and that quickly becomes the *mise-en-scene* for all sorts of hilarious characters and carryings-on. An ex-football hero who does their ironing, the Brazilian navy arriving in force and in a conga line, and a double-talking Greek landlord broadly but well played by funny George Tobias, all become part of the girls' settling-in process. No philosophical sideswipes at "New York types" in this flick: The ladies from the heartland are in the big town to make it. At film's end they are each well on their way. It's all fine fun.

Charles Vidor, another extremely adept hand at comedy, had directed Irene Dunne and Charles Boyer in a funny story about a French sculptor and a lady mayor, called *Together Again*. Then he turned to material that dealt directly with the war. This time Irene is not a widow but the wife of a very much alive although slightly overaged reporter who enlists in the army. Max, played by Alexander Knox, is having trouble keeping up with the younger recruits, so Polly writes the weekly editorials that he has promised his publisher (crotchety old Charles Coburn, who else?) he will continue to dispatch to the failing journal. This leads to the usual screwball type complications, but the story is fresh and lively, the problems during wartime of the *Over 21* set (that's what it was called) striking an unhackneyed calibration midst the young-love-separation-and-sufferings situation that keyed most romantic films of those years. Sidney Buchman produced, from his screenplay based on Ruth Gordon's theater piece. Considering that it was both comedy and wartime, the film has a quiet air about it, much in keeping with the "apple-pie order" that Polly-Irene espouses in the editorials allegedly written by her spouse.

Screwball comedy had peaked earlier and slowly trickled its way down the inevitable decline in popularity that marks the end of a trend. It had been proven a surprisingly durable form, given the meager contents of even the best of them. Directors turned to projects that were of greater interest to themselves, and the studios were naturally reluctant to place top-salaried stars in vehicles of diminishing box-office returns. The screwball comedies

My Sister Eileen: Rosalind Russell, Janet Blair, and the "Brazilian" navy (1942)

had a unique kind of charm that helped ease audiences out of their own troubles for a few hours, and at that task the genre performed admirably.

By the time the world conflict was over, the earth had become a totally different place than anyone had ever known. There was a stridency, a harsher reality, a loss of innocence that had not been as noticeable at the end of World War I three decades before. Then, the world had turned from the ugliness of war to the never-never land of the roaring 20s—the jazz age with the Charleston and bathtub gin; nothing serious, nothing sacred. Just a good time.

The doggie in the window and the Chagall on the wall help spell home sweet home for the sisters from Ohio

But the terrors of New York still throw them sometimes

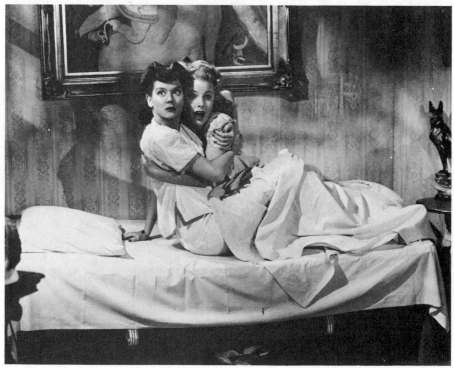

Charles Boyer, Irene Dunne, and Mona Freeman are all *Together Again* (1944)

World War II was to have no such denouement. Comedy will always exist, thank God, but its output was to become only of sporadic interest in films. There would be the isolated funny movies, sometimes better than ever as subject matter was broadened with the new moral leniency, but no outpouring of dozens of predictably funny movies every year. Soon television would demonstrate its insatiable appetite for what became known as situation comedies, but except for their being on film, they had no relationship to the inspired art of the screwball comedies at their zaniest best.

It was fun while it lasted, and for fun, it lasted a very long time.

The Screwball Comedies : Appendix
TWENTIETH CENTURY

(Released: May 11, 1934)

Director: Howard Hawks
Editor: Gene Havlick
Based on the Play by:
  Charles MacArthur, Ben Hecht,
  Charles Mulholland
Screen Play;
  Charles MacArthur
  Ben Hecht
Cameraman: Joseph August, A.S.C.

Footage: 8485 ft.

Cast:
John Barrymore
Walter Connolly
Charles Levison
Dale Fuller
Billie Seward
Clifford Thomson
James B. Burtis
Gi-Gi Parrish
Edgar Kennedy

Carole Lombard
Roscoe Karns
Etienne Giradot
Ed Gargan
Snowflake
Herman Bing
Lee Kohlmer
Pat Flagherty

LADY BY CHOICE

(Released: October 2, 1934)

Director: David Burton
Editor: Viola Lawrence
Based on the Story by:
  Dwight Taylor
Screen Play: Jo Swerling
Cameraman: Ted Tetzlaff

Footage: 7039 ft.

Cast:
Carole Lombard
Roger Pryor
Walter Connolly
Arthur Hohl
Raymond Walburn

James Burke
Henry Kolker
Mariska Aldrich
John Boyle

THE WHOLE TOWN'S TALKING

(Released: February 7, 1935)

Director: John Ford
Editor: Viola Lawrence
Based on the Story by:
  W. R. Burnett
Screen Play:
  Jo Swerling
  Robert Riskin
Cameraman: Joseph August, A.S.C.

Footage: 8305 ft.

Cast:
Edward G. Robinson
Arthur Hohl
Arthur Byron
Paul Harvey
Etienne Giradot
J. Farrel McDonald
Effie Ellsler

Jean Arthur
Wallace Ford
Donald Meek
Ed Brophy
James Donlan
John Wray

SHE MARRIED HER BOSS

(Released: August 19, 1935)

Director: Gregory La Cava
Editor: Richard Cahoon
Story: Thyra Samter Winslow
Screen Play: Sidney Buchman
Art Director: Stephen Goosson
Cameraman: Leon Shamroy, A.S.C.

Footage: 8147 ft.

Cast:
Claudette Colbert
Melvyn Douglas
Michael Bartlett
Raymond Walburn
Jean Dixon
Katherine Alexander

Edith Fellows
Grace Hale
Clara Kimball Young
Charles E. Arnt
Schuyler Shaw

SHE COULDN'T TAKE IT

(Released: October 9, 1935)

Director: Tay Garnett
Editor: Gene Havlick
Story: Gene Town and
   Graham Baker
Art Director: Stephen Goosson
Cameraman: Leon Shamroy

Cast:
George Raft
Joan Bennett
Walter Connolly
Billie Burke
Lloyd Nolan

Wallace Ford
James Blakely
Alan Mowbray
William Tannen
Donald Meek

Footage: 7148 ft.

THEODORA GOES WILD

(Released: November 5, 1936)

Director: Richard Boleslawski
Associate Producer: Everett Riskin
Editor: Otto Meyer
Story: Mary McCarthy
Screen Play: Sidney Buchman
Art Director: Stephen Goosson
Music Director: M. W. Stoloff
Gowns: Bernard Newman

Cast:
Irene Dunne
Melvyn Douglas
Thomas Mitchell
Thurston Hall
Elisabeth Risdon
Margaret McWade

Spring Byington
Nana Bryant
Henry Kolker
Leona Marich
Robert Craig
Frederick Burton

Footage: 8788 ft.

IT'S ALL YOURS

(Released: July 26, 1937)

Director: Elliot Nugent
Producer: William Perlberg
Editor: Gene Havlick
Story: Adelaide Heilbron
Screen Play: Mary C. McCall, Jr.
Art Director: Stephen Goosson
Music Director: M. W. Stoloff
Gowns: Kalloch
Jewelry: Talbert & Hoeller, Inc.

Director of Photography:
   Henry Freulich, A.S.C.

Footage: 7373 ft.

Cast:
Madeleine Carroll
Francis Lederer
Mischa Auer
Grace Bradley
Victor Kilian
George McKay
Charles Waldron
J. C. Nugent
Richard Carle
Arthur Hoyt

THE AWFUL TRUTH

(Released: October 15, 1937)

Director: Leo McCarey
Associate Producer:
   Everett Riskin
Editor: Al Clark
Based on the Play by:
   Arthur Richman
Screen Play: Vina Delmar

Interiors: Babs Johnstone
Gowns: Kalloch
Cameraman:
   Joe Walker, A.S.C.

Footage: 8376 ft.

Cast:
Irene Dunne
Cary Grant
Ralph Bellamy
Alexander D'Arcy
Cecil Cunningham
Molly Lamont

Music: Ben Oakland
Lyrics: Milton Drake
Art Directors:
  Stephen Goosson
  Lionel Banks
Music Director: M. W. Stoloff

Esther Dale
Joyce Compton
Robert Allen
Robert Warwick
Mary Forbes

THERE'S ALWAYS A WOMAN

(Released: March 16, 1938)

Director: Alexander Hall
Editor: Viola Lawrence
Story: Wilson Collison
Screen Play: Gladys Lehman
Art Director: Stephen Goosson
Associate: Lionel Banks
Music Director: M. W. Stoloff
Gowns: Kalloch

Director of Photography:
  Henry Freulich, A.S.C.

Footage: 7442 ft.

Cast:
Joan Blondell
Melvyn Douglas
Mary Astor
Frances Drake
Jerome Cowan
Robert Paige
Thurston Hall
Pierre Watkin
Walter Kingsford
Lester Mathews

HOLIDAY

(Released: May 24, 1938)

Director: George Cukor
Producer: Everett Riskin
Editors:
  Otto Meyer
  Al Clark
Based on the Play by:
  Philip Barry
Screen Play:
  Donald Ogden Stewart
  Sidney Buchman
Art Director: Stephen Goosson

Assistant Art Director:
  Lionel Banks
Music Director:
  M. W. Stoloff
Interiors: Babs Johnstone
Gowns: Kalloch
Jewelry: Paul Flato
Cameraman: Franz Planer

Footage: 8376 ft.

Cast:
Katharine Hepburn
Cary Grant
Doris Nolan
Lew Ayres
Edward Everett
  Horton
Henry Kolker
Binnie Barnes
Jean Dixon
Henry Daniell

THERE'S THAT WOMAN AGAIN

(Released: December 15, 1938)

Director: Alexander Hall
Assistant Producer:
  B. B. Kahane
Editor: Viola Lawrence
Story: Gladys Lehman
Screen Play:
  Philip G. Epstein
  James Edward Grant
Art Director: Lionel Banks
Music Director: M. W. Stoloff
Interior Decorations:
  Babs Johnstone

Director of Photography:
  Joe Walker, A.S.C.

Footage: 6719 ft.

Cast:
Melvyn Douglas
Virginia Bruce
Margaret Lindsay
Stanley Ridges
Gordon Oliver
Tom Dugan
Don Beddoe
Jonathan Hale
Pierre Watkin
Paul Harvey

116

GOOD GIRLS GO TO PARIS

(Released: June 20, 1939)

Director: Alexander Hall
Producer: William Perlberg
Editor: Al Clark
Original Story:
  Lenore Coffee
  William Joyce Cowen
Screen Play:
  Gladys Lehman
  Ken Englund
Art Director: Lionel Banks
Music Director: M. W. Stoloff
Gowns: Kalloch

Director of Photography:
  Henry Freulich, A.S.C.

Footage: 7039 ft.

Cast:
Melvyn Douglas
Joan Blondell
Walter Connolly
Alan Curtis
Joan Perry
Isabel Jeans
Stanley Brown
Alexander D'Arcy
Henry Hunter
Clarence Kolb
Howard Hickman

HIS GIRL FRIDAY

(Released: December 29, 1939)

Director: Howard Hawks
Editor: Gene Havlick
Based on the Play, *The Front Page*
  by: Ben Hecht and
  Charles MacArthur
Screen Play: Charles Lederer
Art Director: Lionel Banks
Music Director: M. W. Stoloff
Gowns: Kalloch
Cameraman: Joe Walker, A.S.C.

Footage: 8430 ft.

Cast:
Cary Grant
Rosalind Russell
Ralph Bellamy
Gene Lockhart
Porter Hall
Ernest Truex
Cliff Edwards
Clarence Kolb
Roscoe Karns
Frank Jenks

Regis Toomey
Abner Biberman
Frank Orth
John Qualen
Helen Mack
Alma Kruger
Billy Gilbert
Pat West
Edwin Maxwell

TOO MANY HUSBANDS

(Released: March 21, 1940)

Director: Wesley Ruggles
Assistant Director: Arthur Black
Editors:
  Otto Mayer
  William Lyon
Based on the Play by:
  Somerset Maugham
Screen Play: Claude Binyon
Musical Score:
  Frederick Hollander

Art Director:
  Lionel Banks
Music Director:
  M. W. Stoloff
Director of Photography:
  Joe Walker, A.S.C.

Footage: 7475 ft.

Cast:
Jean Arthur
Fred MacMurray
Melvyn Douglas
Harry Davenport
Dorothy Peterson
Melville Cooper
Edgar Buchanan
Tom Dugan

HE STAYED FOR BREAKFAST

(Released: August 22, 1940)

Director: Alexander Hall
Assistant Director:
  William Mull

Musical Score:
  Werner R. Heyman
Art Director: Lionel Banks

Cast:
Loretta Young
Melvin Douglas

Producer: B. P. Schulberg
Editor: Viola Lawrence
Based on the Play, *Liberte
    Provisoire,* by: Michel Duran
Adaptation: Sidney Howard
Screen Play:
    P. J. Wolfson
    Michael Fressier
    Ernest Vadja

Music Director:
    M. W. Stoloff
Gowns: Irene
    Kalloch
Director of Photography:
    Joe Walker, A.S.C.

Footage: 8075 ft.

Alan Marshal
Eugene Pallette
Una O'Connor
Curt Bois
Leonid Kinskey

THIS THING CALLED LOVE

(Released: January 2, 1941)

Director: Alexander Hall
Assistant Director:
    William Mull
Producer: William Perlberg
Editor: Viola Lawrence
Based on the Play by:
    Edwin Burke
Screen Play:
    George Seaton
    Ken Englund
    P. J. Wolfson
Art Director: Lionel Banks
Music Director: M. W. Stoloff
Miss Russell's Gowns: Irene

Director of Photography:
    Joe Walker, A.S.C.

Footage: 8664 ft.

Cast:
Rosalind Russell
Melvyn Douglas
Binnie Barnes
Allyn Joslyn
Gloria Dickson
Lee J. Cobb
Gloria Holden
Paul McGrath
Leona Maricle
Don Beddoe
Rosina Galli
Sig Arno

HERE COMES MR. JORDAN

(Released: July 23, 1941)

Director: Alexander Hall
Producer: Everett Riskin
Editor: Viola Lawrence
Based on the Play by:
    Harry Segall
Screen Play: Sidney Buchman
Music: Frederick Hollander
Art Director: Lionel Banks
Assistant Art Director:
    William Mull
Music Director: M. W. Stoloff

Gowns: Edith Head
Cameraman:
    Joe Walker, A.S.C.

Cast:
Robert Montgomery
Evelyn Keyes
Claude Rains
Rita Johnson
Edward Everett
    Horton
James Gleason
John Emery
Donald MacBride
Don Costello
Halliwell Hobbes
Benny Rubin

OUR WIFE

(Released: August 4, 1941)

Director: John M. Stahl
Assistant Director:
    Ridgeway Callow
Associate Producer: Irving Starr

Screen Play:
    P. J. Wolfson
Musical Score:
    Leo Shuken

Cast:
Melvyn Douglas
Ruth Hussey
Ellen Drew

118

Editor: Gene Havlick
Based on the Play by:
  Lillian Day
  Lyon Mearson

Music Director:
  M. W. Stoloff
Director of Photography:
  Franz E. Planer

Charles Coburn
John Hubbard
Harvey Stephens
Theresa Harris

THEY ALL KISSED THE BRIDE

(Released: June 1, 1942)

Director: Alexander Hall
Assistant Director: William Mull
Producer: Edward Kaufman
Editor: Viola Lawrence
Based on the Story by:
  Gina Kaus
  Andrew P. Solt
Screen Play: P. J. Wolfson
Music: Werner R. Heyman
Art Director: Lionel Banks
Associate: Cary Odell
Music Director: M. W. Stoloff
Gowns: Irene
Director of Photography:
  Joe Walker, A.S.C.

Cast:
Joan Crawford
Melvyn Douglas
Roland Young
Billie Burke
Allen Jenkins
Andrew Tombes
Helen Parrish

Emory Parnell
Mary Treen
Nydia Westman
Ivan Simpson
Roger Clark
Gordon Jones
Edward Gargan

THE TALK OF THE TOWN

(Released: July 21, 1942)

Director: George Stevens
Assistant Director:
  Norman Demins
Producer: George Stevens
Associate Producer: Fred Guiol
Editor: Otto Meyer
Based on the Story by:
  Sidney Harmon
Screen Play:
  Irwin Shaw
  Sidney Buchman
Adaptation: Dale Van Every
Music: Frederick Hollander
Art Director: Lionel Banks

Associate Art Director:
  Rudolph Sternad
Music Director:
  M. W. Stoloff
Montage Effects:
  Donald Starling
Gowns for Miss Arthur:
  Irene
Cameraman:
  Ted Tetzlaff, A.S.C.

Cast:
Cary Grant
Jean Arthur
Ronald Colman
Edgar Buchanan
Glenda Farrell
Charles Dingle
Emma Dunn
Rex Ingram
Leonid Kinskey
Tom Tyler
Don Beddoe

MY SISTER EILEEN

(Released: August 27, 1942)

Director: Alexander Hall
Assistant Director:
  William Mull
Producer: Max Gordon
Editor: Viola Lawrence

Music Director:
  M. W. Stoloff
Interiors: Ray Babcock
Cameraman:
  Joe Walker, A.S.C.

Cast:
Rosalind Russell
Brian Aherne
Janet Blair
George Tobias

Based on the Play by:
Joseph Fields
and Jerome Chodorov
Adopted from the Stories by:
Ruth McKenny
Screen Play:
Joseph Fields
Jerome Chodorov
Art Director: Lionel Banks
Associate Art Director:
Cary Odell

Grant Mitchell
Elizabeth Patterson
June Havoc
Frank Sully
Allyn Joslyn
Gordon Jones
Richard Quine
Donald MacBride
Clyde Fillmore
Miss Jeff Donnell

THE MORE THE MERRIER

(Released: March 26, 1943)

Director: George Stevens
Assistant Director:
Norman Demings
Producer: George Stevens
Associate Producer: Fred Guiol
Editor: Otto Meyer
Story:
Robert Russell
Frank Ross
Screen Play:
Robert Russell
Frank Ross
Richard Flournoy
Lewis R. Foster
Music: Leigh Harline

Torpedo Song:
Henry Myers
Edward Eliscu
Jay Gorney
Art Director: Lionel Banks
Associate Art Director:
Rudolph Sternard
Music Director
M. W. Stoloff
Interiors: Ray Babcock
Cameraman:
Ted Tetzlaff, A.S.C.

Cast:
Jean Arthur
Joel McCrea
Charles Coburn
Richard Gaines
Bruce Bennett
Frank Sully
Don Douglas
Clyde Fillmore
Stanley Clements

TOGETHER AGAIN

(Released: October 30, 1944)

Director: Charles Vidor
Editor: Otto Meyer
Story: Stanley Russell and
Herbert Biberman
Screen Play:
Virginia Van Upp
F. Hugh Herbert
Musical Score:
Werner R. Heyman
Art Directors:
Stephen Goosson
Van Nest Polglase

Set Director: Ray Babcock
Gowns: Jean Louis
Director of Photography:
Joe Walker, A.S.C.

Cast:
Irene Dunne
Charles Boyer
Charles Coburn
Mona Freeman
Jerome Courtland
Elizabeth Patterson
Charles Dingle

OVER 21

(Released: July 25, 1945)

Director: Charles Vidor
Assistant Director: Ray Nazarro

Music Director:
M. W. Stoloff

Cast:
Irene Dunne

120

Producer: Sidney Buchman
Editor: Otto Meyer
Based on the Play by:
  Ruth Gordon
Screen Play: Sidney Buchman
Musical Score: Marlin Skiles
Art Director: Stephen Goosson

Set Director: Louis Diage
Gowns: Jean Louis
Cameraman:
  Rudolph Mate, A.S.C.

Footage: 6332 ft.

Alexander Knox
Charles Coburn
Jeff Donnell
Loren Patrick
Phil Brown
Cora Witherspoon
Charles Evans

4 | The Stars

"What's in a name?"
 —William Shakespeare in *Romeo and Juliet*
"What's in a name?"
 —Harry Cohn in his front office

HARRIET LAKE BECAME ANN SOTHERN, BILL BEEDLE became William Holden, Margarita Cansino became Rita Hayworth, Marilyn Novak became Kim Novak. They all became stars.*

Harry Cohn liked to change people's names. It added to his feeling of control over them. It also enhanced the new image he was creating. And he did create images, some of them incredibly long lasting and pervasive: the Love Goddess (numbers one and two—Hayworth and Novak respectively), Golden Boy (after the actor became a millionaire, the moniker Golden Holden really stuck).

Columbia films had done much to advance the careers of stars it had employed on loan-out. When Clark Gable returned to MGM from his supposed exile at Columbia for *It Happened One Night*, his salary was tripled. Similar things happened to

---

*Betty Miller became Joan Perry. She never became a star, but she did become Mrs. Harry Cohn, and later Mrs. Laurence Harvey.

Before the golden girl, there was a *Golden Boy*—William Holden as the fighter, Adolph Menjou as his manager (1939)

The romantic interest in the Clifford Odets-based drama—Barbara Stanwyck and William Holden in *Golden Boy* (1939)

many other names. But the only star whom Columbia had added to the cinematic firmament and retained on its own lot was Jean Arthur.

Cohn didn't want to be just a filmmaker. He wanted to be a star-maker, too. Columbia's burgeoning fortunes during the 30s and early 40s could be both utilized and increased by some home-grown talent. All of the other major studios had stables of glamorous actresses, and now Cohn wanted his.

Surprisingly, he was to develop a major male star first. William Holden got a lot of attention as Cohn's *Golden Boy* lead, and Columbia owned half of his contract, in partnership with Paramount. He made a number of pictures on loan-out as well as for Columbia, but his was a slowly rising career which was not aided by much effort from Harry Cohn on Holden's behalf.

It wasn't until after the war that Holden made much impact on anybody. He was solid and reliable, never the dashing hero of the Gable-Grant-Power type, nor the wholesome hero of Cooper-Stewart proportions. But he did figure in some of the most important of Columbia's post-war films: *Born Yesterday* in 1950, playing well to Judy Holliday's unforgettable Billie Dawn; *Picnic* in 1956, very macho, especially dancing sans shirt with Kim Novak; *The Bridge on the River Kwai* in 1957, his heroics in the latter part of the film somewhat out of tune with the low-key drama of the rest.

Appearing in such prestigious pictures enhanced his career greatly, and Holden was able to write his own ticket. The Cohns' mills ground slowly, but in some cases, they ground exceedingly fine. Never a headline-maker, Holden made his consistency work to build a sizeable personal fortune.

Of much more moment to Cohn and the rest of the world was his next creation—the glamour queen he had always wanted. With Rita Hayworth, nee Margarita Cansino, Columbia had a star. And she could be lent to other studios—a satisfying role-reversal for Harry Cohn—making Columbia the beneficiary of all the promotion behind her loan-out films. And like a true star, she would soon attract the kind and quantity of publicity that money couldn't buy.

But Columbia started her off slowly. The public saw a peep of her in Howard Hawks' *Only Angels Have Wings*, but it was a showy little part that brought her attention. She had bit parts in some smaller films, such as *Blondie on a Budget*, and other studios had given her a few "also-appearing" parts. In 1941, though, Warners did well by her with *Strawberry Blonde*, which featured James Cagney, as did 20th with *Blood and Sand*, starring Tyrone Power.

The momentum had begun, and Harry Cohn picked it up. Margarita Cansino had been a dark-haired Spanish dancer; Rita Hayworth was an auburn-tressed star. Somewhere along the line during the transformation, Harry Cohn remembered that she had been a Spanish dancer in her former life and decided to star her in a musical. (The singing had to be dubbed, but so what? She already had a brand new hairline, two inches farther back than the old Margarita's, so the far more common Hollywood operation of transplanting vocal chords on-screen was a simple matter.)

Cohn was ready to go all the way with a big film for his new star, and that meant some big spending. Cohn understood this perfectly. The movie was called *You'll Never Get Rich*, contrary to Cohn's way of life, perhaps, but okay for a title. For the co-star, Fred Astaire. Who could make a dancing girl look better than that master? Nobody. To write the songs, Cole Porter. Again, none better. Cohn had grasped the idea that only top production values, as well as top productions, could make an actress *seem* like a star.

But it was no hoax. The flood of publicity pictures the studio sent out became fast pin-up favorites with American servicemen all over the globe. *Life* magazine featured one that became among the most celebrated of all glamour poses: The sexy star on the satin sheets was the last word in forties sensuality. *Life* dubbed her the Love Goddess and assured the public that her popularity would far outlast that of the other unremembered starlet they contrasted her with. It was like getting official documentation.

Along with her fandango skirts and black mantillas, it was time to start shedding husbands as well. Hayworth was one of the first of the big divorcers. (Lana Turner was another. Elizabeth Taylor made it a high art, but eventually the grabby Gabor sisters made it farcical and of declining public interest.) Now everything Rita did drew attention. When the first Astaire-Hayworth musical premiered, the publicity department gave her an honor guard of servicemen who escorted her everywhere.

Alleged love affairs with her co-stars also stirred the public's interest. Throughout the war years, she swung from straight films to musicals, but it was generally her off-screen antics that were the big attention-getters.

She was great box-office. Another even more lavish film with Astaire was scheduled for the following year, 1942. *You Were Never Lovelier* put her in marvelous clothes, aroused to youthful romance by Jerome Kern-Johnny Mercer songs like "I'm Old-Fashioned" and "Dearly Beloved," now considered perennials, and all filmed in a sumptuous setting.

After a tumultuous battle, her divorce from Edward Judson came through. Her next husband was to be Hollywood's resident genius, Orson Welles. It was a clear-cut case of Beauty and the Brain, a favorite Hollywood plot. For a while, they seemed to be happy. He even directed her in a non-musical, *The Lady from Shanghai*, an intense mystery in which she performed very well.

But it was in musicals that Rita was to shine brightest. And the very brightest one she made came along soon after *The Lady from Shanghai*. It was the sparkling *Cover Girl*, her best movie. She got top billing for this; her co-star was the still somewhat unknown Gene Kelly.

Second husband Orson Welles turned Rita blonde and dramatic as *The Lady from Shanghai* (1947)

Rita dances with Astaire in *You'll Never Get Rich* and . . .

You Were Never Lovelier (1942)

So many of the integral Columbia factors came together in the making of this one. The overall concept was Sidney Buchman's, more and more Cohn's alter ego (in a positive way since the absence of Capra). It was scripted by Virginia Van Upp, who was later to head up all production at Columbia after she wrote all Hayworth's best pictures. Charles Vidor directed still another of his successes for the studio. The glories of Technicolor were fully explored and the technical finesse of the Columbia crew had one of its finest hours. The big sound stages that were used for the filming of production numbers at the major studios still didn't exist at Columbia. Gene Kelly, who choreographed as well as co-starred, fell right in with the ingenuity and "making do" that had long been Gower Street trademarks. Once again, the physical limitations of the studio gave rise to inspired creativity, filling the screen with an enchanting freshness that money couldn't buy, but merely obliterate. Jerome Kern paired with Ira Gershwin to provide the songs. The offbeat personality of Phil Silvers shone through it all, allowing much more genuine comedy than musicals usually did. And though she was hardly noticed in all the excitement, a budding actress debuted here: Shelley Winters' first on-screen appearance.

Cover Girl was one of the sunniest movies made during the gloom of World War II; audiences everywhere loved it.* The Cohn trademark of quality had never been more clearly discernible. Its production during wartime restrictions was a minor miracle.

The story involved night club shenanigans in an out-of-the-way place in Brooklyn, but it was remarkably free of most of the show-biz backstage clichés that such films were usually cluttered with. Oh, the old story of lost love refound and lost again, with all its convolutions, is here in one of its endless variations. But it really doesn't matter, because not once in the proceeding is a silly story allowed to get in the way of the fun.

And the fun is what counts. Kelly and Silvers seem to be telling Rita—and us—even a love goddess can have a good time.

As a real goddess, in the follow-up movie to *Cover Girl* and sequel to *Here Comes Mr. Jordan*, Rita didn't have nearly as good a time. Neither did the audiences. It was called *Down to Earth*, and it was a passable pastiche of some of the elements in both earlier films. James Gleason was back to play his original

_____
*Noted English filmmaker Basil Wright notes in his book, *The Long View*, that the head of the Films Division of the British Ministry of Information ran *Cover Girl* each morning to "revive his own and his staff's morale."

130

With Gene Kelly in *Cover Girl* (1944)

role of Max Corkle, and Edward Everett Horton his part as the Messenger from the *Jordan* script. Rita got to wear a lot of chiffon and spout a lot of nonsense as she portrayed the Muse of the dance.

After a few other trifling films, she got down to real business again. It was a straight story this time, with only one musical number. But with that number, Hayworth was to make history. The film was *Gilda* and it established her as the reigning sexpot in Hollywood. The story was a sordid, not terribly interesting melodrama about a nightclub entertainer, but then, it wasn't written to garner any literary prizes. It was written as a display piece for Rita Hayworth. The writing and the production as well were tailored totally for her talents by Virginia Van Upp. Her leading man was the just-home-from-the-wars Glenn Ford, who never got in any actress' way.

One of the all-time great movie ads (1946)

132

As *The Lady in Question*, made in 1940, Rita Hayworth is flanked by Brian Aherne and Glenn Ford

Aside from being a Rita Hayworth starrer, the picture would have most likely surfaced briefly and then sunk like a stone. But somewhere during the proceedings, Hayworth sang a torchy number called "Put the Blame on Mame" while shedding some of her black satin wardrobe. It was one of the most frankly sexual provocations ever to scorch celluloid and it was more than enough to land Rita at the top of the list of Hollywood's most alluring ladies.

"There never was a woman like Gilda!" the ad headlines screamed, and for once they didn't exaggerate. The movie was exploited to its fullest potential. The star herself did everything she could to help sustain the Gilda image: she eventually separated from Welles and ran off to Europe to join Prince Aly Khan. Their international high jinks made headlines jump like a Slavko Vorkapich newspaper montage. Every public move the couple made was leaped upon by the papers; they were followed all over the continent and then back to Mexico. The usual voices of moral outrage spoke out against her, but the equally forceful American attraction to royalty worked in Rita's favor. Besides, she married the guy eventually. Harry Cohn didn't exactly love it, but he didn't hate it either. As long as the new princess was willing to work and fulfill her contractual obligations to Columbia, all would be well.

How to bill—and build—a star; Hayworth gets top treatment: co-star, music, settings, costumes all the very best

Enticing Glenn Ford in *Gilda*, Rita Hayworth's greatest triumph (1946)

©D-RITA HAYWORTH

Pin-ups, glamour, publicity—that's what Hollywood's little girls are made of

But she didn't and it wasn't. Early on, Rita should have saved some of the passion she was spending on her Aly Khan liaison for her career. After the 1948 film, *Loves of Carmen*, which Columbia put together for her and Ford in order to capitalize on the *Gilda* spillover, she flounced back to Europe with her prince and her entourage (which included her first baby—Rebecca—by Orson Welles).

The most publicized marriage of a decade lasted for two years.

Rita was back in Hollywood with two daughters (number two, by Aly—Yasmin) and little else besides the need to work.

1952 netted her one film—a hastily constructed piece that again attempted a nod to *Gilda*, pairing her with Ford. *Affair in Trinidad* didn't do badly, but neither it nor her subsequent films would catch fire like *Gilda* had. Put the blame on—who? Harry Cohn for not giving his star the star treatment? Not really, because he put up a pile of money for a huge Biblical epic, starring Hayworth. It was *Salome*, and it surrounded her with supporting players like Charles Laughton, Judith Anderson, Sir Cedric Hardwicke, Maurice Schwartz, and Stewart Granger. Perhaps he should have spent less; a big budget doesn't necessarily make an ex-Spanish dancer emote like a powerhouse.

Miss Sadie Thompson wasn't any better. It was an update of Somerset Maugham's classic *Rain*, with Jose Ferrer as the reverend and Rita as the umbrella carrier.

In about the same league with those two movies was her next step to the altar. Number four was a no-longer popular singer named Dick Haymes, who inexplicably decided that, having sent his own career down the drain, he could ably perform the same function for his new wife.

Haymes' dicta to Columbia on everything concerning Rita made Welles seem like a disinterested bystander by comparison. This was not exactly Harry Cohn's cup of tea. He was seldom inclined to listen to the advice of his own hirelings, let alone the fourth husband of a star he had single-handedly created from a hank of hair and a bag of possibilities.

Had her films continued to draw well, Harry might have listened, or at least gone through the motions. But they weren't, and Mrs. Hayworth-Haymes wasn't getting any younger. It was time to start another twinkle.

Through the 50s, Rita Hayworth would continue to make films for the studio. But they were of decreasing interest, both to Cohn and to the paying public. It wasn't until she was teamed up with the new goddess-to-be, that some of the old fire and by then, well-burnished glamour, shone again.

She did do an interesting movie in 1959 with Gary Cooper, directed by Robert Rossen. *They Came to Cordura* is one of those films that should be much better than it is. The stars are there, the story line is interesting, but something fails to spark, and the result is a failed film instead of a big success. Hayworth's part was straight dramatic, and she handled it well.

But in the meantime, while Hayworth was finishing her contract and freelancing elsewhere, Columbia scouts presented Harry Cohn with a nervous, but breathtakingly beautiful girl. Twinkle, twinkle. He was more than a little dubious. When Hayworth had been spotted, she had already played a load of bit parts in movies, and night-club exposure had strengthened her poise. Marilyn Novak was promoting refrigerators at the time, but her looks suggested so much that Cohn decided to try. After all, 20th Century-Fox wasn't doing too badly with another blonde named Marilyn who had somehow managed to slip through his hands.

First he changed her name to Kim. She went through the conveyor belt for make-up, hair, and figure changes. But she did not come out looking like a standardized Hollywood package. The uniqueness of her looks had been softened, modified a bit, but were basically unchanged. Cohn knew when he had a good thing.

Soon the public knew it, too. He started her off, a la Hayworth, with small but showy parts, meanwhile flooding the publicity and personal appearance circuits. She was famous in the papers and periodicals before she was prominent on the screen. But that was a carefully engendered campaign to build up both demand and recognition.

After two years of the most polished schedule, Kim Novak placed Number One in popularity among all American movie stars. Small parts in unimportant pictures like *Pushover* and *Five Against the House* and a chance to be seen with the other Columbia rising and talented stars—Judy Holliday and Jack Lemmon, in *Phffft*—provided the impetus. It was an important movie that gave her the big push.

When Kim danced with William Holden in *Picnic*, they both started moving quickly. But, as we've noted, his is a career that was a long time abuilding, while hers was created overnight.

But so well had all the necessary components been assembled that Kim Novak was the longest lasting of any of the so-called "manufactured" stars. And for a while at least, she was right up

Holden was to help make a star,
Kim Novak, in *Picnic* (1955) As they
looked in the ads . . .

. . . and on screen

The famous dance scene from *Picnic*

there. It had been tried before with far less success than Harry Cohn achieved.

Sam Goldwyn had tried it back in the 30s with a Russian import named Anna Sten. He spent a fortune trying to popularize her with the American public, but to no avail. (The fact that she couldn't speak much English may have been a hindrance.)

Alfred Hitchcock tried twice to replace Grace Kelly after she skipped to m'lou all the way to Monaco. But the public neither bought nor fancied Vera Miles nor Tippi Hedren, even after the fantastic buildups mounted for them. And both of those girls spoke English.

Once more Harry Cohn out-angled the bigger boys and fished out the prize catch. But nothing lasts forever.

Kim went into a string of flossier and costlier productions. Maybe Cohn had overreached, but suddenly something wasn't going as it should have. For most of her career, Rita Hayworth had achieved no great dramatic breakthroughs, but she was always interesting to watch. Moreover, in her movies, she sparkled with the best of them. She danced with Astaire and Kelly, the two finest male partners ever to appear on screen. Her *Gilda*

150

Kim Novak publicity photos . . . ▶

Kim Novak publicity photos, continued

had been electrifying. She had great powers of arousal in those heavily censored days, and conveyed something to the audience almost instinctively, or so it seemed. But Kim was getting bad notices.

She had been put into parts where looking good just wasn't enough. There was a degree of emoting required and it just wasn't coming off.

When Marilyn Monroe came off the calendar and onto the screen, she was warm and appealing, and eventually showed that she was very adept at handling light comedy. Kim of the glamour-lit stills might just as well have stayed on the walls.

A top roster of leading men didn't help: Kirk Douglas, James Stewart, Tyrone Power, Jeff Chandler. Neither did a director selected for his degree of simpatico, nor Rita Hayworth's old dressing room. Harry Cohn could make a star and push her to the top. But once there, only the public's sustaining interest could keep her at the top. A few more mediocre films, mostly made elsewhere, and that interest dribbled to nothingness.

Ironically, the star shining brightest at Columbia during the fifties was one Cohn hadn't wanted at all. He had bought the

Kim in *The Eddie Duchin Story* with James Whitmore and Tyrone Power (at the piano) (1956)

smash Broadway play, *Born Yesterday*, but he didn't want Judy Holliday, who had scored heavily in it. And Cohn hadn't merely bought *Born Yesterday*; he had paid a million dollars for it. At a time when the movie business was in one of its worst periodic slumps, the publicity that such a move garnered had a good deal of positive psychological value. But he wanted this hot property protected. He didn't think the general public was going to react favorably to a night club comedienne on the screen.

Garson Kanin, who wrote the play, finagled a part for Holliday in another movie at another studio. It constituted the most elaborate screen test in history. But with well-wishers like Katharine Hepburn and Spencer Tracy, the co-stars of all time, rooting for her, Judy Holliday pulled it off. She gathered great notices for her part in *Adam's Rib* and one of the noticers was her former detractor but now her boss-to-be, H. Cohn of Columbia.

Her unforgettable dumb blonde Billie Dawn earned Judy the Best Actress Oscar in her very first starring role. Harry Cohn had been pushed, yelling and protesting, to do it, but now he had another star. Not a sex idol maybe, but a warm, endearing and talented actress whom the public doted on.

She was to make five films for Columbia. George Cukor, who had been part of the *Adam's Rib* conspiracy, directed *Born Yesterday* as well as her next two films. (Kanin and his wife Ruth Gordon worked on these two scripts, too.) In *The Marrying Kind*, she was cast opposite Aldo Ray, whom Cohn was grooming for bigger things until the two personalities collided, as happened so often with Cohn and actors.

But Cukor found another nice young man for her next picture, *It Should Happen to You*. It was Jack Lemmon, and Harry Cohn had the expected reaction to that name. But Lemmon held his ground. He refused to let Cohn hang another name on him, even if it meant forfeiting a contract. In the end, it was Cohn who gave in. Lemmon signed, and his next assignment with Columbia was with Judy Holliday again.

Born Yesterday and Judy Holliday had started something at Columbia—the best run of comedies since the dear gone days of the screwballs. *It Should Happen to You* was a marvelously funny film that kept the string going, after the weaker *Marrying Kind*. Lemmon had quickly shown his enormous charm and capabilities. Maybe there was another dream team in the making.

But alas, their next film was almost as bad as its title.

156

Broderick Crawford, William Holden, Judy Holliday, and a plush Washington hotel suite—the setting for *Born Yesterday* (1950)

It Should Happen to You—Judy Holliday getting kissed by Peter Lawford (1954)

But Judy's real love is a newcomer in his first film—Jack Lemmon; here . . .

. . . and here, Jack seems to need convincing

Judy is the girl who becomes famous
for putting her name on a giant
billboard

People didn't know how to say *Phffft*, so how could they suggest to each other to go and see it? "Don't say it—see it!" the ads begged, but people weren't going to plunk down money for something they couldn't pronounce. It didn't do well. Lemmon went on to other things (as we shall soon see) and Judy played another role that had been written especially for her, again a Broadway comedy bought for the screen, and once more her leading man was the original Harry Brock of *Born Yesterday*, Paul Douglas. Now they were reunited in *The Solid Gold Cadillac*, an awfully funny yarn about a dithery lady who owns a few shares of stock in a major corporation. With little else to claim her time, she spends a great deal of it, all out of proportion to her holdings but nonetheless within her legal rights, on the affairs of the company. This, of course, to the consternation of its chief executive officer, Paul Douglas, who has something of his own in mind for the company. It's almost Capra-like in its structuring of the small individual against the giant corporation, but the sophistication of the situations, dialogue, and resolution are light years away from the simpler Capra philosophy.

Most importantly, it was Judy Holliday back at the top of her form, speculating on vaster questions than were posed by her set of little domestic comedies. Unfortunately, it was back behind the apron again for her next and last Columbia fixture; sadly, it was the next to last picture she was ever to make, the funny, tender, and under-rated *Full of Life*.

The tragedy was that Judy didn't live up to that title. In 1965, she died from cancer of the throat. She was only 43. A light, a very bright light, went out.

But all the lights were shining for her former co-star, the man Harry Cohn said was the nicest actor who had ever worked at Columbia. Jack Lemmon arrived at the right time for an actor to hit Hollywood. Stars were getting more and more powerful in the workings of the system, forming their own production companies and dictating choice of directors and other integral elements of picture-making that had always been the prerogatives of the studios. Lemmon asked for, and got, clauses in his contract that would have been unthinkable a decade earlier.

But Cohn acceded to the actor's desire to be able to do a play or even a movie for someone else every year. And he was never able to direct or in any way influence Lemmon's private life, the way he had done with the two earlier male stars whose careers he had developed, William Holden and Glenn Ford. Ford especially had been maintained by Columbia to perform secondary

It seems Judy has some ideas of her own. (The Capitol dome seems to be held over from *Mr. Smith Goes to Washington*)

functions, underlining Rita Hayworth in many of her efforts. He had never been expected to carry a major feature on his own. He was essentially Mr. Nice Guy, inoffensive, the utility outfielder. But Jack Lemmon was (and is) something else.

He could play light comedy as well as heavy drama, and make a poor film seem much better than it actually was. His versatility was formed and confirmed by the dozen Columbia pictures he made. Unfortunately, most of his better movies were made away from the studio, and he went on to become the only actor ever to graduate from a Best Supporting Oscar to the top award.*

It remains one of the ironies of the star system that so many played their most notable performances away from the "home" studios with which they were associated. Clark Gable reigned for decades as the undisputed king of the MGM lot, yet his one and only Oscar came for his one and only Columbia loan-out. Likewise, the biggest box-office attraction that Columbia ever developed for itself, Rita Hayworth, enhanced her early career most markedly with two loan-out performances, *Strawberry*

---

*The first was for his role as Ensign Pulver in *Mr. Roberts* (1955) which brought him his initial public acclaim, and he was Best Actor in 1973 for *Save the Tiger*.

In *The Solid Gold Cadillac* Paul Douglas has Judy Holliday all wrapped up, or so he thinks (1956)

Judy the minority stockholder announces her victory; That's Arthur O'Connell at right looking pleased

Blonde and *Blood and Sand*. (But after the successes of *Cover Girl* and *Gilda*, Harry Cohn was to change his mind and keep her exclusively on Gower Street.)

Hayworth, Holden, Holliday, Novak, Lemmon. For a studio that never maintained a stable of stars or stock players, Columbia added some great names (or Cohn some great re-names) to theater marquees all over the world. Additionally, there was scarcely a star of any magnitude who didn't work at the studio at one time or another with singularly fine results. (These will be discussed at greater length in a subsequent chapter.) Therefore, Columbia's "star power" at any given time in its history far surpassed what a superficial perusal of its resources would have indicated.

"We get them on the way up and we get them on the way down," Harry Cohn was fond of saying about the ever-available reservoir of kissable feet that Hollywood provided. But this was part of his courtship routine, and not part of the marriage con-

Judy faces pregnancy in the warm and funny *Full of Life*

In addition to the Hayworth films,
Glenn Ford also made some good
westerns; here with Felicia Farr in
Jubal, which also featured Ernest
Borgnine and Rod Steiger (1956)

Glenn Ford and Van Heflin in *3:10 to Yuma*, one of the classic westerns; filmed in 1957

In the 1955 remake of *My Sister Eileen*, Jack Lemmon and Betty Garrett are rather romantically inclined

Another lady brought out at the studio for a stint with Jack Lemmon was a sneakered Doris Day in *It Happened to Jane* (1959)

tract, under which his "own" stars were wedded to Columbia. Those feet had to toe the mark and dance according to Cohn's tune. He strove to control every aspect of their lives, from the cosmetic name changes to facial adjustments to dating and mating regulations. Rita Hayworth's scandals were great box-office, and so permissible, but the semi-secret gossip that raged around Kim Novak was poison, or so Cohn thought, and strong-arm tactics were employed to force her to cease and desist from a liaison that Cohn thought would destroy her career and sink Columbia's investment in her.*

---

*No threats were made to Kim directly, but the man was told he'd never work again if the affair didn't end immediately. It did.

JUVENILE COURT

(Released: September 7, 1938)

Director: Ross Lederman
Editor: Byron Robinson
Screen Play:
  Michael L. Simmons
  Robert E. Kent
  Henry Taylor
Music Director: M. W. Stoloff
Cameraman:
  Benjamin Kline, A.S.C.

Cast:
Paul Kelly
Rita Hayworth
Frankie Darro
Halley Chester
Don Latorre
David Gorcey
Dick Selzer

Allan Ramsey
Charles Hart
Howard Hickman

GOLDEN BOY

(Released: August, 1939)

Director: Reuben Mamoulian
Producer: William Perlberg
Editor: Otto Meyer
Musical Score: Victor Young
Based on the Play by:
  Clifford Odets
Screen Play:
  Lewis Meltzer
  Daniel Taradash
  Sarah Y. Mason
  Victor Heerman
Art Director: Lionel Banks

Music Director:
  M. W. Stoloff
Montage Effects:
  D. W. Starling
Cameramen:
  Mick Muauraca, A.S.C.
  Karl Freund, A.S.C.

Footage: 9105 ft.

Cast:
Barbara Stanwyck
Adolph Menjou
William Holden
Lee J. Cobb
Joseph Calleia
Sam Levene
Edward S. Brophy
Beatrice Blinn
William H. Strauss
Don Beddoe

THE LADY IN QUESTION

(Released: July 31, 1940)

Director: Charles Vidor
Producer: B. B. Kahane
Editor: Al Clark
Story: Marcel Achard
Screen Play: Lewis Meltzer
Music: Lucien Moraweck
Art Director: Lionel Banks
Music Director: M. W. Stoloff
Cameraman: Lucien Adroit, A.S.C.

Footage: 7843 ft.

Cast:
Brian Aherne
Rita Hayworth
Glenn Ford
Irene Rich
George Coulouris
Lloyd Corrigan
Evelyn Keyes
Edward Norris

Curt Bois
Frank Reicher
Sumner Getchall
Nicholas Bela

ANGELS OVER BROADWAY

(Released: September 27, 1940)

Director: Ben Hecht
Co-Director: Lee Charms
Producer: Ben Hecht
Associate Producer:
Douglas Fairbanks, Jr.
Editor: Gene Havlick
Screen Play: Ben Hecht
Music: George Antheil
Art Director: Lionel Banks
Music Director: M. W. Stoloff

Gowns: Kalloch
Cameraman:
Lee Garmes, A.S.C.

Footage: 7235 ft.

Cast:
Douglas Fairbanks, Jr.
Rita Hayworth
Thomas Mitchell
John Qualen
George Watts
Ralph Theodore
Eddie Foster
Jack Roper
Constance Worth

ARIZONA

(Released: Dec. 25, 1940)

Director: Wesley Ruggles
Assistant Director: Norman Deming
Editors:
Otto Meyer
William Lyon
Based on the Story by:
Clarence Budington Kelland
Screen Play: Claude Binyon
Music: Victor Young
Art Director: Lionel Banks
Associate Art Director:
Robert Peterson
Music Director: M. W. Stoloff
Set Decorations: Frank Tuttle
Second Unit Direction:
Sam Nelson
Miss Arthur's Gowns: Kalloch
Directors of Photography:
Joe Walker, A.S.C. (Interiors)
Harry Hallenberger, A.S.C.
(Exteriors)
Fayte Browne, A.S.C. (Exteriors)

Cast:
Jean Arthur
William Holden
Warren William
Porter Hail
Edgar Buchanan
Paul Harvey
George Chandler
Byron Foulger
Regis Toomey
Paul Lopez
Colin Tapley

Uvaldo Varela
Earl Crawford
Griff Barnette
Ludwig Hardt
Patrick Moriarity
Frank Darien
Syd Sayler
Wade Crosby
Frank Hill
Nina Campina
Addison Richards

TONIGHT AND EVERY NIGHT

(Released: January 9, 1945)

Director: Victor Saville
Producer: Victor Saville
Assistant Producer:
Norman Deming
Editor: Viola Lawrence
Based on the Play, *Heart of
a City;* **Stage Production:**
Gilbert Miller

Assistant Directors:
Rex Bailey
Louis Germonprez
Choreographies:
Val Rasel
Special Effects:
Lawrence W. Butler
Montages: John Hoffman

Cast:
Rita Hayworth
Lee Bowman
Janet Blair
Marc Platt
Leslie Brooks
Professor Lomberti
Dusty Anderson

169

Screen Play:
  Lesser Samuels
  Abem Finkel
Music: Jules Styne
Lyrics: Sammy Cahn
Orchestra Arrangement:
  Martin Skiles
Vocal Arrangement:
  Saul Champlin
Art Directors:
  Stephen Goosson
  Rudolph Sternad
  Lionel Banks
Music Directors:
  M. W. Stoloff
  Jack Cole
Set Director: Frank Tuttle

Gowns and Costumes:
  Jean Louis
  Marcel Vertes
Make-up: Clay Campbell
Hairstyles: Helen Hunt
Director of Photography:
  Rudolph Mate, A.S.C.
Cameraman:
  Fayte M. Browne
Technicolor Director:
  Natalie Kalmus

Footage: 8579 ft.

Stephen Crane
Jim Bannon
Florence Bates
Ernest Cossart
Richard Haydon
Philip Merivale
Patrick Moon

GILDA

(Released: February, 1946)

Director: Charles Vidor
Assistant Director: Arthuros Black
Producer: Virginia Van Upp
Assistant Producer:
  Norman Deming
Editor: Charles Nelson
Story: E. A. Ellington
Screen Play: Marion Parsonnet
Adaptation: Jo Eisinger
Music: Allan Roberts
  Doris Fisher
Art Directors: Stephen Goosson
  Van Nest Polglase

Music Directors:
  M. W. Stoloff
  Marlin Skiles
Set Decorations:
  Robert Priestley
Gowns: Jean Louis
Make-up: Clay Campbell
Hairstyles: Helen Hunt
Director of Photography:
  Rudolph Mate, A.S.C.

Footage: 8951 ft.

Cast:
Rita Hayworth
Glenn Ford
George MacReady
Joseph Calleia
Steven Geray
Joe Sawyer
Gerald Mohr
Robert Scott
Ludwig Donath
Don Douglas

THE LADY FROM SHANGHAI

(Released: October, 1947)

Director: Orson Welles
Assistant Director: Sam Nelson
Producer: Orson Welles
Associate Producers:
  Richard Wilson
  William Castle
Editor: Viola Lawrence
Based on the Novel by:
  Sherwood King
Screen Play: Orson Welles
Musical Score: Heinz Roemheld
"Please Don't Kiss Me" Song:
  Allan Roberts
  Doris Fisher

Art Directors:
  Stephen Goosson
  Sturges Carne
Music Director:
  M. W. Stoloff
Set Decorations:
  Wilbur Menefee
  Herman Schoenbrun
Gowns: Jean Louis
Director of Photography:
  Charles Lawton, Jr.,
  A.S.C.

Cast:
Rita Hayworth
Orson Welles
Everett Sloane
Glenn Anders
Ted DeCorsia
Erskine Sangord
Gus Schilling
Carl Frank
Louis Merril
Evelyn Ellis
Harry Shannon

170

LOVES OF CARMEN

(Released: August, 1948)

Director: Charles Vidor
Assistant Director:
 Earl Bellamy
Producer:
 Charles Vidor,
 The Beckworth Corp.
Editor: Charles Nelson
Based on the Story, *Carmen,*
 by: Prosper Merimee
Screen Play: Helen Deutsch
Musical Score:
 Marco Castlenuolo-Tedesco
Art Directors: Stephen Goosson
 Cary Odell
Music Director: M. W. Stoloff
Choreography: Robert Sidney
Associate: Eduardo Cansino

Set Decorations:
 Wilbur Menefee
 William Kiernan
Gowns: Jean Louis
Make-up: Clay Campbell
Hairstyles: Helen Hunt
Director of Photography:
 William Snyder, A.S.C.
Technicolor Director:
 Natalie Kalmus
Associate: Francis Cugat

Footage: 8685 ft.

Cast:
Rita Hayworth
Glenn Ford
Ron Randell
Victor Jory
Luther Adler
Arnold Moss
Joseph Buloff
Margaret Wycherly
Bernard Nedell
John Baragrey

BORN YESTERDAY

(Released: November 20, 1950)

Director: George Cukor
Assistant Director:
 Earl Bellamy
Producer: S. Sylvan Simon
Editor: Charles Nelson, A.C.E.
Play: Garson Kanin
Screen Play:
 Albert Mannheimer
Art Director: Harry Horner
Set Decorations:
 William Kiernan
Dialogue Supervision:
 David Pardoll

Make-up:
 Clay Campbell, S.M.A.
Hairstyles: Helen Hunt
Director of Photography:
 Joe Walker, A.S.C.
Sound Engineer:
 Jack Goodrich

Cast:
Judy Holliday
Broderick Crawford
William Holden
Howard St. John
Frank Otto
Larry Oliver
Barbara Brown
Grandon Rhodes
Claire Carleton

AFFAIR IN TRINIDAD

(Released: June, 1952)

Director: Vincent Sherman
Assistant Director: Sam Nelson
Producer: Vincent Sherman
Editor: Viola Lawrence, A.C.E.
Story: Virginia Van Upp
 Bernie Giler
Screen Play: Oscar Saul
 James Gunn
Art Director:
 Walter Holscher
Music Director: M. W. Stoloff
 George Duning

Miss Hayworth's
 Choreography:
 Valerie Bettis
Set Decorations:
 William Kiernan
Gowns: Jean Louis
Make-up Clay Campbell
Hairstyles: Helen Hunt
Director of Photography:
 Joe Walker, A.S.C.

Footage: 9029 ft.

Cast:
Rita Hayworth
Glenn Ford
Alexander Scourby
Valerie Bettis
Torin Thatcher
Howard Wendell
Karel Stepanek
George Voskovek
Steven Geray
Walter Kohler
Juanita Moore

SALOME

(Released: February, 1953)

Director: William Dieterle
Assistant Director:
Earl Bellamy
Producer: Buddy Adler
Editor: Viola Lawrence, A.C.E.
Story:
Jesse L. Lasky, Jr.
Harry Kleiner
Screen Play: Harry Kleiner
Music:
George Duning
Daniele Amfitheatrof
Orchestrations: Arthur Morton
Choral Music:
Roger Wagner Chorale
Music Director: M. W. Stoloff
Choreography: Valerie Bettis

Set Decorations:
William Kiernan
Gowns: Jean Louis
Men's Costumes:
Emile Santiago
Make-up: Clay Campbell
Hairstyles: Helen Hunt
Director of Photography:
Charles Lang, A.S.C.
Technical Consultant:
Millard Sheets
Technicolor Consultant:
Francis Cugat

Cast:
Rita Hayworth
Stewart Granger
Charles Laughton
Judith Anderson
Sir Cedric
Hardwicke
Basil Sidney
Maurice Schwartz
Arnold Moss
Alan Badel
Sujata and Asoka
(Oriental Dancers)

THE BIG HEAT

(Released: July, 1953)

Director: Fritz Lang
Assistant Director:
Milton Feldman
Producer: Robert Arthur
Editor: Charles Nelson, A.S.C.
Based on the *Saturday Evening
Post* **Serial by:**
William P. McGovern
Screen Play: Sydney Boehm
Art Director: Robert Peterson

Music Director:
Mischa Bakaleinikoff
Set Decorations:
William Kiernan
Gowns: Jean Louis
Hairstyles: Helen Hunt
Make-up:
Clay Campbell, S.M.A.
Director of Photography:
Charles Lang, A.S.C.

Cast:
Glenn Ford
Gloria Grahame
Jocelyn Brando
Alexander Scourby
Lee Marvin
Jeanette Nolan
Peter Whitney
Willis Bouchey
Robert Burton
Adam Williams
Howard Wendell

MISS SADIE THOMPSON

(Released: October, 1953)

Director: Curtis Bernhardt
Assistant Director: Sam Nelson
Producer: Jerry Wald
Associate Producer:
Lewis J. Rachmil
Editor: Viola Lawrence, A.C.E.
Screen Play: Harry Kleiner
Music: George Duning
Songs:
Lester Lee
Ned Washington
Allan Roberts
Art Director: Carl Anderson
Music Director: M. W. Stoloff

Choreography: Lee Scott
Set Decorations:
Louis Diage
Gowns: Jean Louis
Make-up: Clay Campbell
Hairstyles: Helen Hunt
Director of Photography:
Charles Lawton, Jr.,
A.S.C.
Technicolor Consultant:
Francis Cugat

Cast:
Rita Hayworth
Jose Ferrer
Aldo Ray
Russell Collins
Diosa Costello

172

PUSHOVER

(Released: June 11, 1954)

Director: Richard Quine
Assistant Director: Jack Corrick
Producer: Jules Shermer
Associate Producer:
Philip A. Waxman
Editor: Jerome Thoms, A.C.E.
Based on Stories by:
Thomas Walsh
William S. Ballinger
Screen Play: Roy Huggins
Musical Score: Arthur Morton
Art Director: Walter Holscher

Music Director:
M. W. Stoloff
Set Decorations:
James Crowe
Gowns: Jean Louis
Make-up:
Clay Campbell, S.M.A.
Hairstyles: Helen Hunt
Director of Photography:
Lester H. White, A.S.C.
Recording Supervision:
John Livadary

Cast:
Fred MacMurray
Phil Carey
Kim Novak
Dorothy Malone
E. G. Marshall
Allen Nourse

FIVE AGAINST THE HOUSE

(Released: March 2, 1955)

Director: Phil Karlson
Assistant Director:
Milton Feldman
Producer: Stirling Silliphant
Associate Producer:
John Barnwell
Helen Ainsworth
Editor: Jerome Thoms, A.C.E.
**Based on the Good Housekeeping
Magazine Short Story by:**
Jack Finney
Screen Play:
Stirling Silliphant
William Bowers
John Barnwell
Musical Composition:
George Duning

Art Director:
Robert Peterson
Music Director:
M. W. Stoloff
Set Decorations:
Frank Tuttle
Gowns: Jean Louis
Director of Photography:
Leslie White, A.S.C.
Sound: Harry Smith
Recording Supervision:
John Livadary

Cast:
Guy Madison
Kim Novak
Brian Keith
Alvy Moore
Kerwin Mathews
William Conrad
Jack Diamond
Jean Willes

JUBAL

(Released: January, 1956)

Director: Delmar Daves
Assistant Director: Eddie Saeta
Producer: William Fadiman
Editor: Al Clark, A.C.E.
Based on the Novel by:
Paul I. Wellman
Screen Play:
Russel S. Hughes
Delmar Daves
Musical Score: David Raskin
Orchestration: Arthur Morton
Music Director: M. W. Stoloff

Set Decorations:
Louis Diage
Gowns: Jean Louis
Hairstyles: Helen Hunt
Make-up:
Clay Campbell, S.M.A.
Director of Photography:
Charles Lawton, Jr.,
A.S.C.
Color Consultant:
Henri Jaffa

Cast:
Glenn Ford
Ernest Borgnine
Rod Steiger
Valerie French
Felicia Farr

THE EDDIE DUCHIN STORY

(Released: February, 1956)

Director: George Sidney
Producer: Jerry Wald
Associate Producer: Jonie Taps
Story: Leo Katcher
Screen Play: Samuel Taylor
Original Music: George Duning
Gowns: Jean Louis
Jewels: Lakinetcie
Director of Photography:
  Harry Stradling
Color Consultant: Henri Jaffa
Piano Recordings: Carmen Cavallaro

Cast:
Tyrone Power
Kim Novak
James Whitmore
Victoria Shaw
Rex Thompson
Mickey Maga
Shepperd Strudwick
Frieda Inescort
Gloria Holden
Larry Keating
John Mylong
Gregory Gay
Warren Hsieh
Jack Albertson
Carlyle Mitchell
Richard Sternberg
Andy Smith
Lois Kimbrell

PICNIC

(Released: November, 1956)

Director: Joshua Logan
Assistant Director:
  Carter DeHaven, Jr.
Producer: Fred Kohlmar
Editors:
  Charles Nelson, A.C.E.
  William A. Lyon, A.C.E.
Based on the Play by:
  William Inge
Screen Play: Daniel Taradash
Music: George Duning
Orchestrations: Arthur Morton
Art Director: William Flannery
Music Director: M. W. Stoloff
Music Advisor: Fred Karger

Set Decorations:
  Robert Priestley
Gowns: Jean Louis
Make-up: Clay Campbell
Hairstyles: Helen Hunt
Director of Photography:
  James Wong Howe,
  A.S.C.
Second Unit Photography:
  Ray Cory, A.S.C.
Color Consultant:
  Henri Jaffa

Cast:
William Holden
Kim Novak
Betty Field
Susan Strasberg
Cliff Robertson
Arthur O'Connell
Verna Felton
Reta Shaw
Nick Adams
Raymond Bailey
Elizabeth W. Wilson
Rosalind Russell

FIRE DOWN BELOW

(Released: May, 1957)

Director: Robert Parrish
Assistant Directors:
  Gus Agosti
  Bluey Hill
Producers:
  Irving Allen
  Albert R. Broccoli
Associate Producer:
  Ronald Kinnoch
Editors:
  Jack Slade
  David Elliott (Sound)
Based on the Novel by: Max Catto
Screen Play: Irwin Shaw

Steel Band:
  The Katzenjammers
  of Trinidad
Assistant Art Director:
  Syd Cain
Set Decorations:
  John Box
Choreography:
  Tutte Lemkow
Special Effects:
  Cliff Richardson
Wardrobe: John McCrory
Make-up: Fred Williamson
Director of Photography:
  Desmond Dickinson, B.S.C.

Cast:
Rita Hayworth
Jack Lemmon
Robert Mitchum
Herbert Lom
Ronar Colleano

174

Continuity:
Angela Martelli
Kay Rawlings
Music: Arthur Benjamin
Orchestra: London Sinfonia,
Muir Mathieson
"Fire Down Below" Theme:
Jack Lemmon
Music for Miss Hayworth's Dances:
Vivian Comma

Second Unit Photography:
Cyril Knowles, B.S.C.
Cameramen:
Ernest Day
Gerald Turpin

3:10 TO YUMA

(Released: July, 1957)

Director: Delmer Daves
Editor: Al Clark
Screen Play: Halsted Welles
From a Story by:
Elmore Leonard
Art Director: Frank Hotaling
Music Composed by:
George Duning
Music Director: M. W. Stoloff
Title Song by: Ned Washington and
George Duning

Running time: 92 minutes

Cast:
Glenn Ford
Van Heflin
Felicia Farr
Leora Dana
Henry Jones
Richard Jaeckel
Robert Emhardt

Sheridan Comerate
George Mitchell
Robert Ellenstein
Ford Rainey
Barry Curtis
Jerry Hartleben

BELL, BOOK AND CANDLE

(Released: October, 1958)

Director: Richard Quine
Assistant Director: Irving Moore
Producer: Julian Blaustien
Editor: Charles Nelson, A.C.E.
Based on the Play by:
John Van Druten
Screen Play: Daniel Taradash
Musical Score: George Duning
Art Director: Cary Odell
Set Decorations: Louis Diage
Gowns: Jean Louis
Hairstyles: Helen Hunt
Make-up: Ben Lane, S.M.A.

Native Primitive Art:
Carelebach Gallery,
New York
Director of Photography:
James Wong Howe,
A.S.C.
Special Color Consultant:
Eliot Elifson
Technicolor Consultant:
Henri Jaffa

Cast:
James Stewart
Kim Novak
Jack Lemmon
Ernie Kovacs
Hermione Gingold
Elsa Lancaster
Janice Rule
Philippe Clay
Bek Nelson

IT HAPPENED TO JANE

(Released: May, 1959)

Produced and Directed by:
Richard Quine
Screen Play: Norman Katkov

Cast:
Doris Day
Jack Lemmon

Guest Stars:
Bill Cullen

Based on a Story by:
Max Wilk and Norman Katkov
Executive Producer: Martin Melcher
Art Direction: Cary Odell
Photography: Charles Lawton, Jr.
Color Consultant: Henri Jaffa
Set Decoration: Louis Diage
Editor: Charles Nelson
Assistant Director:
Carter DeHaven, Jr.
Music Composed by: George Duning
Music Director: M. W. Stoloff

Ernie Kovacs
Steve Forrest
Teddy Rooney
Russ Brown
Walter Greaza
Parker Fennelly
Mary Wickes
Philip Coolidge
Casey Adams
John Cecil Holm
Gina Gillespie
Dick Crockett
Napoleon Whiting

Dave Garroway
Steve McCormick
Jayne Meadows
Garry Moore
Henry Morgan
Bob Paige
Betsy Palmer
Gene Raeburn

THEY CAME TO CORDURA

(Released: June, 1959)

Director: Robert Rossen
Assistant Director:
Carter DeHaven, Jr.
Producer: William Goetz
Editor: William A. Lyon, A.C.E.
Based on the Novel by:
Glendon Stewart
Screen Play:
Ivan Moffat
Robert Rossen
Music: Elie Siegmeister
Orchestration: Arthur Morton
Music Director: M. W. Stoloff
Set Decorations: Frank A. Tuttle
Assistant Director:
Milton Feldman

Make-up:
Clay Campbell, S.M.A.
Hairstyles: Helen Hunt
Director of Photography:
Burnett Guffey, A.S.C.
Second Unit Director:
James Havens
Cameraman:
Frank G. Carson
Technical Consultant:
Col. Paul Davison,
USA, Ret'd.
Color Consultant:
Henri Jaffa

Cast:
Gary Cooper
Rita Hayworth
Van Heflin
Tab Hunter
Richard Conte
Michael Callan
Dick York
Robert Keith

THE NOTORIOUS LANDLADY

(Released: February, 1962)

Director: Richard Quine
Assistant Director:
Carter DeHaven, Jr.
Producer: Fred Kohlmar
Editor: Charles Nelson, A.C.E.
Based on the Story by:
Margery Sharp
Screen Play:
Larry Gelbart
Blake Edwards
Musical Score: George Duning
Orchestration: Arthur Morton
Art Director: Cary Odell

Set Decorations:
Louis Diage
Miss Novak's Gowns:
Miss Novak
Executed by:
Elizabeth Courtney
Make-up
Ben Lane, S.M.A.
Director of Photography:
Arthur Arling, A.S.C.

Cast:
Kim Novak
Jack Lemmon
Fred Astaire
Lionel Jeffries
Estelle Winwood
Maxwell Reed
Philippa Bevan
Henry Daniell
Ronald Long
Richard Peel
Doris Lloyd

THE MARRYING KIND

(Released: February, 1952)

Director: George Cukor
Assistant Director: Earl Bellamy
Producer: Bert Granet
Editor: Charles Nelson, A.C.E.
Screen Play:
  Ruth Gordon
  Garson Kanin
Musical Score: Hugo Friedhofer
Art Director: John Meehan
Music Director: M. W. Stoloff
Set Decorations: William Kiernan

Gowns: Jean Louis
Hairstyles: Helen Hunt
Make-up: Clay Campbell
Director of Photography:
  Joe Walker, A.S.C.
Second Unit Direction:
  Harry Horner

Cast:
Judy Holliday
Aldo Ray
Madge Kennedy
Sheila Bond
John Alexander
Rex Williams
Phyllis Povah
Mickey Shaughnessy
Griff Barnett

IT SHOULD HAPPEN TO YOU

(Released: December, 1953)

Director: George Cukor
Assistant Director:
  Earl Bellamy
Producer: Fred Kohlmar
Editor: Charles Nelson, A.C.E.
Story and Screen Play:
  Garson Kanin
Art Director: John Meehan
Musical Score:
  Frederick Hollander
Orchestrations: Arthur Morton

Music Director:
  M. W. Stoloff
Set Decorations:
  William Kiernan
Gowns: Jean Louis
Hairstyles: Helen Hunt
Make-up: Clay Campbell
Director of Photography:
  Charles Lang, A.S.C.

Cast:
Judy Holliday
Peter Lawford
Jack Lemmon
Michael O'Shea
Vaughn Taylor
Connie Gilchrist
Walter Klavun
Whit Bissell

PHFFFT

(Released: December, 1954)

Director: Mark Robson
Producer: Fred Kohlmar
Editor: Charles Nelson, A.S.C.
Story and Screen Play:
  George Axelrod
Musical Score: Frederick Hollander
Music Director: M. W. Stoloff
Set Decorations: William Kiernan
Director of Photography:
  Charles Lang, A.S.C.

Cast:
Judy Holliday
Jack Lemmon
Jack Carson
Kim Novak
Luella Gear

Donald Randolph
Donald Curtis
Arny Freeman
Merry Anders
Eddie Searles

THE SOLID GOLD CADILLAC

(Released: July, 1957)

Director: Richard Quine
Assistant Director: Irving Moore
Producer: Fred Kohlmar

Music Director:
  Lionel Newman
Set Decorations:

Cast:
Judy Holliday
Paul Douglas

Editor: Charles Nelson, A.C.E.
Based on the Play by:
  George S. Kaufman
  and Howard Teichmann
Screen Play: Abe Burrows
Musical Score:
  Cyril J. Mockridge
Orchestration: Bernard Mayers
Art Director: Ross Bellah

William Kiernan
Louis Diage
Gowns: Jean Louis
Hairstyles: Helen Hunt
Make-up:
  Clay Campbell, S.M.A.
Director of Photography:
  Charles Lang, A.S.C.

Fred Clarke
Hiram Sherman
Ralph Dumke
John Williams
Neva Patterson
Ray Collins
Arthur O'Connell
Narration:
  George Burns

FULL OF LIFE

(Released: April, 1957)

Director: Richard Quine
Assistant Director:
  Herb Wallerstein
Producer: Fred Kohlmar
Based on the Novel by:
  John Fante
Screen Play: John Fante
Musical Score: George Duning
Orchestrations: Arthur Morton
Art Director: William Flannery
Music Director: M. W. Stoloff

Set Decorations:
  William Kiernan
  Louis Diage
Hairstyles: Helen Hunt
Make-up:
  Clay Campbell, S.M.A.
Director of Photography:
  Charles Lawton, A.S.C.

Cast:
Judy Holliday
Richard Conte
Salvatore Baccaloni
Esther Minciotti
Joe De Santis
Silvio Minciotti
Penny Santon
Arthur Lovejoy
Eleanor Audley
Trudy Marshall
Walter Conrad
Sam Gilman

FUNNY LADY

Producer: Ray Stark
Director: Herbert Ross
Musical Numbers Directed by:
  Herbert Ross
Screenplay by:
  Jay Presson Allen
  Arnold Schulman
Story by: Arnold Schulman
Director of Photography:
  James Wong Howe, A.S.C.
Music and Lyrics to
  Original Songs:
  John Kander
  Fred Ebb
Music Arranged and Conducted
  by:
  Peter Matz
Production Design:
  George Jenkins
Costume Design:
  Ray Aghayan
  Bob Mackie
Film Editor: Marion Rothman

Choral Supervision:
  Ray Charles
Music Editor:
  William Saracino
Title Design
  Wayne Fitzgerald
Assistant Director:
  Jack Roe
Second Assistant Directors:
  Stu Fleming
Assistant Art Director:
  David Haber
Sound: Jack Solomon
Sound Effects:
  Richard Oswald
Re-Recording:
  Richard Portman
Aerial Photography:
  Tyler Camera Systems
Assistant to the Producer:
  Frank Bueno

Cast:
Barbra Streisand
James Caan
Omar Sharif
Roddy McDowall
Ben Vereen
Carole Wells
Larry Gates
Heidi O'Rourke
Samantha Huffaker
Matt Emery
Joshua Shelley
Corey Fischer
Garrett Lewis
Don Torres
Raymond Guth
Gene Troobnick
Royce Wallace
Byron Webster
Lilyan Chauvin
Cliff Norton
Ken Sansom
Colleen Camp

Unit Production Manager:
  Howard Pine
Assistant to Mr. Ross:
  Nora Kaye
Casting: Jennifer Shull
Camera Operator: Dick Johnson
Special Effects: Phil Cory
Mens Wardrobe: Seth Banks
Ladies Wardrobe: Edna Taylor
Miss Streisand's Wardrobe:
  Shirlee Strahm
Script Supervisor:
  Marshall Schlom
Set Decorator: Audrey Blasdel
Properties: Richard M. Rubin
Make-up: Don Cash
Hairstyles: Kay Pownall
Special Photographic Effects:
  Albert Whitlock
Key Grip: Bob Moore
Gaffer: Bill Shaw
Unit Publicist: Regina Gruss
Assistant Film Editors:
  David Ramirez
  Michael Polakow
Make-up Supervision:
  Ben Lane
Associate Choreographer:
  Howard Jeffrey
Dance Arranger: Betty Walberg
Dance Assistant: Lester Wilson
Aquatic Sequence:
  Oak Park Marionettes,
  Supervised by Marion Kane

Alana Collins
Jackie Stoloff
Bert May
Bea Busch
Maggie Malooly
Jodean Russo
Larry Arnold
Shirley Kirkes
Jerry Trent
Toni Kaye
Gary Menteer
Deborah Sherman
Dick Winslow
Dick De Benedictis
Louis Da Pron
Hank Stohl
Diane Wyatt
Tom Northam
Tod Durwood
Paul Bryar
Brett Hadley
Jack Frey
Jadeen Vaughn
Ben Freedman
Maralyn Thoma
Phil Gray
Frank L. Pine
Bill Baldwin

Gene Kelly in *Cover Girl*—a publicity shot

5 | The Musicals

THE MUSICALS THAT WERE MADE BY COLUMBIA WERE comparatively few in number, measured against, say, the MGM or Warner's output. But the standout films were extremely innovative, and the major studios were quick to duplicate the Gower Street successes in numbers that constituted sometimes a temporary trend, and sometimes a distinct new sub-genre of musical films.

It is little less than astounding that it was Columbia, long before it achieved anything near major studio status, that introduced grand opera into films. But it did, in a pulled-together picture called *One Night of Love*. This pastiche, combining some popular ballads with several well-known arias, was an emergency vehicle for Grace Moore. After a few filmic flops for MGM, the temperamental diva gave up movies (or rather they gave her up) and she returned to the New York stage, shifting back and forth between opera and Broadway musicals. It was in one of the latter that Harry Cohn spotted her, and induced her to return to Hollywood.

Miss Grace Moore, as she was billed, and Tullio Carminati making *One Night of Love* (1934)

She had another brief flirtation with MGM, but they didn't know what to do with her, so she signed with Cohn. He didn't know what to do with her either. Her previous films had been operettas of the sort that would later prove successful for the Jeanette MacDonald-Nelson Eddy team.

But Moore had a trained operatic voice and Cohn had a director, Victor Schertzinger, a trained classical conductor, and so they took the plunge, mixing lumps of Puccini and the like into a pancake batter of plot thickeners such as the nice American girl, European settings, playboys, yachts, and glamour.

The incredible result was that, like the proverbial hotcakes, the public ate it up. The picture and Grace Moore were both nominees for Oscars. But it was the year of Columbia's big breakthrough, *It Happened One Night*, and *One Night of Love* got lost in the voting, at least for the major awards. Nevertheless, the score was cited for one of those gold statuettes, and Columbia also received a special award for the technical advances made by its sound department in recording the track for the film.

It was a triumph of many sorts for Harry Cohn. He had made a star out of a Louis Mayer reject, and made a pile of money with a film that his New York office said could never sell. While doing it, he had introduced a new element of artistry into films, bringing opera to millions who had never paid it any attention previously. True, it was opera staged in the most *kitschy-* koo manner imaginable, but, to former Tin Pan Alley song plugger Cohn, it was as satisfying an accomplishment as one could hope for.

Grace Moore was starred in a succession of similar movies for the studio. In *Love Me Forever*, both the director, Victor Schertzinger, and the cameraman, Joseph Walker, noted for his glamorous photography of Columbia leading ladies, were on the set again. The string of voices to back Miss Moore was expanded to regimental proportions. Then *The King Steps Out* featured a dashing young man to co-star in the title role, Franchot Tone, music to order by Fritz Kreisler, and superb direction by Josef von Sternberg. But the bubbles, in spite of this immense injection of talent, began to go flat.

When You're in Love, in 1937, gave Grace both Cary Grant and an opportunity for the most extraordinary screen vocalizing since Ginger Rogers sang "We're in the Money" in pig-Latin in *Gold Diggers of 1933*. In what has to stand for all time as the pinnacle of popularizing, of bringing "high culture" to the lowly screen, the former pet of the Met sang "Minnie the Moocher."

Nothing could follow an act like that, even though Melvyn Douglas tried gamely in *I'll Take Romance*. By then, the public wasn't taking anything having to do with opera, even though almost all the studios had jumped on the bandwagon. Gladys Swarthout, Rise Stevens, Lily Pons, Marion Talley, and other lesser names made quick and unmemorable sojourns through Hollywood, but none of them ever enjoyed even brief movie stardom. Columbia had stumbled on the successful formula and made the best imitations of the original model. But that didn't last beyond the 30s. It was a novelty at best, and best is exactly what the operatic-aspiring musical seldom was. Still, it was a major accomplishment for a studio with the size and limitations of Columbia during its struggling second decade.

If *One Night of Love* and its production was a saga of a star in need of a story, another important Columbia innovation had exactly the reverse problem. For a long time Cohn had been toying with the idea of doing a picture based on the life of Chopin. At one point, it was going to be a Frank Capra project. Sidney Buchman had provided a scenario, but something or

Miss Moore with lace, pleats, trills and Cary Grant in *When You're In Love* (1937)

Fred Astaire has joined the army in 1941's *You'll Never Get Rich*

other always managed to delay putting the thing into production. Too, the New York office argued against the project, saying that the public didn't want classical music in its movies, forgetting the lesson, of which Harry Cohn was quick to remind them, of *One Night of Love.*

But by the end of World War II, Columbia was scrambling for story material. The Chopin screenplay was resurrected. The company's major incursion into Technicolor, *Cover Girl,* had been an enormous success. The sound and music departments had proven themselves at least the equals of their counterparts at the bigger studios. Harry Cohn felt ready to forge ahead with the Chopin biography as a large-scale effort.

Cornel Wilde was chosen for the lead. He had been around Hollywood for a number of years without attracting much attention. Fox hadn't succeeded in making him the new Tyrone Power, but Columbia managed to make him a star. As the tragically ill composer, in a story which made much of his love of freedom and democracy (popular ideas after the war against fascism) as well as his sufferings from tuberculosis, all set against Chopin's keyboard, Wilde was in a brilliantly romantic pose which captured the public fancy.

Cohn was right again. The public loved it. After the relative austerity of many of the war movies, the market for schmaltz had reopened. Seldom had the goo been so elegantly garnished. Merle Oberon played George Sand, the role that Capra had insisted only Marlene Dietrich could play. But when Oberon made her first appearance in the film, clad in man's clothes and a top hat, the effect was unforgettable. It was classic movie magic, an entrance that filmgoers will always remember, out of a movie that was not anywhere near as good as it looked. Oberon's tailcoat and the tubercular blood on the keyboard were cinematic effects, making the parts being greater than the whole of a movie that otherwise didn't really earn its applause. The acting was pretty atrocious, as befitted the dialogue. One of the biggest clinkers was Paul Muni's performance, probably the only bad one of a long and celebrated career. Jose Iturbi, who sat in for Cornel Wilde's fingers, ran through Chopin at just the correct speed for keeping a mass audience awake.

But silly as the whole enterprise seems now, in 1945 it was wonderful. *A Song to Remember* was nominated for six Academy Awards—including Best Actor for Cornel Wilde—but didn't win any of them. The movie made a lot of money and spawned

Here he is with co-star Rita Hayworth . . .

. . . whom he courts in their next venture, *You Were Never Lovelier* (1942)

Cover Girl boasted only 15 lovelies (besides star Hayworth) instead of the hundreds massed in other musicals; they were led by Leslie Brooks, front . . .

. . . and center; Jinx Falkenburg was also featured in the film. (1944)

Cornel Wilde and Merle Oberon in *A Song to Remember*—as George Sand to his Chopin, she was helpful on stage . . .

. . . and off as well; it was an elegant production (1944)

a whole slew of imitators. Again, all of them flopped. Hollywood is quite accomplished at producing pretentiousness, but somehow the public only buys it the first time around. Directors are still trying to make the lives of the great composers palatable (*vide* Ken Russell and Tchaikovsky, an inevitable disaster) but only *A Song to Remember* was a commercial success.

Hot on the heels of the Wilde-Chopin film came a musical in a more familiar vein, *The Jolson Story*. Once again, the east coast scoffed; although Al Jolson had been the number one entertainer of his day, his popularity had disappeared by 1946. It was felt that here was a has-been in whom the public would have no interest whatsoever. They were wrong. Not only was the dubbed-in voice of Jolson refreshing after years of monotonous vocalists, the story itself was very heartwarming, very America. A young unknown, Larry Parks, made a thoroughly convincing Jolson. The songs were the highlights of what had been a truly fabulous career, worth their weight in memories to the older audience and in novelty to the younger one.

The production was originally set for a one and a half million dollars, but within the first few weeks of filming it became evident that it would quickly exceed that budget. Sidney Buchman, persuaded by Cohn to make the film, was given the go-ahead to spend whatever he had to. There were to be no shortcuts on any of the elements of *The Jolson Story*. It was to be a big, first quality film. A great deal of love and care—and a final dollar figure of two million eight hundred thousand—went into its making.

It paid off handsomely. The picture grossed more than eight million dollars, Al Jolson began a whole new career, and Columbia squeezed out a sequel, *Jolson Sings Again*, the following year. As was to be expected, that didn't do as well as the original, but it didn't do badly, either.

Yet, all this success with musicals didn't result in the studio rushing headlong into yearly multiple extravaganzas. Properties were still selected as carefully as ever, before large amounts of money were earmarked for production and promotion. Columbia had achieved its success and durability by concentrating on two or three major movies each year, the balance of the output being fillers for the bottom half of the double bill that

The Jolson Story—Larry Parks (as Jolson), with William Demarest and Bill Goodwin, watches Evelyn Keyes, his wife-to-be, imitate him (1946)

"My mammy-y-y!" Parks recreating Jolie's days in vaudeville

Production number in *The Jolson Story* with Larry Parks

Rita Hayworth, as Terpsichore, has come *Down to Earth*, and Larry Parks (right) has come down to this; Marc Platt is his rival (1947)

The Mount Olympus number, from *Down to Earth*

was still the format for most theaters. Their next noteworthy musical to be released wasn't until 1957.*

That was *Pal Joey*. The John O'Hara story of a heel had been filmed before, but not as a musical. For Gene Kelly, Joey had been transformed into a dancer. But now, he was once more a singer—for Frank Sinatra. He was also a bridge—for Rita Hayworth and Kim Novak. Both love goddess number one *and* number two were to vie for Frank's film favors. Interestingly, this was another property which, like *A Song to Remember*, Cohn had had his eye on for a long time. Similarly, he had envisioned Marlene Dietrich for the Vera Simpson role. Again, he couldn't get her and the project hung fire for a while.

When it was finally set, top talent was brought in to provide the opulent production values that are hallmarks of all the studio's best musicals. George Sidney directed with a lavish hand. Jean Louis designed the costumes, and Hermes Pan did the choreography. Even the character of O'Hara's original tough

---

*This is not to suggest that the musicals were on the wane. There were a couple of minor Hayworth pieces, already noted, but most musicals of the period were black-and-white "B" features of small import.

The Love Goddesses fought for Sinatra in *Pal Joey*, but Novak, though younger, wasn't a dancer and had trouble keeping up with Hayworth (1957)

little anti-hero was somewhat glossed over. But the gritty lyrics of some of Lorenz Hart's best tunes retained the incisiveness of the original story.

Sinatra fitted his role better than either of his leading ladies did theirs, and thus came out looking best of all three stars. Cast as the still glamorous older woman, it was clearly Rita Hayworth's swan song to genuine glamour-girl roles of the type she had thrived on. As the ingenue, Kim Novak looked—and acted—like a department store mannequin. Her nearly perfect face was never marred by anything resembling an expression. The happy ending tacked on to the screeplay was about as convincing as her performance.

All in all, it was a rather typical example of what Hollywood often did when it dolled up a hit from another medium—play, book, whatever—and redid it to movie standards. It was too bad in this case, because *Pal Joey* was merely a hit, and it easily could have been much more, especially on the basis of Sinatra's performance.

In 1963 came *Bye Bye Birdie*. Strictly for fun, this item, about an Elvis Presley-type singer about to enter the army to the consternation of his legions of young fans, did very well. It was bright and bouncy and did not require anything to be taken too seriously. While it did nothing for Janet Leigh, who was terribly miscast, it brought rave notices and star status to both Dick Van Dyke and Ann-Margret. Van Dyke repeated his stage role, as did Paul Lynde. It is the kind of musical that Hollywood generally is best at, and it made a nice splash.

Because the subject matter is fluff to begin with, the mount-

Sidney Poitier, Sammy Davis, Jr., Dorothy Dandridge, Brock Peters and Pearl Bailey (on steps) in the Gershwin opera, *Porgy and Bess* (1959)

Poitier was Porgy, and the lady comforting him is Pearl Bailey

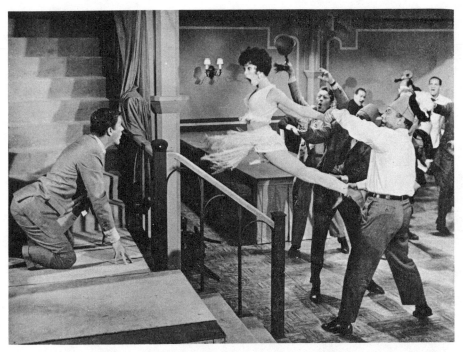

Dick Van Dyke and Janet Leigh at a Shriners' convention in *Bye Bye Birdie*; Leigh's part was cut down to make way for the new girl in town . . .

ing of a musical comedy, as opposed to a *musical*, which may not be comedy at all (like much of *Pal Joey*, *Carousel*, and *The Most Happy Fella*, to cite a near-miss and a couple of casualties), is much more Hollywood's forte. However, the costs of production are such that the giant musical extravaganza is very nearly a dinosaur at the present time, and supposedly we should be grateful for anything we get. The paucity of such films in the 70s may make the 60s biggies look better as time passes.

Before the decade drew to its close, there were to be other musicals produced by Columbia, which for sheer size exceeded anything the studio had put out during the heyday of the form. By the late 60s, choreographers no longer had to improvise routines that a twosome or trio could handle, a la *Cover Girl*. The studio was big enough and rich enough in its physical capabilities to give all the needed scope to any production.

Now everything could be bigger, but was it better?

Some, but not all, of the lessons of *Pal Joey* were absorbed in the mounting of two blockbuster musicals. Also imports from Broadway, both *Oliver!* and *Funny Girl* burst on the big

. . . Ann-Margret, who really took off in this role

Here's Ann-Margret with Jesse Pearson, who played the teen-age idol in the film (1963)

screens of 1968, during another Golden Age at Columbia. Both were very elaborate versions of stories that were essentially steeped in poverty. Neither New York's lower east side nor the poorhouses of Charles Dickens' London ever looked lovelier. But in musicals, credibility is supposed to be stretched anyway.

Oliver! was transported from Broadway with none of the original cast intact, and no real star power to carry it, yet it became the Best Picture of the year; *Funny Girl* was primarily the means for bringing Barbra Streisand to the movies, and *she* was named Best Actress of the year. Thus, both films very neatly performing exactly as they were intended to.

Where *Oliver!* came a cropper was in the early scenes; its poor little orphans just a little too cute and a little too lusty in their demands for more food. Once those few sticky moments were past, the film started to work. The primary relationship between Oliver and Fagin, the rough-hewn love affair of Nancy and Sykes, the camaraderie of the gang of boy-thieves are believable because they are expressed by not overly familiar faces. The Lionel Bart

Sheila White and Shani Wallis lead *Oliver!*—Mark Lester—and the other boys in an impromptu round of "I'd Do Anything" . . .

. . . and even Fagin joins in the fun; Ron Moody is Fagin (1968)

Two views of John Box's recreated London—here is the lower-class street market . . .

. . . and lovely, aristocratic Bloomsbury

score is lively and pertinent and the big dance scenes convey a sense of . . . big dance scenes. They could scarcely be expected to provide a sense of the poor and dismal London of that time. That is hardly the sort of thing that would entertain musical comedy audiences in the supermarket sixties.

On the other hand, the laundering of the Second Avenue tenements in *Funny Girl* didn't matter much because nothing in that film mattered much except Barbra Streisand. There was one hit song ("People") included in the score, and one or two semimemorables. Cast opposite Barbra was Omar Sharif, and in this case the word *opposite* was never more appropriate. She was lively, he was wooden. She glowed, he faded. She sounded authentically New York (why not?). He sounded stranded somewhere in eastern Europe (why?).

An authentic star was born with this first screen role. Her performance dominates the action so totally that the film is well on its way before the realization sneaks up on one that it's not a very good movie. The dialogue is trite, cliché-loaded, the situations and solutions predictable. The moment (all 146 of them) is clearly Barbra's. She is able to extract a wide inventory of emotions from the proceedings and make the audience share them with her. She plays the comedy for all its worth, sings marvelously, letting the instrument of her voice wield itself as if the screen held no limits, and carries the dramatic scenes virtually solo.*

Prior to this film, Barbra Streisand was well-established as a first-rank star in the other media she had tackled: recordings, theater, nightclubs, and television. With this one performance, she became the hottest property to hit the movies in years. Her next film, for double the money, was at another studio, but she came back to Columbia for some of her best dramatic roles, like *The Owl and the Pussycat* and *The Way We Were*.

The 70s also witnessed another kind of musical besides the super-star Streisand hit. A soulful celebration of black wit and music was called *Wattstax '72*. The film included some of the top vocalists and groups of the day, performing at a day-long free concert in the Los Angeles ghetto. Interspersed with the music were rap sessions with comedian Richard Pryor and non-actor community people. *Let the Good Times Roll* tried for something similar in a nostalgia-drenched 50s vein. After these two all-star line-ups came the exuberant *Godspell*, with no stars but a lot of 70s style music and themes.

---

*She would recap the triumph with *Funny Lady*, the Brice-based sequel.

Instant identification for a movie title and instant stardom for its star

As the ebullient Fanny Brice, Barbra Streisand skates her way across the stage; *Funny Girl* brought her an Oscar (1968)

Dramatic turns in the story gave Barbra ample room to display her incredible acting range

Room for romance too, as in this tender scene with co-star Omar Sharif

Production number from *Funny Lady* (1975)

In *Funny Lady*, Barbra is back again as Fanny Brice—shades of Baby Snooks

No show business musical is complete without a rehearsal scene, replete with chorus kids and piano player, in this case, James Caan (right)—but this isn't just any 88'er; as Barbra soon learns, it's Billy Rose

The Staple Singers do their own kind of gospel-based music in *Wattstax* (1973)

Isaac Hayes, "Black Moses" of music, brings *Wattstax* to a powerful climax

The spirited cast of *Godspell* (1973)

Thus the musicals. They were often innovative, and therefore imitated, all out of proportion to the money and physical expense Columbia was usually able to give its films. Technically, they were always superb, making up in quality what was lacking in the physical facilities the studio afforded. By not fashioning musicals mechanically, like so many of the formula standards of the bigger companies, Columbia was to set new standards for the entire genre.

210

ONE NIGHT OF LOVE

(Released: September 6, 1934)

Director: Victor Schertzinger
Editor: Gene Milford
Story:
  Dorothy Speare
  Charles Beqhan
Screen Play: S. K. Lauren
Music: Louis Silvers
Thematic Music: Victor Schertzinger
  and Gus Kahn
Music Director: Dr. Pietro Cimini

Cameraman:
  Joe Walker, A.S.C.

Footage: 7296 ft.

Cast:
Grace Moore
Tullio Carminati
Lyle Talbot
Mona Barrie
Jessie Raph
Luis Alberni
Andres de Segurola
Rosemary Glosz
Nydia Westman

LOVE ME FOREVER

(Released: June 26, 1936)

Director: Victor Schertzinger
Editors: Gene Milford,
  Viola Lawrence
Story: Victor Schertzinger
Screen Play:
  Jo Swerling
  Sidney Buchman
Operatic Numbers Conducted by:
  Gaetano Muola
Lyrics: Gus Kahn
Music Director: Louis Silvers

Photography:
  Joe Walker, A.S.C.

Footage: 8349 ft.

Cast:
Grace Moore
Leo Carillo
Robert Allen
Spring Byington
Michael Bartlett
Louis Alberni
Douglas Dumbrille
Thurston Hall

THE KING STEPS OUT

(Released: May 12, 1936)

Director: Joseph Von Sternberg
Associate Director: William Thiele
Associate Producer:
  William Perlberg
Editor: Viola Lawrence
Story:
  Gustav Holm
  Ernest Decsey
  Hubert Marischa
Screen Play: Sidney Buchman
Musical Score: Howard Jackson
Music Composer: Fritz Kriesler
Lyrics: Dorothy Fields
Art Director: Stephen Goosson

Vocal Music Director:
  Joseph A. Pasternack
Ballet:
  Albertina Rasch
Costumes:
  Ernest Dryden
Director of Photography:
  Lucien Ballard, A.S.C.

Cast:
Grace Moore
Franchot Tone
Walter Connolly
Raymond Walburn
Elisabeth Risdon
Nana Bryant
Victor Jory
Frieda Inescourt
Thurston Hall
Herman Bing
George Russell
John Arthur

WHEN YOU'RE IN LOVE

(Released: February 16, 1937)

Director: Robert Riskin
Editor: Gene Milford
Screen Play: Robert Riskin
Story: Ethel Hill, Cedric Worth
Original Music: Jerome Kern
Lyrics: Dorothy Fields
Music Director: Alfred Newman
Ensemble staged by: Leon Leonidoff
Director of Photography:
  Joe Walker, A.S.C.

Cast:
Grace Moore
Cary Grant
Aline MacMahon
Henry Stephenson
Thomas Mitchell
Catherine Doucet
Luis Alberni
Gerald Oliver Smith
Emma Dunn
George Pearce
Frank Puglia

Footage: 9447 ft.

I'LL TAKE ROMANCE

(Released: November 17, 1937)

Director: Edward H. Griffith
Producer: Everett Riskin
Editors:
  Otto Meyer
  William Lyon
Story: Stephen Morehouse Avery
Screen Play:
  George Oppenheimer
  Jane Murfin
Songs:
  Oscar Hammerstein, II
  Ben Oakland
Opera Sequences Staged by:
  William Von Wymetal, Jr.
Opera Sequences Conducted by:
  Isaac Van Grove
Art Directors:
  Stephen Goosson
  Lionel Banks
Music Director: M. W. Stoloff

Interiors:
  Babs Johnstone
Gowns: Kalloch
Director of Photography:
  Lucien Andriot, A.S.C.

Cast:
Grace Moore
Melvyn Douglas
Helen Westley
Stuart Erwin
Margaret Hamilton
Walter Kingsford
Richard Carle
Ferdinand Gottschalk
Esther Muir
Frank Forest
Walter Stahl
Barry Norton
Lucio Villeges
Gennaro Curci
Marek Windheim

YOU'LL NEVER GET RICH

(Released: September 12, 1941)

Director: Sidney Lanfield
Assistant Director: Gene Anderson
Producer: Samuel Bischoff
Editor: Otto Meyer
Screen Play:
  Michael Fessier
  Ernest Pagano
Songs: Cole Porter
Musical Director: M. W. Stoloff

Cast:
Fred Astaire
Rita Hayworth
Robert Benchley
John Hubbard
Osa Massen
Freida Inescort
Guinn Williams
Donald MacBride
Cliff Nazarro
Marjorie Gateson
Ann Shoemaker
Boyd Davis

212

Art Director: Lionel Banks
Dances staged by: Robert Alton
Director of Photography:
  Phillip Tannura, A.S.C.
Musical Recording: P. J. Faulkner

YOU WERE NEVER LOVELIER

(Released: October 5, 1942)

Director: William A. Seiter
Assistant Director:
  Norman Deming
Producer: Louis F. Edelman
Editor: William Lyon
Story:
  Carlos Olivari
  Sixto Pondal Rios
Screen Play:
  Michael Fessier
  Ernest Pagano
  Delmer Daves
Music: Jerome Kern
Lyrics: Johnny Mercer
Art Director: Lionel Banks
Associate Art Director:
  Rudolph Sternad

Music Director:
  Leigh Harline
Assistant Music Director:
  Paul Meroz
Musical Arrangements:
  Conrad Salinger
Dance Director:
  Val Raset
Interior Decorator:
  Frank Tuttle
Director of Photography:
  Frank Tuttle
Gowns: Irene
Director of Photography:
  Ted Teztlaff, A.S.C.

Cast:
Fred Astaire
Rita Hayworth
Adolphe Menjou
Isobel Elsom
Leslie Brooks
Adele Mara
Gus Schilling
Barbara Brown
Douglas Leavitt
Xavier Cugat and
  his Orchestra

A SONG TO REMEMBER

(Released: August 16, 1944)

Director: Charles Vidor
Assistant Director: Abby Berlin
Producer: Louis F. Edelman
Editor: Charles Nelson
Screen Play: Sidney Buchman
Based on the Story by:
  Ernst Mareschka
Musical Adaptation: Niklos Rozsa
Art Directors:
  Lionel Banks
  Van Nest Polglase
Music Director: M. W. Stoloff
Musical Supervisor: Mario Silva
Set Decorations: Frank Tuttle

Costumes:
  Walter Plumkett
Miss Oberon's Costumes:
  Travis Banton
Make-up:
  Clay Campbell, S.M.A.
Hair Styles: Helen Hunt
Directors of Photography:
  Tony Gaudio, A.S.C.
  Allen M. Davey, A.S.C.
Cameraman:
  Fayte M. Browne
Technicolor Director:
  Natalie Kalmus
Music Recording by:
  William Randell

Footage: 10,426 ft.

Cast:
Paul Muni
Merle Oberon
Cornel Wilde
Nina Foch
George Coulouris
Howard Freeman
Stephen Bekassy

COVER GIRL

(Released: April, 1944)

Director: Charles Vidor
Assistant Director:
 Oscar Boetticher, Jr.
Editor: Viola Lawrence
Story: Erwin Gelsey
Screen Play: Virginia Van Upp
Adaptation:
 Marion Parsonnet
 Paul Gangelin
Music: Jerome Kern
Lyrics: Ira Gershwin
 Songs: "Make Way for
 Tomorrow," "Poor John,"
 "Sure Thing," "Put Me to the
 Test," "That's the Best of All,"
 "The Show Must Go On,"
 "Cover Girl," "Long Ago,"
 "Who's Complaining."
Song: "Poor John":
 Fred W. Leigh,
 Henry E. Pether
Orchestrations: Carmen Dragon
Art Directors:
 Lionel Banks
 Cary Odell
Music Director: M. W. Stoloff
Set Decoration: Ray Babcock
Dance Numbers Staged by:
 Val Raset, Seymour Felix
Magazine Covers Created by:
 Hoffman and Coburn
Magazines Photographed by:
 Robert Coburn

Gowns:
 Travis Benton
 Gwen Wakeling
 Muriel King
Make-up:
 Clay Campbell, S.M.A.
Hairstyles: Helen Hunt
Directors of Photography:
 Rudolph Mate, A.S.C.
 Allen M. Davey, A.S.C.
Technicolor Director:
 Natalie Kalmus
Associate:
 Morgan Padelford
Technical Consultants:
 Harry Conover
 Anita Colby
Music Recording:
 P. J. Faulkner

Cast:
Gene Kelley
Lee Bowman
Phil Silvers
Jinx Falkenburg
Leslie Brooks
Eve Arden
Otto Kruger
Jess Barker
Anita Colby
Curt Bois
Ed Brophy
Thurston Hall
The Cover Girls:
Jean Colleran
Francine Counihan
Helen Mueller
Cecilia Meagher
Betty Jane Hess
Dusty Anderson
Eileen McCleary
Dicki
Karen X. Gaylord
Cheryl Archer
Peggy Floyd
Betty Jane Graham
Martha Outlaw
Susan Shaw
Rose May Robson

THE JOLSON STORY

(Released: July, 1946)

Director: Sidney Buchman
Assistant Director:
 Wilbur McGaugh
Producer: Sidney Skolsky
Editor: William Lyon
Screen Play: Stephen Longstreet
Adaptation:
 Harry Chandlee
 Andrew Solt
Vocal Arrangements:
 Saul Chaplin
Orchestral Arrangements:
 Martin Fried
Art Directors:
 Stephen Goosson

Director of Photography:
 Joe Walker, A.S.C.
Technicolor Director:
 Natalie Kalmus
Associate:
 Morgan Padelford
Sound Recording:
 Hugh McDowell
Music Recording:
 Edwin Wetzel
Re-recording:
 Richard Olson

Cast:
Larry Parks
Evelyn Keyes
William Demarest
Bill Goodwin
Ludwig Donath
Scotty Beckett
Tamara Shayne
Jo-Carroll Dennison
John Alexander
Ernest Cossart
The Mitchell Boy Choir
William Forrest
Ann E. Todd
Edwin Maxwell

Walter Holscher
Music Director: M. W. Stoloff
Set Decorations:
  William Kiernan
  Louis Diag
Dances Staged by: Jack Cole
Production Numbers Directed by:
  Joseph H. Lewis
Montage Director:
  Lawrence W. Butler
Gowns: Jean Louis
Make-up: Clay Campbell, S.M.A.
Hairstyles: Helen Hunt

Emmett Vogan
Eddie Kane
Jimmy Lloyd
Adele Roberts
Franklyn Farnum

DOWN TO EARTH

(Released: March, 1947)

Director: Alexander Hall
Assistant Director:
  Wilbur McGaugh
Producer: Don Hartman
Assistant Producer:
  Norman Deming
Editor: Viola Lawrence
Screen Play:
  Edwin Blum
  Don Hartman
The "Jordan" Characters:
  From the play, "Heaven Can Wait," by Henry Segal
Songs:
  Allan Roberts
  Doris Fisher
Additional Music:
  George Duning
  Heins Roemheid
Art Directors:
  Stephen Goosson
  Rudolph Sternad
Music Director:
  M. W. Stoloff
Set Decorations: William Kiernan
Dances Staged by: Jack Cole

Production Arrangement:
  Charles Chaplin
  Fred Karger
  Earl Hagan
Greek Ballet:
  Castelnuova-Tedesco
Gowns: Jean Louis
Make-up
  Clay Campbell, S.M.A.
Hairstyles: Helen Hunt
Director of Photography:
  Rudolph Mate, A.S.C.
Technicolor Director:
  Natalie Kalmus
Associate:
  Francisco Cugat
Sound Recording:
  George Cooper
Music Recording:
  Philip Faulkner

Cast:
Rita Hayworth
Larry Parks
Marc Platt
Roland Culver
James Gleason
Edward Everett
  Horton
Adele Jergens
George Macready
William Frawley

JOLSON SINGS AGAIN

(Released: August, 1949)

Producer: Sidney Buchman
Associate: Francis Cugat
Director of Photography:
  William Snyder
Technicolor Direction:
  Natalie Kalmus

Cast:
Larry Parks
Barbara Hale
William Demarest
Ludwig Donath

Bill Goodwin
Myron McCormick
Tamara Shayne

215

PAL JOEY

(Released: October, 1957)

Director: George Sidney
Assistant Director: Art Black
Producer: Fred Kohlmar
Editors:
  Viola Lawrence, A.C.E.
  Jerome Thoms, A.C.E.
Screen Play: Dorothy Kingsley
**Based on the Musical Play and
  Book by** John O'Hara
Music: Richard Rodgers
Lyrics: Lorenz Hart
Music Adaptation:
  George Duning
  Nelson Riddle
Musical Arrangements:
  Nelson Riddle
Music Advisor: Fred Karger
Orchestration:
  Arthur Morton
Art Director:
  Walter Holscher
Music Director: M. W. Stoloff

Set Decorators:
  William Kiernan
  Louis Diage
Choreography:
  Hermes Pan
Gowns: Jean Louis
Make-up: Ben Lane,
  S.M.A.
Hairstyles: Helen Hunt
**Technicolor Director of
  Photography:**
  Harold Lipstein, A.S.C.
Technicolor Consultant:
  Henri Jaffa
Sound: Franklin Hansen
Recording Supervisor:
  John Livadary

Cast
Rita Hayworth
Frank Sinatra
Kim Novak
Barbara Nichols
Bobby Sherwood
Hank Henry
Elizabeth Patterson
Robin Morse
Frank Wilcox
Pierre Watson
Barry Bernard
Ellie Kent
Franklyn Farnum

PORGY AND BESS

(Released: June, 1959)

Director: Otto Preminger
Assistant Director: Paul Helmick
Producer: Samuel Goldwyn
Editor: Daniel Mandel, A.C.E.
Based on the Play by:
  DuBose and Dorothy Heyward
Screen Play: N. Richard Nash
Music: George Gershwin
Lyrics:
  DuBose Heyward
  Ira Gershwin
Libretto: DuBose Heyward
Orchestrations:
  Alexander Courage
  Conrad Salinger
  Robert Franklyn
  Al Woodbury
Music Editor: Richard Carruth
Art Directors:
  Serge Krizman
  Joseph Wright
Music Director: Andre Previn
Associate: Ken Darby
Set Decorations: Howard Bristol
Production Design: Oliver Smith

Choreography:
  Hermes Pan
Production Manager:
  Doc Merman
Dialogue Coach:
  Max Slater
Costumes: Irene Sharaff
Make-up:
  Frank McCoy, S.M.A.
  Layne Britton, H.S.U.
Hairstyles:
  Jean St. Oegger, C.H.S.
Director of Photography:
  Leon Shamroy, A.S.C.
**Sound Recording
  Supervision:**
  Gordon Sawyer
  Fred Hynes
Sound Editor:
  Don Hall, Jr.
Music Recording:
  Murry Spivak
  Vinton Vernon

Cast:
Sidney Poitier
Dorothy Dandridge
Sammy Davis, Jr.
Brock Peters
Diahann Carroll
Leslie Scott
Ruth Attaway
Claude Atkins
Pearl Bailey
Clarence Muse
Everdinne Wilson
Joel Fluellen
Earl Jackson
Moses LaMarr
Margaret Hairston
Ivan Dixon

216

BYE BYE BIRDIE

(Released: April, 1963)

Director: George Sidney
Assistant Director: Dave Silver
Producer: Fred Kohlmar
Editor: Charles Nelson, A.C.E.
Based on the Play and Book
  by: Michael Stewart
Screen Play: Irving Brecher
Music and Lyrics:
  Charles Strouse
  Lee Adams
Orchestration:
  Johnny Green
  Al Woodbury
Music Coordinator:
  Fred Karger
Music Supervision and
  Arrangement: Johnny Green
Set Decorations: Arthur Krams
Production Design: Paul Groesse
Choreography: Onna White
Assistant Choreography:
  Tommy Panko

Miss Leigh's Costumes:
  Pat Barto
Wardrobe Coordinator:
  Marjorie B. Wahl
Make-up:
  Ben Lane, S.M.A.
Teenage Make-up
  Created by:
  Helena Rubenstein
Miss Leigh's Hairstyles:
  Larry Germain
Production Assistant:
  Milton Feldman
Director of Photography:
  Joseph Biric, A.S.C.
Sound Supervision:
  Charles J. Rice
Sound:
  James Z. Flaster

Cast:
Janet Leigh
Dick Van Dyke
Ann-Margret
Maureen Stapleton
Bobby Rydell
Jesse Pearson
Paul Lynde
Mary Larouche
Michael Evans
Robert Paige
Gregory Morton
Bryan Russell
Milton Fromme
Ed Sullivan

FUNNY GIRL

(Released: September, 1968)

Director: William Wyler
Assistant Directors:
  Jack Roe
  Ray Gosnell
Producer: Ray Stark
Assistant Producers:
  David Dworski
  Lorry McCauley
Editors:
  Maury Winetrobe
  William Sands
Based on the Play and Book by:
  Isobel Lennart
Screen Play: Isobel Lennart
Musical Numbers:
  Music: Jule Styne
  Lyrics: Bob Merrill
  Director: Herbert Ross
Song, "My Man":
  Music: Maurice Yvain
  French Lyrics:
    A. Willemetz
    Jacques Charles
  English Adaptation:
    Channing Pollack

Music Director:
  Walter Scharf
Set Decorations:
  William Kiernan
Production Design:
  Gene Callahan
Properties:
  Richard M. Rubin
Vocal-Dance
  Arrangements:
  Betty Walberg
Script Supervisor:
  Marshall Schlom
Miss Streisand's
  Costumes:
  Irene Sharoff
Furs: Reiss & Fabrizio
Make-up Supervision:
  Ben Lane, S.M.A.
Make-up Artist:
  Frank McCoy
Hairstyles:
  Virginia Darcy
  Vivienne Walker

Cast:
Barbra Streisand
Omar Sharif
Kay Medford
Anne Francis
Walter Pidgeon
Lee Allen
Mae Questral
Gerald Mohr
Frank Faylen
Mittie Lawrence
Gertrude Flynn
Penny Santon
John Harmon
The Ziegfield Girls:
Thoris Brandt
Bettina Brenna
Virginia Ann Ford
Alena Johnston
Karen Lee
Mary Jane Mangler
Inga Neilsen
Sharon Vaughn

Song, "Second Hand Rose":
  James F. Hanley
  Grant Clarke
Song, "I'd Rather be Blue":
  Fred Fisher
  Billy Rose
Orchestration:
  Jack Hayes
  Walter Scharf
  Leo Shuken
  Herbert Spencer
  Lepard Newhart
Music Editor: Ted Sebern
Art Director: Robert Luthardt

Unit Production
  Manager:
  Paul Helmick
Director of Photography:
  Harry Stradling, A.S.C.
Sound Supervision:
  Charles J. Rice
Sound:
  Arthur Piantadosi
  Jack Solomon
Sound Editor:
  Joe Henrie

WATTSTAX

(Released: February, 1973)

Director: Mel Stuart
Assistant Director:
  Charles Washburn
Producers:
  Larry Shaw
  Mel Stuart
Executive Producers:
  Al Bell
  David L. Wolper
Associate Producer:
  Forest Hamilton, H.N.I.C.
Editors:
  Robert Lambert
  David Newhouse
  David Blewitt
Assistant Editors:
  Joseph Calloway
  Chuck Montgomery
Concert Artist Staging:
  Melvin van Peebles,
  Yeah, Inc.
Music Supervisor: Terry Manning
Music Editor:
  Neiman-Tillar Associates
Concert Unit Supervisors:
  Rick Holmes
  Buster Jones
  Larry McCormick
  Johnny Williams
  Wesley Buford
Concert Unit Director:
  Sid McCoy
Music Director: Dale Warren

Consultants:
  Rev. Jesse Jackson
  Tommy Jacquette
  Mafundi Institute
  Rev. Jesse Boyd
  Teddy Stewart
  Richard Thomas
  John W. Smith
  Sylvester Williams
  Carol Hall
Research Assistant:
  Alex Pomasonoff
Dubbing:
  Samuel Goldwyn Studio
Opticals:
  Cinema Research
Location Sound:
  Richard Wells
Additional Location Sound:
  Leroy Joseph
  Ed Rue
  Thomas Washington
Sound Consultants:
  Ivan Kruglak
  Bruce Bizans
Sound Effects:
  Edit-Rite
Music Recording:
  Wally Heider, Inc.
Supervisors:
  Gabriel Gradney
  Artie King
Lighting: Acey Dcey
Librarian: Bea Dennis

Cast:
  The Dramatics
  The Staple Singers
  Kim Weston
  Jimmy Jones
  Rance Allen Group
  William Bell
  Louise McCord
  Debra Manning
  Eric Mercury
  Freddy Robinson
  Lee Sain
  Ernie Hines
  Little Sonny
  The Newcomers
  Eddie Floyd
  The Temprees
  Frederick Knight
  The Emotions
  The Bar Kays
  Albert King
  Little Milton
  Johnnie Taylor
  Mel & Tim
  Carla Thomas
  Rufus Thomas
  Luther Ingram
  Isaac Hayes
  Richard Pryor
  Ted Lange
  Elizabeth Cleveland
  Raymond Allen
  Andre Edwards
  Patricia Henley

218

Production Associates:
Cassius Weathersby
Jet Set, Inc.
Boom, Boom
J.D. of Hollywood
Production Assistants:
Lou Harris, Matthew Ford
Post Production Supervision:
Phil Wyley
Production Coordinator:
David Oyster
Directors of Photography:
Roderick Young
Robert Marks
Jose Mignone
Larry Clark
Concert Photography:
John Alonzo, D.P.
David Blewitt
Robert Grant
Hal Grier
Roy Lewis
Howard Morehead
Joe Wilcotts

Eric Kilpatrick
Ernest King
Michael Gibson

LET THE GOOD TIMES ROLL

(Released: 1973)

Directors:
Sid Levin
Robert Abel
Director of Photography:
Robert Thomas
Executive Producer: Charles Fries
Produced by: Gerald I. Isenberg
Supervising Film Editor: Sid Levin

Cast:
Chuck Berry
Little Richard
Fats Domino
Chubby Checker
Bo Diddley
The Shirelles
The Five Satins
The Coasters

Danny and
  the Juniors
The Bobby Comstock
Rock and Roll Band
Bill Haley
  and the Comets
Richard Nader

GODSPELL

(Released 1973)

Director: David Greene
Associated Director:
John-Michael Tebelak
Screen Play by: David Greene and
John-Michael Tebelak
Music and Lyrics by:
Stephen Schwartz
Director of Photography:
Richard G. Helmann
Editor: Alan Helm
Producer: Edgar Lansbury

Cast:
Victor Garber
David Haskell
Jerry Sroka
Lynne Thigpen
Katie Hanley

Robin Lamont
Gilmer McCormick
Joanne Jonas
Merrell Jackson
Jeffrey Mylett

6 | The Oscars

GOWER STREET WAS FESTOONED WITH ITS FIRST ARMLOAD of Oscars in 1934 when *It Happened One Night* took all five major awards. Another Capra feature, *You Can't Take It with You,* was Best Picture four years later. Throughout the ensuing time, Columbia was to win Oscars and acclaim for the achievements of its stars, directors, writers, and technical people, but it wasn't until 1949 that its unprecedented domination of the Academy's Best Picture Award began.

The film was *All the King's Men* and it also brought Oscars to its star, Broderick Crawford, and supporting actress, Mercedes McCambridge.* Based on a best-selling novel by Robert Penn Warren, the picture was fashioned by Robert Rossen, who produced, directed, and wrote the screenplay. The story, the rise to power of a southern demagogue, was said to be based on the career and person of Huey Long, murdered Louisiana politician. Elements in the character of the protagonist, Willie Stark, were

---

*The three Oscars were among thirty major awards that the film won internationally.

ul Scofield wrestles with his conscience as Sir—later, St.—Thomas More, *A an For All Seasons* (1966)

more than faintly visible to many around Columbia as more than passingly similar to the head man on Gower Street. Rossen was to admit openly that Willie incorporated many of the traits of one H. Cohn.**

Cohn found it all highly flattering. He could identify with Willie and thus had a deep feeling for the film. For once, he let all the credit accrue where it belonged—to Rossen. The two men fought before and after *All the King's Men*, but the film itself represented an important peak for both of them.

For Robert Rossen, it was the pinnacle of his career. Although he made many fine films afterwards, (including *The Hustler* with Paul Newman) he would never have such total control over such exceptional material as he did here. One of the prominent victims of Hollywood's McCarthy-inspired blacklisting, his work was thwarted for a long period in the 50s and none of his later films had the dramatic and political punch of *All the King's Men*.

For Columbia, it was another breakthrough, comparable to the crowning point of Capra's career years before. Although the company had produced some good films during the war years and

---

**Garson Kanin said the same of Harry Brock, millionaire junk man of *Born Yesterday*. Harry Cohn loved that character, too.

Crawford, with John Ireland as a chief henchman, reviews the troops

222

the post-war period, the times were lean throughout the industry. Public interest in movies, and thereby the grosses, was down. Television was influencing the entertainment habits of the nation; the war had sharpened both the sophistication and awareness of the audience. With the small screen at home requiring no admission price, selectivity became an all-important factor at the box-office. Mediocrity couldn't make it anymore, not for Columbia or anyone else. What the public wanted was not the escape fare of the Depression and war years, but something worth leaving home and plunking down money for.

Setting for a demagogue, American-style, keynotes the authenticity of the production

With the enormous pull of *All the King's Men*, Columbia found the answer. Quality films, even with controversial subject matter long considered above the heads of mass audiences, had a waiting market. The company's long-standing policy of producing two or three top-flight pictures a year, brought to the screen some of the qualitatively finest films to come out of Hollywood in the 50s.

The list of 50s' films that *didn't* win the Oscar for the Best Picture of the Year is almost as impressive as the list of winners: *The Last Angry Man, The Caine Mutiny, Death of a Salesman, Anatomy of a Murder, The Last Hurrah,* and *The Goddess* all number among the Columbia output of this period. So do three with fine appearances by Humphrey Bogart—*Knock on Any*

Door, *In a Lonely Place,* and *The Harder They Fall.* (*The Wild One,* with Brando, is discussed in a later chapter.)

The pattern had been set. Once again, the markets were searched for the best properties—the best-selling novels, hit plays, and occasionally, original screenplays. Oscar time came again in 1953, with one of the longest shots Harry Cohn had ever played.

From Here to Eternity was a breakthrough novel, as explicit in its language and situations as the literary standards of the time would allow. The biggest book to come out of the Second World War, it dealt with the conditions in the army, not under fire, but prior to the outbreak of hostilities. It was widely read for its seamy love scenes and for its vivid depiction of men under stress.

Against the advice of everyone in the company, Harry Cohn bought the screen rights and proceeded to put the project together.

Buddy Adler was the producer, but there is no question that Cohn had a special feeling for *From Here to Eternity.* He worked closely on the developing screenplay with writer Daniel Taradash, director Fred Zinnemann, and Adler.

The film was in production as a Columbia sales meeting was being held. From his bed, Cohn was holding court. To the men present, as to most of Columbia, the feasibility of *Eternity* was still very much in doubt. But Cohn quoted a single line from the book—the adulterous Karen being told by Warden that he knew of a deserted beach. In his moviemaker's eye, Cohn had already translated that simple line into one of the most famous sequences in all of film: Burt Lancaster and Deborah Kerr locked in embrace on the sand as the waves ebb and flow over their joined bodies. Perhaps as much as anything that has been written or said about him, this incident graphically demonstrates Harry Cohn's instincts about movies.

Including the Best Picture citation, *From Here to Eternity* garnered eight Oscars, tying the record with *Gone With the Wind.* It cast gold not only into Columbia's coffers, but into the careers of just about everyone connected with it. It brought Frank Sinatra back; it got Ernest Borgnine started. The singer won the Best Supporting Actor award, and Donna Reed, Best Supporting Actress, for her portrayal of Lorene, the hooker. Fred Zinnemann was named Best Director; Burnett Guffey, won for Best Cinematography; William Lyon for Best Editing, Dan Taradash for Best

---

*Filmography in Appendix to Chapter Nine

Broderick Crawford as Willie Stark in *All the King's Men* (1949)

Shocking for its time, the famous love scene between Deborah Kerr and Burt Lancaster in *From Here to Eternity* (1953)

The Japanese have bombed Pearl Harbor—Burt Lancaster goes into action

Screenplay, and the Columbia sound department for its recording work were all rewarded with the gold statuette.

Harry Cohn used his name in the ads for the film; his only such venture in direct exploitation of one of his movies.

It was a tough act to follow. It would take the best director of the decade, plus the best film actor of at least the decade, plus a topnotch writer, *plus* a producer with total autonomy, to match the impact of *From Here to Eternity*.

Frank Sinatra's dramatic comeback was one of the high points of the film; here he faces off against Ernest Borgnine

That meant Elia Kazan, Marlon Brando, Budd Schulberg, and Sam Spiegel. It meant the hardest-hitting story about the working class to reach the screen since *The Grapes of Wrath*. It meant *On the Waterfront*. The material was woven together expertly by Schulberg from a series of newspaper exposes of conditions on the Brooklyn docks. The illegal dealings of both union and company provide the background for the story, but it is in the characters that the movie makes its fullest impact. It is the faces, both the well-known and the unknown, that utterly absorb the viewer.

Brando is at the height of his powers here; he would have to be, in order not to be overshadowed by the gifted supporting cast —Karl Malden, Lee J. Cobb, Rod Steiger. After the actors', it is the faces of the milling crowds that arrest the audience's attention. They are no less authentic than the raw docks and brittle neighborhood streets in which the film was shot.

Rod Steiger is Marlon Brando's older brother and mentor in *On the Waterfront* (1954)

Brando wrestles with Lee J. Cobb, labor boss of the docks

Eva Marie Saint makes her screen debut as a neighborhood girl who befriends Brando

Karl Malden is the priest whose humanity encourages Brando and Eva Marie after his brutal beating and her brother's death

In two consecutive years, Columbia released two black-and-white conventionally sized motion pictures, and each walked off with eight Academy Awards. All the other studios were vying for attention (and attendance) with bigger screens and louder sounds, but Columbia had stayed out of the technology war and concentrated on quality films. It was a one-two punch that sent the company stock soaring.

For the record, the 1954 awards went this way. Brando, Best Actor; Elia Kazan, Best Director; Eva Marie Saint (in her film debut) Best Supporting Actress; Richard Day, Art Direction; Boris Kaufman, Cinematography; Gene Milford, Editing; Budd Schulberg, Best Story and Screenplay. Best Picture—*On the Waterfront*.

This movie signaled something else that was happening in Hollywood in the 50s—the advent of the independent producer. By 1954, it was more than just a trend, it was becoming the rule rather than the exception at all of the studios. Sam Spiegel could make a deal with Columbia to produce *On the Waterfront* that excluded any participation in the filming by the head of the studio. Thus, the picture was completely out of Cohn's hands. In this case, it was just as well, because he didn't care for it and didn't expect much from it.

And a few years later, when Spiegel brought in another major production, Harry Cohn was busying himself with *Pal Joey*. But 1957 was to be the year of *The Bridge on the River Kwai*. Instead of the old Rodgers-and-Hart standards, the world would be whistling "The Colonel Bogey March."

It was another war story that built on characters rather than combat. The primary fascination of critics and audiences was with the immovable characterization of the British army officer played by Alec Guinness, who carried out orders even to the detriment of his own side. Guinness is marvelous, well deserving of his Oscar. But from his first confrontation with his Japanese counterpart, Sessue Hayakawa, there is evidence of a subtle undercurrent that is thoroughly understood by director David Lean, but never spelled out to the audience. It is racism as much as military discipline that motivates the colonel all the way into his final madness.

"You speak English, of course?" he queries Hayakawa.

"Do you speak Japanese?" Hayakawa retorts and strikes him across the face.

The first encounter between Sessue Hayakawa and Alec Guinness in *The Bridge on the River Kwai* (1957)

Hayakawa learns that not even solitary confinement can break the stiff-necked officer

Even after brutal torture, he is still his own man . . .

. . . a stickler for regulations and discipline at any odds

Alec Guinness, William Holden, and Jack Hawkins are posed in front of the just-completed "bridge"

From this point, the film builds the confrontation between the two as the English war prisoners build the bridge of the title. It's a fine film, although some all-American heroics by William Holden in the final reel seem to have been slapped on as a sop to the American audience expected to turn out in huge numbers to see this largely foreign-made production.

The orchestra got to play "The Colonel Bogey March" seven times at the Academy's ceremony. For the picture itself, of course, and as mentioned, for Alec Guinness as Best Actor. Then, Pierre Boulle, who wrote the novel and the screenplay based on it, David Lean for Best Director, Jack Hildyard for Best Cinematography, Peter Taylor for Best Editing, and Malcolm Arnold for the musical score. (Now Getty uses the movie's theme march to sell gasoline.)

It was the sixth Columbia film to be named Best Picture by the Academy during the reign of Harry Cohn, and it was to be the last. He died just before the Oscar ceremonies, two years after his brother Jack. A succession of changes took place, but so entrenched had the independent producers and stars' production companies become that the company output continued strong. Three more Bests awaited Columbia.

The Spiegel-Lean team brought in the next one, too. It dealt with an English officer in strange surroundings once again. But here the similarity to *Kwai* ends. The setting is largely desert and *Lawrence of Arabia* is in full charge here. The colonialism is muted here, too, as Lawrence is portrayed as a loonily romantic figure, a political nincompoop. He loves the desert, he loves the

The Britishers in the cast include Peter O'Toole, Alec Guinness (as Prince Feisal), Claude Rains, Jack Hawkins, and Anthony Quayle

Arabs, he loves to blow up trains. When he unwittingly outlives his usefulness to His Majesty's Government, he is yanked back to leafy English lanes. The movie does little to clarify one of history's more enigmatic figures, but he was a great grosser, at least as played by Peter O'Toole. (O'Toole is as blond and tall

Monumental scenes such as these made *Lawrence of Arabia* the greatest spectacular of its time (1962)

as the real T. E. Lawrence was short and dark, but who really cares?) *Lawrence of Arabia* bagged seven Oscars: Best Picture, Best Director (Lean), Art Direction (John Box, John Stoll), Cinematography (Fred Young), Editing (Anne Coates), Music (Maurice Jarre), Sound (Shepperton Studio sound department).

Quinn in battle

O'Toole as Lawrence

O'Toole and his comrade-in-arms, Omar Sharif

The next Oscar winner was an import from England, via Broadway. *A Man for All Seasons* had been a stage smash on two continents, although its theme didn't seem to be the most commercially promising for that medium or for movies. Sir Thomas More is the lord chancellor to King Henry the Eighth. When Henry wants to divorce his current wife, Sir Thomas' Catholic conscience cannot go along. Since the pushy monarch wants total approval, all sorts of pressures are put upon Sir Thomas, but in the end, his will does not falter, even in the face of death. The character is only slightly more realistic than is usually the case in these pageantry dramas, but that was enough to earn Paul Scofield the Best Actor award, and Fred Zinnemann his second Columbia picture Best Director award. In addition, cameraman Ted Moore, costume designers Elizabeth Haffenden and Joan Bridge, and Robert Bolt, who adapted the screenplay from his own drama, all were cited Best in their respective categories for the cinema year of 1966.

This ad came, of course, after the fact that it was the year's biggest winner in the Oscar sweepstakes

240

Robert Shaw is Sir Thomas' king, Henry the Eighth; he wants a new queen, and Sir Thomas' approval for his divorce

Susannah York is Sir Thomas' daughter, Margaret . . .

. . . and Wendy Hiller his wife, Alice

The movie's climactic scene, the trial of Sir Thomas More by the king's court—Leo McKern is the accusing prosecutor, Cromwell

Orson Welles (back to camera) is Cardinal Wolsey in this drama

The 60s were crowned for the studio with another thoroughly English property that also went the West End-Broadway route before coming to Hollywood. But *Oliver!* was centuries away in content as well as concept. It was at least the fourth screen translation of the Dickens novel and far and away the most successful. Mark Lester played the title character without being too much the child star. Jack Wild was a believable Artful Dodger. As the equally artful codger who trains little boys to steal, Ron Moody carried most of the weight of the film. The overall effect was just a little too pretty for the dreary slums of 19th century London, but people liked it.

Oliver! won six Academy Awards. Producer John Woolf accepted the Best Picture Oscar and Carol Reed was named Best Director. John Green for his scoring of the original Lionel Bart music, Onna White's choreography, John Box among others for art direction, and the Shepperton sound department were all cited Bests for 1968.

Seven Best Pictures in a nineteen-year span—a fine accomplishment, especially noteworthy in that the time included the years of Hollywood's greatest problems: the inroads television was making on movie attendance, the McCarthy investigations, the rebuilding of foreign competitive companies, the break-up of the old autocratic studio system. Instead of looking for new technical features to exploit, Columbia concentrated on making the best films possible. During the 50s and 60s, the policy paid off handsomely.

The latter decade saw the release of, in addition to the Bests cited above, such films as *Guess Who's Coming to Dinner?, In Cold Blood, The L-Shaped Room, Dr. Strangelove, Fail-Safe, Requiem for a Heavyweight, Suddenly Last Summer, Georgy Girl, Advise and Consent,* and *A Raisin in the Sun.* It was the decade of *The Guns of Navarone* and Elsa the Lion of *Born Free* and *Bob and Carol and Ted and Alice,** among other trendsetters. It was a second Golden Age for the company and there was now a roomful of trophies, silent and golden, to prove it.

---

*Filmographies in Chapter Nine Appendix.

IT HAPPENED ONE NIGHT

(Released: 1934)

Director: Frank Capra
Assistant Director: C. C. Coleman
Producer: Harry Cohn
Editor: Gene Havlick
Based on the Short Story "Night Bus" by: Samuel Hopkins Adams
Screen Play: Robert Riskin
Art Director: Stephen Goosson
Music Director: Louis Silvers
Costumes: Robert Kolloch
Director of Photography: Joe Walker, A.S.C.
Sound: E. E. Bernds

Cast:
Clark Gable
Claudette Colbert
Roscoe Karns
Walter Connolly
Alan Hale
Ward Bond
Eddie Chandler
Jameson Thomas
Wallis Clark
Arthur Hoyt
Blanche Frederici
Charles C. Wilson
Charles D. Brown
Harry C. Bradley
Harry Holman
Maidel Turner
Irving Bacon
Harry Todd
Frank Wyaconell
Henry Wadsworth
Claire McDowell
Ky Robinson

Frank Holliday
James Burke
Joseph Crehan
Milton Kibbee
Mickey Daniel
Oliver Eckhardt
George Breakston
Bess Flowers
Edmunds Burns
Ethel Sykes
Tom Ricketts
Eddie Kane
Ernie Adams
Kit Guard
Billie Engel
Allen Fox
Marvin Loback
Dave Wengren
Burt Starky
Rita Ross
Hal Price

ALL THE KING'S MEN

(Released: October, 1949)

Director: Robert Rossen
Assistant Director: Sam Nelson
Editor: Al Clark
Editorial Adviser: Robert Parrish
Based on the Novel by: Robert Penn Warren
Screen Play: Robert Rossen
Musical Score: Louis Gruenberg
Art Director: Sturges Carne
Music Director: M. W. Stoloff
Set Decorations: Louis Diage
Montages: Donald W. Starling
Gowns: Jean Louis
Make-up: Clay Campbell, S.M.A.

Hairstyles: Helen Hunt
Director of Photography: Burnett Guffey, A.S.C.
Sound Engineer: Frank Goodwin

Cast:
Broderick Crawford
John Ireland
Joanne Dru
John Derek
Mercedes McCambridge
Shepperd Strudwick
Ralph Dumke
Anne Seymour
Katharine Warren
Raymond Greenleaf
Walter Burke
Will Wright
Grandon Rhodes

FROM HERE TO ETERNITY

(Released: September, 1953)

Director: Fred Zinneman
Assistant Director: Earl Bellamy
Producer: Buddy Adler
Editor: William Lyon, A.C.E.
Based on the Novel by:
  James Jones
Screen Play: Daniel Taradash
Background Music: George Duning
Song, "Re-enlistment Blues":
  James Jones
  Fred Karger
  Robert Wells
Orchestrations: Arthur Morton
Art Director: Cary Odell
Music Director: M. W. Stoloff
Set Decorations: Frank Tuttle
Gowns: Jean Louis
Make-up: Clay Campbell, S.M.A.
Hairstyles: Helen Hunt
Director of Photography:
  Burnett Guffey, A.S.C.
Technical Advisor:
  Brig. Gen. Kendall J. Fielder, Ret.
Sound Engineer: Lodge Cunningham

Cast:

Burt Lancaster	Arthur Keegan
Montgomery Clift	Barbara Morrison
Deborah Kerr	Jean Willis
Frank Sinatra	Claude Akins
Donna Reed	Robert Karnes
Philip Ober	Robert Wilke
Mickey Shaughnessy	Douglas Henderson
Harry Bellaver	George Reeves
Ernest Borgnine	Don Dubbins
Jack Warden	John Cason
John Dennis	Kristine Miller
Merle Travis	John Bryant
Tim Ryan	

ON THE WATERFRONT

(Released: October, 1955)

Director: Elia Kazan
Assistant Director:
  Charles H. Maguire
Producer: Sam Spiegel
Assistant Producer: San Rheiner
Editor: Gene Milford
Story: Budd Schulberg
  Based on Articles by:
  Malcolm Johnson
Screen Play: Budd Schulberg
Music: Leonard Bernstein
Art Director: Richard Pay
Script Supervision: Robert Hodes
Dialogue Supervision: Guy Thomajan
Wardrobe Supervision:
  Anna Hill Johnstone
Wardrobe Mistress: Flo Tansfield
Make-up: Fred Ryle
Hairstyles: Mary Roche
Production Manager: George Justin
Director of Photography:
  Boris Kaufman
Sound: James Shields

Cast:

Marlon Brando	John Heldabrand
Karl Malden	Rudy Bond
Lee J. Cobb	Don Blackman
Rod Steiger	Arthur Keegan
Pat Henning	Abe Simon
Eva Marie Saint	Barry Macollum
Leif Erickson	Mike O'Dowd
James Westerfield	Marty Balsam
Tony Galento	Fred Gwynne
Tami Mauriello	Thomas Hanley
John Hamilton	Anne Hegira

THE BRIDGE ON THE RIVER KWAI

(Released: December 1957)

Director: David Lean
Assistant Directors:
Gus Agosti
Ted Sturgis
Producer: Sam Speigel
Chief Editor: Peter Taylor
Based on the Novel by:
Pierre Boulle
Screen Play: Pierre Boulle
Continuity: Angela Martelli
Music: Malcolm Arnold
Music Played by:
The Royal Philharmonic
Orchestra
Art Director: Daniel M. Ashton
Assistant Art Director:
Geoffrey Drake
Wardrobe: John Apperson
Make-up: Stuart Freeborn
George Parfleton
Production Executive:
William N. Graf
Production Manager:
Cecil F. Ford

Construction Manager:
Peter Kukelow
Director of Photography:
Jack Hildyard, B.S.C.
Cameraman:
Peter Newbrook
Photographed in Ceylon
Technical Advisor:
Major-General L.E.M.
Perowne, C.B., C.B.E.
Sound:
John Cox
John Mitchell
Chief Sound Editor:
Winston Ryder
Chief Electrician:
Archie Danise

Cast:
William Holden
Alec Guinness
Jack Hawkins
Sessue Hayakawa
James Dohald
Geoffrey Horne
Andre Morell
Peter Williams
John Boxer
Percy Herbert
Harold Goodwin
Ann Sears
Henry Okawa
K. Katsumoto
M.R.B. Chakrabandhu
Vilaiwan
  Seeboonreaung
Ngamta Suphaphongs
Javanart Punynchoti
Kannikar Dowklee

LAWRENCE OF ARABIA

(Released: December, 1962)

Director: David Lean
Assistant Director: Roy Stevens
Producer: Sam Speigel
Editor: Anne Coates
Screen Play: Robert Bolt
Continuity: Barbara Cole
Musical Composition:
Maurice Jarre
Arrangement:
Gerard Schurmann
Music Played by: The London
Philharmonic Orchestra
Conductor: Sir Adrian Boult
Art Director: John Stoll
Assistant Art Directors:
Roy Rossotti
George Richardson
Terry Marsh
Anthony Rimmington
Music Director: M. W. Stoloff
Production Design: John Box

Make-up: Charles Parker
Hairstyles: A. G. Scott
Second Unit Directors:
Andre Smagghe
Noel Howard
Properties: Eddie Fowlie
Production Manager:
John Palmer
Location Manager:
Douglas Twiddy
Construction Manager:
Peter Dukelow
Director of Photography:
F. A. Young, B.S.C.
Cameraman: Ernest Day
Second Unit
Photography:
Skeets Kelly
Nicholas Roeg
Peter Newbrook
Sound: Paddy Cunningham

Cast:
Peter O'Toole
Alec Guinness
Anthony Quinn
Jack Hawkins
Jose Ferrer
Anthony Quayle
Claude Rains
Arthur Kennedy
Donald Wolfit
Omar Sharif
I. S. Johar
Gamil Ratib
Michel Ray
Zia Mohyeddin
John Dimech
Howard Marion
  Crawford
Jack Gwillim
Hugh Miller

Set Dresser: Dario Simoni
Casting Direction:
Maude Spector
Costumes: Phyllis Dalton
Wardrobe: John Apperson

Sound Editor:
Winston Ryder
Chief Electrician:
Archie Dansie

A MAN FOR ALL SEASONS

(Released: April, 1966)

Director: Fred Zinneman
Assistant Director: Peter Boulton
Producer: Fred Zinneman
Executive Producer:
William N. Graf
Editor: Ralph Kemplen
Based on the Play by:
Robert Bolt
Screen Play: Robert Bolt
Continuity: Constance Willis
Music: Georges Delerue
Art Director: Terence Marsh
Assistant Art Director:
Roy Walker
Music Director:
Georges Delerue
Production Design: John Box
Set Dresser: Josie MacAvin
Casting: Robert Lennard
Wardrobe: Jackie Cummins
Color Costume Design:
Elizabeth Haffendon
Joan Bridge
Make-up:
George Frost
Eric Allwright
Second Unit Direction:
Patrick Carey

Production Supervisor:
William Kirby
Construction Manager:
Peter Kukelow
Director of Photography:
Ted Moore, B.S.C.
Cameraman:
Robert Kindred
Sound: Buster Ambler
Bob Jones
Dubbing: Harry Miller
Dubbing Assistant:
Marcel Durham

Cast:
Paul Scofield
Wendy Hiller
Leo McKern
Robert Shaw
Orson Welles
Susannah York
Nigel Davenport
John Hurt
Corin Redgrave
Colin Blakely
Cyril Luckham
Jack Gwillim
Thomas Heathcote
Yootha Joyce
Anthony Nichols
John Nettleton
Eira Heath
Molly Urquhart
Paul Hardwick
Michael Latimer
Philip Brack
Martin Boddey
Eric Mason
Matt Zinnerman

OLIVER!

(Released: December, 1968)

Director: Carol Reed
Assistant Director: Colin Brewer
Producer: John Woolf
Editor: Ralph Kemplen
Assistant Editor: Marcel Durham
Freely Adapted from
Oliver Twist **by:**
Charles Dickens
Screen Play: Vernon Harris
Continuity: Pamela Davies

Choreographic Music
Layouts: Ray Holder
Special Effects:
Allan Bryce
Casting: Jenia Reissar
Costumes: Phyllis Dalton
Wardrobe Supervision:
John Wilson-Apperson
Make-up: George Frost
Hairstyles: Bobbie Smith

Cast:
Ron Moody
Shani Wallis
Oliver Reed
Harry Secombe
Mark Lester
Jack Wild
Hugh Griffith
Joseph O'Conor
Peggy Mount

Music and Lyrics: Lionel Bart
Orchestrations and Choral
   Arrangements: John Green
Additional Orchestration:
   Eric Rogers
Music Editor: Kenneth Runyon
Associate Music Editor:
   Robert Hathaway
Music Coordinator: Dusty Buck
Art Director: Terence Marsh
Assistant Art Directors:
   Ray Walker
   Bob Cartwright
Music Director: John Green
Associate Music Director:
   Eric Rogers
Production Design: John Box
Set Dressers:
   Vernon Dixon
   Ken Mugglestone
Choreography and Musical
   Sequences: Onna White
Associate Choreography:
   Tom Panke
Assistant Choreography:
   Larry Oaks
   George Baron

Second Unit Assistant
   Direction: Ray Corbett
Production Supervisor:
   Denis Johnson
Construction Manager:
   Peter Dukelow
Unit Production Manager:
   Denis Johnson, Jr.
Title Backgrounds:
   Graham Barkley
Director of Photography:
   Oswald Morris, B.S.C.
Cameraman:
   Freddie Cooper
Second Unit Photography:
   Brian West
Sound Supervision:
   John Cox
Sound Recording:
   Buster Ambler
   Bob Jones
Sound Editor:
   Jim Groom

Leonard Rossiter
Hylda Baker
Kenneth Cranham
Megs Jenkins
Sheila White
Wensley Pithey
James Hayter
Elizabeth Knight
Fred Emney
Edwin Flynn
Roy Evans
Norman Mitchell
Graham Buttrose
Dempsey Cook
Nigel Grice
Nigel Kingsley
Brian Lloyd
Clive Moss
Peter Renn
Kim Smith
Raymond Ward

The Oscars: Appendix II

COLUMBIA'S ACADEMY AWARDS

1934

Best Picture:	*It Happened One Night*
Best Actor:	Clark Gable, *It Happened One Night*
Best Actress:	Claudette Colbert, *It Happened One Night*
Best Director:	Frank Capra, *It Happened One Night*
Writing (Adaptation):	Robert Riskin, *It Happened One Night*
Sound Recording:	Paul Neal, *One Night of Love*
Music (Score):	Louis Silvers, *One Night of Love*
Scientific or Technical (Class III):	Columbia Pictures Corp.

1936

Best Director:	Frank Capra, *Mr. Deeds Goes to Town*

1937

Best Director:	Leo McCarey, *The Awful Truth*
Interior Decoration:	Stephen Goosson, *Lost Horizon*
Film Editing:	Gene Havlick, Gene Milford, *Lost Horizon*
Scientific or Technical (Class III):	John P. Livadary, Director of Sound Recording for Columbia Pictures

1938

Best Picture: *You Can't Take it with You*
Best Director: Frank Capra, *You Can't Take It with You*

1939

Writing (Original Story):   Lewis R. Foster, *Mr. Smith Goes to Washington*

1941

Writing (Original Story):   Harry Segall, *Here Comes Mr. Jordan*
Writing (Screenplay):   Sidney Buchman, Seton I. Miller,
                                      Here Comes Mr. Jordan

1942

Writing (Original Story):   Emeric Pressburger, *The Invaders*

1943

Best Supporting Actor: Charles Coburn, *The More the Merrier*

1944

Music (Scoring of a Musical):   Morris Stoloff, *Cover Girl*
Scientific or Technical (Class III): Bernard B. Brown, John P. Livadary

1945

Documentary: Govts. of Great Britain and U.S.A.,
                                      The True Glory

1946

Sound Recording: John P. Livadary, *The Jolson Story*
Music (Scoring of a   Morris Stoloff, *The Jolson Story*
  Musical Picture):

1949

Best Picture: *All the King's Men*
Best Actor: Broderick Crawford, *All the King's Men*
Best Supporting Actress: Mercedes McCambridge, *All the King's Men*

1950

Best Actress: Judy Holliday, *Born Yesterday*
Cartoon: *Gerald McBoing-Boing*
Scientific or Technical (Class II): John P. Livadary, Floyd Campbell, L. W. Russell
                                      and Columbia Studio Sound Dept.

1953

Best Picture: *From Here to Eternity*
Best Supporting Actor: Frank Sinatra, *From Here to Eternity*
Best Supporting Actress: Donna Reed, *From Here to Eternity*
Best Director: Fred Zinnemann, *From Here to Eternity*
Writing (Screenplay):   Daniel Taradash, *From Here to Eternity*
Cinematography (Black and White): Burnett Guffey, *From Here to Eternity*
Sound Recording: Columbia Sound Dept., *From Here to Eternity*
Film Editing: William Lyon, *From Here to Eternity*

1954

Best Picture:	*On the Waterfront*
Best Actor:	Marlon Brando, *On the Waterfront*
Best Supporting Actress:	Eva Marie Saint, *On the Waterfront*
Best Director:	Elia Kazan, *On the Waterfront*
Writing (Story and Screenplay):	Budd Schulberg, *On the Waterfront*
Cinematography (Black and White):	Boris Kaufman, *On the Waterfront*
Art Direction-Set Decoration (Black and (White):	Richard Day, *On the Waterfront*
Film Editing:	*On the Waterfront*
Cartoon	*When Magoo Flew*
Scientific or Technical (Class III):	John P. Livadary, Lloyd Russell and Columbia Studio Sound Dept.

1955

Film Editing:	Charles Nelson, William Lyon, *Picnic*

1956

Documentary:	Jacques Yves-Cousteau, *The Silent World* (France)
Costume Design (Black and White):	Jean Louis, *The Solid Gold Cadillac*
Cartoon:	*Mister Magoo's Puddle Jumper*

1957

Best Picture:	*The Bridge on the River Kwai*
Best Actor:	Alec Guinness, *The Bridge on the River Kwai*
Best Director:	David Lean, *The Bridge on the River Kwai*
Screenplay (Adaptation):	Pierre Boulle, *The Bridge on the River Kwai*
Cinematography:	Jack Hildyard, *The Bridge on the River Kwai*
Music (Scoring):	Malcolm Arnold, *The Bridge on the River Kwai*
Film Editing:	Peter Taylor, *The Bridge on the River Kwai*

1959

Short (Live Action):	*The Golden Fish* (France)
Music (Scoring of a Musical Picture):	Andre Previn, *Porgy and Bess*

1960

Music (Scoring of a Musical Picture):	Morris Stoloff, Harry Sukman, *Song Without End*
Scientific or Technical (Class III):	Arthur Holcoms, Petro Vlahos, and Columbia Studio Camera Dept.

1961

Special Effects:	Bill Warrington, Vivian C. Greenham, *The Guns of Navarone*

1962

Best Picture:	*Lawrence of Arabia*
Best Director:	David Lean, *Lawrence of Arabia*
Cinematography (Color):	Fred A. Young, *Lawrence of Arabia*

Art Direction-Set Decoration (Color):	John Box, John Stoll, Dario Simoni (Color), *Lawrence of Arabia*
Sound:	Shepperton Studio Sound Dept., *Lawrence of Arabia*
Music (Score-Substantially Original):	Maurice Jarre, *Lawrence of Arabia*
Film Editing:	Anne Coates, *Lawrence of Arabia*
Foreign Language Film:	*Sundays and Cybele* (France)

1963

Cartoon:	*The Critic*

1964

Documentary:	Jacques-Yves Cousteau, *World Without Sun* (France)

1965

Best Actor:	Lee Marvin, *Cat Ballou*
Cinematography (Black and White):	Ernest Laszlo, *Ship of Fools*

1966

Best Picture:	*A Man for All Seasons*
Best Actor:	Paul Scofield, *A Man for All Seasons*
Best Director:	Fred Zinnemann, *A Man for All Seasons*
Writing (Screenplay-Adaptation):	Robert Bolt, *A Man for All Seasons*
Cinematography (Color):	Ted Moore, *A Man for All Seasons*
Costume Design (Color):	Elizabeth Haffenden, Joan Bridge, *A Man for All Seasons*
Music (Song):	John Barry, Don Black, *Born Free*
Music (Original Score):	John Barry, *Born Free*

1967

Best Actress:	Katharine Hepburn, *Guess Who's Coming to Dinner*
Writing (Story and Screenplay):	William Rose, *Guess Who's Coming to Dinner*

1968

Best Picture:	*Oliver!*
Best Actress:	Barbra Streisand, *Funny Girl*
Best Director:	Carol Reed, *Oliver!*
Art Direction-Set Direction:	John Box, Terence Marsh, Vernon Dixon, Ken Muggleston, *Oliver!*
Sound:	Shepperton Studio Sound Dept., *Oliver!*
Music (Scoring of a Musical Picture):	John Green, *Oliver!*
Choreography:	Onna White, *Oliver!*

1969

Best Supporting Actress:	Goldie Hawn, *Cactus Flower*
Special Visual Effects:	Robbie Robertson, *Marooned*
Short (Live Action):	*The Magic Machines*

254

1970

Costume Design:	Nino Novarese, *Cromwell*
Foreign Language Film:	*Investigation of a Citizen above Suspicion* (Italy)

1971

Best Supporting Actor:	Ben Johnson, *The Last Picture Show*
Best Supporting Actress:	Cloris Leachman, *The Last Picture Show*
Art Direction-Set Decoration:	John Box, Ernest Archer, Jack Maxsted, Gil Parrando, Vernon Dixon, *Nicholas and Alexandra*
Costume Design:	Yvonne Blake, Antonio Castillo, *Nicholas and Alexandra*

1972

Best Supporting Actress:	Eileen Heckart, *Butterflies Are Free*
Musical Score:	Charles Chaplin, Raymond Rasch, Larry Russell, *Limelight*
Short (Live Action):	*Norman Rockwell's World . . . An American Dream*

1973

Best Song:	Marvin Hamlisch, Marilyn and Alan Bergman, *The Way We Were*
Musical Score:	Marvin Hamlisch, *The Way We Were*

7 | The Road Pictures

It Happened One Night WON SOMETHING ELSE BESIDES its Oscars: a permanent place in American folklore as a work that epitomized its time and place. Without benefit of much promotion, without a concerted effort by its own makers, the film went on to win its audience, who came in droves to see and laugh and identify with Ellie Andrews and Pete Warne.

In each of the five decades of its history so far, there has been a Columbia film that has done much the same—a move that defines a particular period, mentality, and standard. It is probably indicative of one of our constant strongest national impulses—mobility—that each of these films qualifies as what later came to be known as "road" pictures (not to be confused with Bob Hope/Bing Crosby "Road" comedies).

It Happened One Night, the film of and for the 30s, was based on a story called "Night Bus," and much of its action takes place in what was then the principal means of moving long distances for most people in the Depression days. Had the protagonists met a century earlier, it would probably have been on a wagon train, headed from east to west, rather than the south-north flow of the Florida-to-New York bus.

By the end of the 30s, things were looking up, and in more ways than one. Americans had their eyes on the skies, and although civilian commercial aviation was not slated to really get off the ground until after the war, the daredevil pilots who pioneered a new mode of swift movement had already become part legend.

Howard Hawks was a pioneer in making films with exciting aerial photography, and his Columbia movie, *Only Angels Have Wings*, is a classic in the genre. Under his taut direction, the sky lanes became the new "road" in the popular imagination, the way out for the next generation of restless men to escape their humdrum lives.

There was nothing humdrum about this particular crew. Cary Grant ran the makeshift airline in a mythical South American country, which was also the landing place of showgirl Jean Arthur. The supporting cast included Richard Barthelmess,

As the operator of a fledgling airline in a banana republic in *Only Angels Have Wings*, Cary Grant portrayed the age's new kind of hero, the flying daredevil; always in the thick of things, here he separates Rita Hayworth from Jean Arthur . . .

Thomas Mitchell, and Noah Beery, Jr. Aside from the skin-of-our-teeth adventuring, spectacularly filmed by the never-failing Joe Walker, the great added excitement was the small part played by a new young beauty. It was Rita Hayworth, in one of her unheralded early career-building appearances.

Aviation was becoming the major thrust of the war effort, so military and combat pictures dominated the skies for the rest of the 40s, rather than the barnstormers and dare-devils of the sort in *Angels*.

... and Allyn Joslyn from Richard Barthelmess, (with John Carroll and Sig Rumann looking over Barthelmess' shoulders) ...

... and finally, Thomas Mitchell from Richard Barthelmess

Allyn Joslyn and a crowd of extras anxiously await an incoming plane (It really was a banana economy!)

And after that long decade of armed heroics, perhaps it was only natural that a new type of man, a nonhero, should emerge. In books he appeared in many guises, but in the movies, he had one personification that towered above all the others, and he too traveled a different road.

Or at least, he traveled in a different way and for different reasons than any of his predecessors.

He was Marlon Brando, *The Wild One*. And when he pushed his throbbing motorcycle down a stretch of asphalt, he became the archetypal young male of the 50s. For him as for the Kerouac wanderers of the time, the road was not a way of getting somewhere else, but an end in and of itself. Riding was a way of life, and all its accoutrements became the costumes and the props, the language and the attitude of the young audience that came of age in the 50s.

The film came out in 1953, about six months before Columbia released *On the Waterfront* with Brando. *On the Waterfront* got all the awards and critical acclaim, but *The Wild One* created more public attention for its star and its style than any film in years. Brando's black leather jacket with its silver studs, his cap and goggles, became the standard uniform for toughs

Hellbent for black leather, Marlon Brando, *The Wild One*, leads his gang of motor-cyclists into a small town (1953)

Brando is Johnny, and his arch rival Chino is a bearded Lee Marvin, just starting to win attention from movie-goers

As Johnny and Chino square off, the townspeople watch with that "As long as they only kill each other" attitude

Mary Murphy as Kathie, tries to understand the animalistic, inarticulate Johnny, but it's beyond her ken

and would-be toughs all over the world. His Hell's Angels symbolism was *de rigueur* for guys who had never kicked off with a bike in their lives, but had to affect the look.

Never had Brando's monosyllabic style of animalism been more riveting. He said more with the cocking of his head than other actors could convey in expansively worded paragraphs. He was thirty years old when the film was made, but a younger generation looked at the screen and saw itself as it was and as it wanted to be.

One of Stanley Kramer's productions for Columbia, *The Wild One* did not make a great deal of money for the company. But its influence on its audience was incalculable. When the great youth movement of the 60s arrived, it traveled in the dust tracks of *The Wild One*.

But the outlook of Brando's band of semi-outlaws was, in its nihilistic, faintly fascistic tone, not the attitude of the newer generation of runaways. From the beatniks had evolved the flower children of the drug culture. Although their widely differing philosophy was, in the final analysis, no more profound than that of their predecessors, they fell into a totally opposite category. Brando's bunch rode into a town and terrified its inhabitants just for the hell of it, but the hippies, in their own communities or out on the road are the oppressed, not the oppressors.

Such was the theme of *Easy Rider,* the movie that quickly became *the* movie for the kids of the 60s. When Peter Fonda and Dennis Hopper get on their bikes for a surge across America, America becomes the enemy. Their "thing" is not necessarily evil in itself, but it sure is in the eyes of those who warily watch this new pair of motorcyclists take to the open road.

The film spins rather lazily in the earlier sequences, taking the two riders through a series of more or less edifying adventures that seem to build their confidence in reaching their ultimate goal, New Orleans. (They started out from Los Angeles. They should have never left, really.) They make it, but the film ends abruptly, almost amateurishly, when they leave the Queen City and head out on the road again, where they are almost immediately ambushed and killed.

And every young ticket-holder died with them. That was the response of the audience who saw themselves being killed in smaller, different ways by the same controlling, uncomprehending, adult world.

Practically no other movie ever spawned as many imitations as *Easy Rider*. Hopper and Fonda, who respectively produced

The next generation of motorcyclists, exemplified by Dennis Hopper and Peter Fonda, in *Easy Rider*

Peter Fonda went looking for America in *Easy Rider*—he never found it (1969)

and directed it, are still making essentially the same movie five years later. But none of their successive attempts ever caught the essence of the time nearly as well. Whatever its faults as cinema, the movie spoke to its audience in its own voice, saying

Dennis Hopper and Peter Fonda share a jail cell with Jack Nicholson; they decide he can come along on their quest

things the audience wanted to hear. Even in its gritty amateurishness, it rang true to the generation that was so distrustful of everything that came to them via the "establishment."

If the film seems to have dated very quickly, it is because it was of and for its moment, inhaling, exhaling, and expiring with the decade—its movement, its ideas, and its ideals. If it all seems so long ago already, perhaps five years in the nuclear age *is* a long time.

A "freak" by choice, Nicholson will share the same fate as his new companions

In addition to its two main protagonists, *Easy Rider* brought two other interesting personalities to the screen. Karen Black plays a hooker and Jack Nicholson a smalltown lawyer who joins the duo for a stretch of the journey. For both, *Easy Rider* was a prelude to their starring film, which in its own turn is the quintessential picture, thus far, of the 70s.

The title is *Five Easy Pieces*, and it was hailed as the best American film in years by many critics here and overseas. It deals with matters more complex than those posed by *Easy Rider*, and the characters achieve dimensions far beyond those in the earlier film. The two motorcyclists were leaving California primarily for a change of scenery (admittedly cultural and erotic as well as roadside) but in *Five Easy Pieces* Jack Nicholson's Bobby has canceled out on an entire life style, picking up on a new one that is far less attractive to everyone else in the film and presumably in the audience as well. But although Bobby's family life is highbrow, affluent, "worthwhile," it is also dead-end and stultifying. And dead ends are something that Bobby is definitely not interested in.

In *Five Easy Pieces*, Jack Nicholson is first encountered working on an oil rig (1970)

266

Caught in a traffic jam, his slightly dadaistic solution is to jump on a junk truck and bang some Chopin out of a battered old upright

Trained as a classical pianist, a fact that is only toyed with early in the film and confirmed later on, he is working on an oil rig, living with a waitress (Karen Black), and consorting with other blue-collar types. Bobby is restless, Bobby is moody, and naturally none of his new friends can figure out why. Naturally not. He is in with the old three-squares-a-day-and-a-roof-overhead crowd, who theoretically have evolved from a twelfth-century existence of thatched huts and hog-slaughtering to present-day trailer camps and bowling alleys. And actually, they're pretty much the same as their precursors.

When he first appears on-screen, Bobby seems to be pretty much one of them. His most erratic quirk is a dislike for the country music that bloats the soundtrack continuously. But when Bobby splits for home to see his vegetating, moribund father for perhaps the last time, we find out what's bothering Bobby.

He is a modern Ulysses, at home nowhere. The diners and trailer camps are by now obviously not his milieu; neither is his Chopin and Rachmaninoff-filled family manse. Even when he is stalking his brother's fiancée (well played by Susan Anspach) he is not comfortable.

At film's end, Bobby has hopped a ride on still another moving vehicle (after a car ride that weaves up two-thirds the West Coast) headed for a job in a lumber camp. He is still searching for that middle ground somewhere between bowling alleys and baby grands. The long bleak stretch of roadscape that looms

Karen Black is the diner waitress, Rayette, with whom Nicholson (Robert Eroica Dupea) is temporarily—and stormily—domiciled

Sally Struthers (here billed as Sally Ann) and Marlena MacGuire pick Nicholson up in a bowling alley and provide interim diversion from his problems

A much more serious conquest, but no more successful for Nicholson, is Susan
Anspach

before and after him seems to suggest to us that he isn't going to find it up there in the tall timber, either.

Although Bobby's meanderings are sort of extreme, he does embody an increasing number of people who constantly question the hows and whys in their lives. Like most, he has a lot of questions but no real answers. Unlike the quests in *The Wild One* and *Easy Rider*, the road in itself is not the grail, but merely the means of finding it. When he tries to explain to his mute father what he's been doing since he left home, he can only say, "I've moved around a lot." Adding to the frustration is the fact that no one is sure if the father can even hear anymore. His son's statement may be inaudible as well as inarticulate. America's—and thereby Hollywood's—love affair with the road may be just a series of one-night stands, each motel looking alike, each encounter forgotten by the dawn's light. Moving around may not be enough of an answer anymore, either, for Nicholson's Bobby or for the audience.

Maybe a film of the 80s will provide some of these answers. It is much more likely though that it will merely pose some new questions.

Obviously a lot of things have changed from the time "the walls of Jericho" separated Claudette Colbert from Clark Gable to the time Karen Black slipped into bed with Jack Nicholson and pouted, "I can't fall asleep, hint, hint." These five films catalogue many of the changes, but given the limits of the medium, can only "hint, hint" at the causes for the changes. Each one, viewed in the perspective of its time, serves to illustrate what happened, but not why. Those answers are with the audience rather than the film.

ONLY ANGELS HAVE WINGS

(Released: May 15, 1939)

Director: Howard Hawks
Editor: Viola Lawrence
Screen Play: Jules Furthman
Music: Dimitri Tiomkin
Art Director: Lionel Banks
Music Director: M. W. Stoloff
Special Effects: Roy Davison
Director of Photography:
 Joe Walker, A.S.C.
Aerial Photography:
 Ealer Dyer, A.S.C.
Technical Advisor and **Chief Pilot:**
 Paul Mantz

Cast:
Cary Grant
Jean Arthur
Richard Barthelmass
Thomas Mitchell
Allyn Joslyn
Sig Rumann
Victor Killian
John Carroll
Donald Barry
Noah Beery, Jr.
Maciste

Milessa Sierra
Lucio Villegas
Pat Flaherty
Pedro Regas
Pat West

Footage: 11,079 ft.

THE WILD ONE

(Released: November, 1953)

Director: Laslo Benedek
Assistant Director:
 Paul Donnelly
Editor: Al Clark
Story: Frank Rooney
Screen Play: John Paxton
Music: Leith Stephens
Art Director: Walter Holscher
Music Director: M. W. Stoloff

Set Decorations:
 Louis Diage
Production Design:
 Rudolph Sternad
Director of Photography:
 Hal Mohr, A.S.C.
Sound Engineer:
 George Cooper

Cast:
Marlon Brando
Mary Murphy
Robert Keith
Lee Marvin
Peggy Maley
Jay C. Flippen

EASY RIDER

(Released: July, 1969)

Director:
 Dennis Hopper
Producer:
 Peter Fonda
Executive Producer:
 Bert Schneider
Associate Producer:
 William Haywood
Editor: Donn Cambren

Cast:
Peter Fonda
Dennis Hopper
Antonio Mendoza
Phil Spector
Mac Mashourian
Warren Finnerty
Tita Colorado
Luke Askew

Hayward Robillard
Arnold Hess, Jr.
Buddy Causey, Jr.
Duffy LaFront
Blase M. Dawson
Paul Guerdy, Jr.
Suzie Ramagos
Elida Ann Herbert

*Filmography for *It Happened One Night* in Chapter Six Appendix.

Screen Play:
  Peter Fonda
  Dennis Hopper
  Terry Southern
Director of Photography:
  Lazlo Kovacs

Luana Anders
Sabrina Scharf
Sandy Wyeth
Robert Walker
Robert Ball
Carmen Phillips
Ellie Walker
Michael Pataki
Cathi Cozzi
Jack Nicholson
George Fowler
Keith Green

Rose LeBlance
Mary Kaye Herbert
Cynthia Grezaffi
Collette Purpera
Toni Basil
Karen Black
Thea Salerno
Ann McLain
Beatriz Montiel
Marcia Bowman
David Billodeau
Johnny David

Music

Performer:	Song:	Composer:
Steppenwolf	"The Pusher"	Hoyt Axton
Steppenwolf	"Born to be Wild"	Mars Bonfire
The Byrds	"I Wasn't Born to Follow"	Jerry Goffin, Carole King
The Band	"The Weight"	Jaime Robbie Robinson
The Holy Modal Rounders	"If You Want to Be a Bird"	Antonia Duren
Fraternity of Men	"Don't Bogart Me"	Elliott Ingber, Larry Waner
The Jimi Hendrix Experience	"If Six was Nine"	Jimi Hendrix
Little Eva	"Let's Turkey Trot"	Jerry Goffin, Jack Keller
The Electric Prunes	"Kyrie Eleision"	David Axelrod
The Electric Flag, An American Music Band	"Flash, Bam, Pow"	Mike Bloomfield
Roger McGuinn	"It's Alright Ma (I'm Only Bleeding)"	Bob Dylan
Roger McGuinn	"Ballad of Easy Rider"	Bob Dylan, Roger McGuinn

FIVE EASY PIECES

(Released: September, 1970)

Director: Bob Rafelson
Assistant Director:
  Sheldon Schrager
Producer:
  Bob Rafelson
  Richard Wechsler
Associate Producer:
  Harold Schneider
Editors:
  Christopher Holmes
  Gerald Shepard
Assistant Editors:
  Pete Denenberg
  Harold Hazen

Interior Design:
  Toby Rafelson
Production Coordinator:
  Marilyn Schlossberg
Script Supervisor:
  Terr Terrill
Location Representative:
  Kent Remington
Casting: Fred Roos
Prop Master:
  Walter Starkey
Wardrobe: Bucky Rous
Transportation Captain:
  Al Schultz
Director of Photography:
  Lazlo Kovacs

Cast:
Jack Nicholson
Karen Black
Susan Anspach
Billy 'Green" Bush
Fannie Flagg
Sally Ann Struthers
Marlena MacGuire
Richard Stahl
Lois Smith
Helena Kallianiotes
Toni Basil
Lorna Thayer
William Challee
John Ryan
Irene Dailey

272

Screen Play: Adrien Joyce
Songs Performed by:
Tammy Wynette
"Stand by Your Man":
B. Sherrill, T. Wynette
"D-I-V-O-R-C-E":
B. Braddock, C. Putnam
"When There's a Fire in
Your Heart": W. Kilgore,
C. Williams
"Don't Touch Me":
H. Cochran
Pianist: Pearl Kaufman
Fantasy in F Minor Op 49:
Frederic Francois Chopin
Chromatic Fantasy Fugue:
Johann Sebastian Bach
*Piano Concerto in E Flat
Major K. 271:* Wolfgang
Amadeus Mozart
*Prelude in E Minor Op 28
No. 4:* Frederic
Francois Chopin
Fantasy in D Minor K. 397:
Wolfgang Amadeus Mozart

Gaffer: Richard Aguilar
Key Grip: George Hill
Dolly Grip:
Howard Hagadorn
Sound Effects:
Edit-Rite, Inc.
Sound Mixer:
Charles Knight
Re-recording: *Audio Tran*

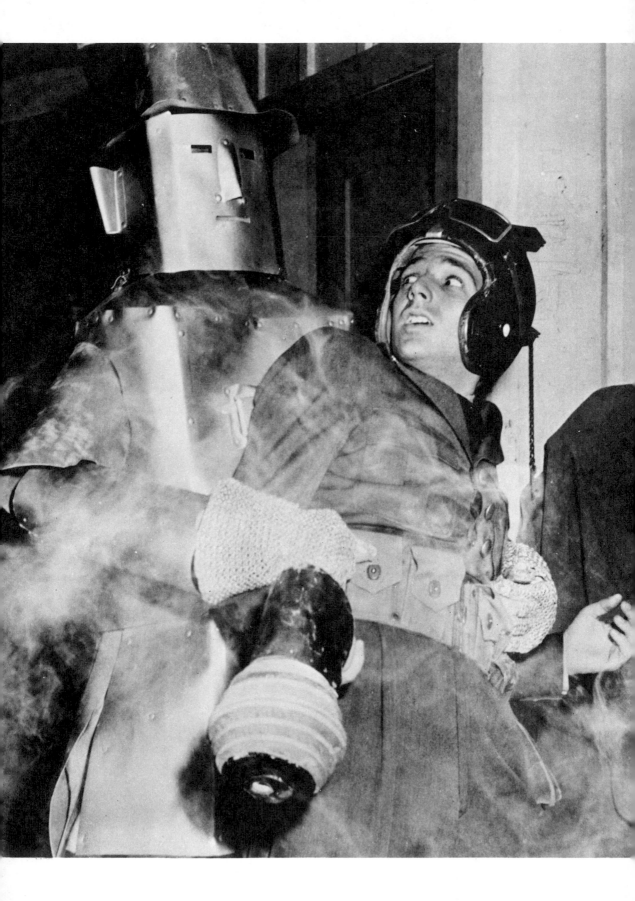

They Also Ran: The B's, The Serials, and Selected Short Subjects

8

Like those other venerated American institutions, pop records and Chinese restaurants, the film industry, too, has its *A* side and its *B* side.

And while Harry Cohn was generally driving half of Gower Street crazy making the two or three major films each year, what was the other half doing?

The *B* side. The bottom half of the mandatory double bill. The programmers. The series. Incredibly, between the mid-30s and the mid-50s, when the demand had died out, Columbia alone was churning out 56* different serials. In addition they were spinning out full-length series films, which ran the gamut from light romance (*Blondie*) to mystery (*Crime Doctor*) to adventure (*Jungle Jim*) to westerns (Ken Maynard) to singing westerns (Gene Autry), and any other category that can be affixed by celluloid.

---

*A list of the serials by title and date of release will be found at the end of this chapter.

Calling Captain Video! Some tinhorn has captured the Ranger!

Then, there are also the short subjects to be considered. The program fillers, a pre-war staple but now long gone, include the cliff-hanger serials, cartoons, and funny, educational, or documentary short subjects.

The *B*'s, singular or series variety, could have stood for bread and butter, even in Hollywood's caviar days. The studios ground them out, selling them as part of the "block," the total output of a given time. They were useful proving grounds for stars (Rita Hayworth was peeped at in *Blondie on a Budget*) as well as fledgling directors. Contract players could be utilized in *B* pictures between *A* assignments. (Dick Haymes showed up in something called *All Ashore* in 1953, presumably to keep him busy and out of Harry Cohn's way in the management of Rita Hayworth, to whom Haymes was married at the time. Aging juvenile Mickey Rooney showed up too, as did Peggy Ryan.)

By the middle of the 50s, whatever it was that *B* pictures did for audiences, television was presumably doing better, or at least doing it for free. Coupled with the disappearance of the double bill and stage shows in movie houses, the no longer very profitable *B's* just about disappeared from the production tables of the major studios. But while they lasted, well, they just seemed to last and last and *last*, especially the series.

There were 28 *Blondie* movies, with Penny Singleton in the title role and Arthur Lake as Dagwood in every single one of them.

There were 10 *Crime Doctors* all with Warner Baxter, but a changing cast that included at various times Lloyd Bridges, Nina Foch, Barton MacLane, Margaret Lindsay, Jerome Cowan, and Ellen Drew.

Gene Autry played himself 32 times on Gower Street, usually accompanied by his familiar sidekick, Smiley Burdette. (How often his famous horse Champion had to be retired and replaced is not even a matter of record.)

Boston Blackie piled up a string of 13 films and the *Lone Wolf* accounted for another 12. There was a great advantage to the series: audience familiarity. If you liked one *Whistler*, you'd like all of them—all 8, hopefully. Johnny Weissmuller, after having worn out the welcome mat as Tarzan, came to Columbia to be Jungle Jim for a string of 16 vine swingers.

Audiences identified actors with their series characters more so than with one-time roles. Chester Morris was a tough-talking wise guy in nearly sixty other features, but it is as Boston Blackie that fans remember him best. The same holds true for Richard

Warner Baxter as the *Crime Doctor* helps Margaret Lindsay to a light in the series originated in 1943

The cliff-hanger serials used every trick in the moviemaking book—Buster Crabbe as Captain Silver in *The Sea Hound* (1947) is victim of the old "let's hang him by the hands in the blazing sun 'til the red ants get him" trick

Then it's the old "hit him over the head with a big rock" trick—that's too simple for Crabbe, so . . .

. . . it's the dastardly complicated machinations of the old "tie them to the water-wheel" trick

Meanwhile, back on the schooner, it's the old "let's get his pal while the Chinese have him distracted" trick; Jimmy Lloyd and Spencer Chan, respectively

But our hero always wins out in the end, especially when the star is a champion swimmer like Crabbe, and can pull his own old "dive off the boat from a height nobody else would dare" trick

Johnny Weissmuller as Jungle Jim with two of his typical adversaries

An early treatment of *Batman* was the serial with Lewis Wilson in the title role and Douglas Croft as his sidekick.

The Man of Steel is another perennial favorite, in episode after episode of *Superman*, the players are Kirk Alyn and Noel Neill

THE REDUCER RAY Chapter 3 SUPERMAN A COLUMBIA SERIAL

By arrangement with National Comics Publications, Inc

284

In the fifties, the serials taste the benefits of technology—a new kind of hero faces intergalactic evil every week

Larry Stewart is Captain Video and Judd Holdren is his assistant and friend, the Ranger (1951)

Typical serials typecasting: the stars of *The Monster and the Ape* (The "civilians" are unidentified) (1944)

Dix, who was The Whistler. His career stretches all the way back to 1929, but his biggest impact was in this 40s series.

Warner Baxter was the only Crime Doctor, for all 10 of the films in that series; it evolved after his long film stint, the highlight of which was *Prisoner of Shark Island*. But other series heroes weren't always portrayed by the same performer: The Lone Wolf part was parceled out among several actors, including Melvyn Douglas (*The Lone Wolf Returns*). No one seems to have minded too much, not Francis Lederer, Warren Williams, or any of the others.

Another basis for audience acceptance of the series was that many of them were based on already familiar sources. *Blondie* and *Jungle Jim* were both comic-strip staples, she being the most widely syndicated strip even today, he having been a best-selling comic book item for years. The *Crime Doctor* was a radio broadcast creation of writer Max Marcin. *The Whistler*, too, was first heard on the airwaves, as was *Boston Blackie*. Ellery Queen came out of detective novels for a long screen career.

But for all the suspense generated by the crime and adventure-oriented series, for popularity and longevity, none of them could touch *Blondie*. All of the characters of the Chic Young strip were brought to the screen versions, and they were played by the same

The Lone Wolf Returns, this time as Melvyn Douglas; there were several silent versions in the late twenties (1936)

Penny Singleton was Blondie and Arthur Lake was Dagwood in the most successful series of all; Larry Simms is their son, Baby Dumpling

actors throughout the long span of the series. Even when Baby Dumpling, the son, outgrew that name and was called Alexander, he continued to be played by Larry Simms, who just grew up in the part in a natural way that Little Orphan Annie, for example, never has.

Although Blondie and Dagwood's offspring matured, it would be hard to say the same of the plots. From 1938 to 1950, there was little change in the elements of a Blondie episode. Dagwood was always the architect of the world's tallest sandwiches, suspended between wife on one hand and boss on the other, high over some seemingly insoluble dilemma not necessarily of his own making.

Surprisingly enough for what was basically family entertainment, Dagwood's difficulties usually involved Blondie's misunderstanding of his contacts with another woman. It was always innocent, of course, even when the brunette in the case turns out to be Rita Hayworth.

Other occasional soon-to-be-stars dropped in from time to time: Lloyd Bridges, Glenn Ford. But for the most part, the cast was essentially a repertory company with Danny Mummert, Jack Rice, Irving Bacon (as the mailman), Eddie Acuff, and Jonathan Hale (as J. C. Dithers, Dagwood's boss, in the first eighteen films, until he was replaced by Jerome Cowan). Marjorie Kent, like her erstwhile brother, was allowed to grow up on-screen in the part of the Bumsteads' daughter, Cookie.

Even the directors stayed. Frank R. Strayer directed the original *Blondie* and turned out the next thirteen. In 1945, Abby Berlin took over for all but the last five, which were directed by Edward Bernds.

When the string of films was finally played out, there were two attempts to relocate the Bumstead menage on television. But neither visit was successful. The films themselves are still run on TV fairly frequently, though.

The comic strip, which started it all, is still highly popular all over the world. *Sic transit gloria* Blondie.

Another domestically oriented series, albeit more short-lived, attained some popularity in the 40s. Its stars were a boy actor named Ted Donaldson* and the Wonder Dog Ace, who had the title role in the *Rusty* adventures. Following in the wake of *Lassie*, there were six pleasant enough bill-bottoms turned out.

---

*Donaldson turned the dog in for a caterpillar named Curley in a whimsical comedy called *Once upon a Time*, with Cary Grant and Janet Blair, in 1944.

Ace the Wonder Dog and Ted Donaldson were pals in *Adventures of Rusty* (1945)

But the dominant category for series was the western, if only in terms of sheer numbers. Although the studio was to turn out some first-class westerns like *Arizona, 3:10 to Yuma, Jubal,* and *Man From Laramie* (while turning down a Stanley Kramer suggestion called *High Noon*), its output of the routine oater was massive. Dozens of films *each* were turned out by such cowboy stars as Charles Starrett, Ken Maynard, Bob Steele, Bill Cody, Fred Scott, Buck Jones, Bill Elliott, Tex Ritter, Bob Allen, and Tim McCoy, among others. Randolph Scott spent a major part of his later career at Columbia, almost exclusively a westerns performer.

Nor were the *B* westerns all series films. Not by a long shot. Singular features of little distinction were made by Rock Hudson, George Montgomery, Broderick Crawford, William Holden, Jon Hall (out of the jungle for once), James Stewart, Richard Widmark, Joseph Cotten, Stewart Granger, Raymond Burr, and countless others who stepped through Columbia's swinging doors.

Others, like Rory Calhoun, Rod Cameron, Phil Carey, and Audie Murphy never got beyond the dusty streets of the *B*'s. Another one who never got better than second-billed westerns made perhaps the greatest fortune ever amassed by any movie performer—singing cowboy Gene Autry, who invested his earnings shrewdly and expanded them into an empire of varied holdings estimated currently to be worth over $100,000,000. And he never got to kiss the girl except in one film! (The fans objected so to this soiling of his super-clean image that he never repeated the act. He has been seen to hug his horse, though.)

The *B*'s did everything the *A* pictures did, only a little worse. Or, as in the case of most of the science fiction turned out, a lot worse. But they could also do a lot less, thus the short subject, so dear to the heart of the money-conscious movie-goer of the Depression. Life needed a lot of escaping from then, and the longer the bill at the neighborhood movie house, the more customers it was likely to lure. Columbia had started its corporate life turning out one- and two-reelers in the silent days, but even with the advent of sound, the production of shorts never stopped.

The range of subject matter presented in the short films through the years is amazing. There was everything from travelogues (always with the inevitable sunset closing shot and affected narrative) that were little more than puff pieces for their respective

Showdown time before the fatal stabbing: Randolph Scott and George Macready; among the onlookers are Forrest Tucker (center) and Sheriff Edgar Buchanan

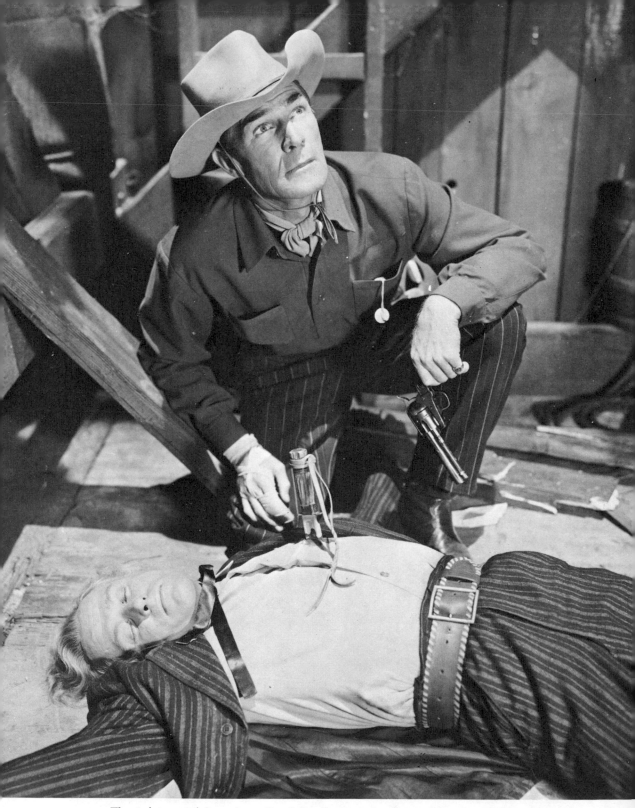

The quintessential cowboy, Randolph Scott, is in *Coroner Creek* with an undone George Macready (1948)

The Walking Hills was a mystery to everyone, including Ella Raines, William Bishop, and Randolph Scott (1949)

You could meet anyone in a Randolph Scott movie—Angela Lansbury's address was *Lawless Street* (1955)

Wild Bill Elliot in a rare moment of repose

Wild Bill in an even rarer moment with a girl—Iris Meredith, toting a gun in *The Return of Wild Bill* (1940)

Double-teaming, western style

Charles Starrett specialized in movies with noisy titles—An ad for *Blazing Six Shooters* (1940)

Starrett in *Thunder Over the Prairie* with Cliff Edwards and unnamed "extra" (1941)

Westerns we always have with us—*The Mine with the Iron Door* struck a small comic vein in 1936; that's Richard Arlen greeting Stanley Fields

The original singing cowboy, Gene Autry

locations. There were singalongs, with the lyrics appearing on-screen for the unhappy audience that may have forgotten the words. In 1942 there was even number one in the projected series, *America Sings with Kate Smith.* But alas, that never ever got as far as number two. Mickey Rooney, before he became Andy Hardy or met Judy Garland, was Mickey McGuire for a series of two-reelers released in 1933 and '34. And the output of comedy shorts, both live and animated, was truly prodigious.

298

Always Your Pal
Gene Autry

A Bullet is Waiting, 1954, paired Rory Calhoun, who always made *B* pictures, with Jean Simmons, who seldom did

Crowning the live comedy shorts was the triumvirate known collectively as the Three Stooges, or to the aficionados, Larry, Moe, and Curly. The trio romped through a parade that never let up, from the mid-30s to the mid-50s. The basic Stooges style never changed in all those years. It was one act that translated

The Three Stooges at the height of their popularity

well to television, where the Stooges proved to be as popular with the video generation as they had been with its parents.

Relying on outrageous slapstick, the predictable reactions that always delight very young audiences, and a cockeyed way of looking at the world, the threesome gagged its way through such screen splendors as *Three Little Pigskins*, where they romped with a lady named Lucille Ball (1934); *Ants in the Pantry*, with Clara Kimball Young (1936); *Three Little Twirps*, with Chester Conklin in 1943. They thrived on punning titles like *Phony Express* and *Busy Buddies* and *Idle Roomers*.

The Stooges knocked out as many as nine comedies in a single year. But there were other players who were equally busy. Classic comedians Buster Keaton and Harry Langdon made shorts

301

for the company well into the 40s. Leon Errol, whose lively antics brightened so many feature films for twenty years, was very active in the earliest days of two-reel talkies. Andy Clyde, Hugh Herbert and Charlie Chase also had careers that spanned the decades from talkies to the demise of the short feature.

Although primarily a comedians' medium, there were ladies present too, most notably Vera Vague, who fluttered her way through a number of silly things. From time to time, the accomplished comedienne Una Merkel showed up. Most of the other women played secondary, not starring roles.

Even more popular than these features was the totally new, purely cinematic art form, the animated cartoon. They held a limited appeal before sound, but when the imaginative little creatures learned to talk, they became irresistible. In 1930, Columbia released a sound cartoon called *Steamboat Willie*, produced by a young artist who had recently arrived on the lot.

Outrageous props and Rude Goldberg contraptions were part of the Andy Clyde action in each film

303

The baggy-pants king of innumerable comedy shorts, Andy Clyde

One of the most lovable comedians in minor films was Joe E. Brown—snacking with June Harris in *The Gladiator*, 1935 (One of the scriptwriters was Philip Wylie)

Willie was the original mouse that roared, for when he changed his name to Mickey, he and his creator, Walt Disney, became world famous.

For the next two years, the studio released all the Mickey product, 43 cartoons in all. They were, and remain, a sheer delight. The characters have changed very little from Disney's initial concepts, the story lines and perky and fun, and it's all underscored by the kind of pleasant music that Disney always used so imaginatively.

In 1929, the *Silly Symphonies* series was started. More Disney characters were born: Pluto, in 1930, though he didn't get his name for another year. Goofy came along in 1932. By now, some of the cartoons, drawn chiefly by Disney's long-time collaborator, Ub Iwerks, were in color.

But this most marvelous of beginnings was not to last. Mickey's boss and Columbia's boss did not see eye-to-eye on many things. At the end of 1932, Disney packed up his brushes and pencils and went elsewhere for his distribution, until his operation grew so large and so successful that he opened his own studio and thereby gained total control of his films.

Columbia's experience with cartoons preceded the Disney years, actually; they lost the mouse, but they still had the cat. Or more accurately, the Kat—Krazy by name. Here was another comic strip character who translated successfully to the screen. During the 30s, there were about 100 little episodes featuring the surprisingly sophisticated antics of Krazy Kat and friends.

The dynamic Krazy Kat, originally created for the comics page by Herriman, brought to the screen as hero of one hundred cartoon shorts

Several other minor cartoon series were forthcoming as the company grew, but the next great breakthrough came after the war. So skilled had techniques become and so demanding of perfection the audience, that the cartoon had become the single most expensive film to produce. Even the Disney people were turning increasingly to live action features and the nature studies they pioneered.

Then came the change-about. Simplification of figures and backgrounds, rather than a wealth of subtle detail, became the order of the day. Limited action, whereby the major portion of a figure did not need to be redrawn for each separate frame, reduced costs considerably. Also reduced was the great charm of the earlier cartoons, alas. Having been brought to the very edge of reality, characters were now pulled back and simplified into near stick figures.

But the new simplification permitted the introduction of many new characters. And the best of them made up in wit and human qualities for what they lost in graphics. At the head of the parade of new favorites marched *Gerald McBoing Boing* and *Mr. Magoo*. Both were the creation of a fresh young company called UPA. They burst on the scene in the 50s and turned the field of film cartooning around with their innovative approach.

Magoo was the crinkle-voiced little man who made a career out of near-sightedness. He walked down holes, into poles, and through every hazard imaginable, but always came out all right. He seemed to personify that mental short-sightedness with which most of us go through life, and perhaps he gave us a little hope that we'd always end rightside up, too.

McBoing Boing was a child, the essence of innocence. He never spoke; he just went "boing boing." But with that simple sound, he managed to express himself very clearly on a number of matters.

One of the wonderfullest of the new wave of cartoons was *Gerald McBoing-Boing;* here, the little boy who couldn't speak is taunted by other youngsters

Gerald's aloneness is poignantly illustrated in simple and enormously effective graphics

But goodness triumphs, as it always must, and Gerald reaps the reward of fame and fortune

UPA's other great hero was lots more vocal, compensation perhaps for his limited vision—typically, Mr. Magoo approaches an insurance company by the way of sky-high scaffolding . . .

. . . shakes hands with a suit of armour, oblivious to the danger behind him . . .

308

. . . and heads for certain trouble with a tow truck—but Magoo too, will come out all right in the end

All of the UPA cartoons dealt with off-beat subjects in a whimsical sort of way. They changed the content of cartoons from the merely slapstick and slapdash to the faintly philosophical, and the content added depth to the flattened-out form of the simplified animation.

Near-sighted or not, Mr. Magoo managed to walk off with two Oscars (1954 and 1956), and Gerald McBoing Boing garnered his statuette in 1950. All told, there were 55 cartoons released under Columbia's banner that bore the UPA imprint.

Then, all the pen-and-ink people went to television, rather than theaters, the small screen demanding ever-increasing amounts of product for its living-room audience. The cameras kept grinding. But theatrical need for cartoons, series, and series pictures had peaked.

This sheer abundance of output should not overshadow the fact that dozens of nonseries full-length *B* pictures were being churned out each year into the 50s. There were westerns, musicals, adventures, comedies—a mishmash of movies that were often noteworthy for their very lassitude. Sometimes, though, they could be fun for the very nuttiness that was permissible in the cockeyed scripts that would never have passed muster in the least *A* production. If nothing made much sense, so what? When the primary purpose of a movie is to empty the theater to make room for the next onslaught of ticketbuyers, then the worse it is, the better it is.

Once in a while a new formula for the *B*'s would come along. An interesting sidelight are the revue-type musicals that sprang up during the early 40s. The war had brought a halt to the recording industry, and filmland stepped into the breach to provide some suitable fare for the pop music fans.

Constructed around a premise rather than a full-grown plot, a variety of entertainers not usually brought before the cameras were suddenly recruited to make movies. In one pasted-together job called *Reveille with Beverly*, Ann Miller is a lady disc jockey. When she announces a song by Frank Sinatra, guess what lanky young singer appears on the screen! Then it's Duke Ellington with the big band! And Count Basie with his aggregation! But none of these entertainers ever appear together in the film. It's just a series of clips glued together without even the benefit of scenery, just musicians photographed against a curtain. Even the talent wasn't as expensive as it would seem: Sinatra hadn't yet made his mark in films, and for bands like the Duke's, there wasn't much work available.

All of these program fillers can be considered as adjuncts to the serious business of movie-making; only the better animated cartoons really made a contribution much beyond that of employing some performers and technicians who otherwise might have stood idle those long decades. To some degree, they do mirror the styles and tastes of their times, if anyone can sit still long enough to catch a glimpse of a reflection of a time gone by.

But the real interest lies in those films which illuminate and shape their time, not merely cast its shadow. It is to those films, great in themselves or in their performers, that we turn our attention in the next chapter.

Surrounded by a lot of ladies is the young Frank Sinatra of *Reveille with Beverly* (1943)

Moving with a multitude of men is Ann Miller, who played the title role of *Beverly* in this wartime entertainment

BLONDIE #1

(Released: November 2, 1938)

Director: Frank R. Strayer
Assistant Producer:
  Robert Sparks
Editor: Gene Havlick
Based on the Comic Strip by:
  Chic Young
Screen Play: Richard Flournoy
Art Director: Lionel Banks
Set Decorations: Babs Johnstone
Director of Photography:
  Henry Freulich, A.S.C.

Cast:
Penny Singleton
Arthur Lake
Gene Lockhart
Ann Doran
Jonathan Hale
Gordon Oliver
Stanley Andrews

Danny Mummert
Kathleen Lockhart
Dorothy Moore
Fay Helm
Richard Fiske
Daisy (Dog)

MEET BOSTON BLACKIE

(Released: February 20, 1941)

Director: Robert Florey
Editor: James Sweeney
Based on the Character Created by:
  Jack Doyle
Screen Play: Jay Dratier
Director of Photography:
  Franz F. Planer, A.S.C.

Cast:
Chester Morris
Rochelle Hudson
Richard Lane
Charles Wegenheim

Jack O'Malley
George Magrill
Michael Rand

REVEILLE WITH BEVERLY

(Released: January 26, 1943)

Director: Charles Barton
Producer: Sam White
Editor: James Sweeney
Screen Play:
  Howard Green
  Jack Henley
  Albert Duffy
Art Director: Lionel Banks
Associate: Paul Murphy
Music Director: M. W. Stoloff
Set Decorations: Joseph Kish
Director of Photography:
  Philip Tannura, A.S.C.
Technical Radio Adviser:
  Jean Ruth

Cast:
Bob Crosby
  and band
Ella Mae Morse
Duke Ellington
  and band
Count Basie
  and band
Frank Sinatra

Mills Brothers
Radio Rogues
Ann Miller
William Wright
Dick Purcell
Larry Parks
Douglas Leavitt
Adele Mara

CRIME DOCTOR

(Released: June 9, 1943)

Director: Michael Gordon
Producer: Ralph Cohn
Editor: Dwight Caldwell
From the Radio Program,
  "Crime Doctor," by:
  Max Marcin
Adaptation: Jerome Odlum
Screen Play:
  Graham Baker
  Louis Lantz

Music: Lee Zahler
Director of Photography:
  James S. Brown,
  A.S.C.

Cast:
Warner Baxter
Margaret Lindsay
John Litel
Ray Collins
Harold Huber
Don Costello
Leon Ames

THE WHISTLER

(Released: March, 1944)

Director: William Castle
Producer: Rudolph C. Flothow
Editor: Jerome Thoms
Story: J. Donald Wilson
Screen Play: Eric Taylor
Music: Wilbur Hatch

Art Director:
  George Van Marter
Set Decorations:
  Sidney Clifford
Director of Photography:
  James S. Brown, A.S.C.

Cast:
Richard Dix
J. Carrol Nash
Gloria Stuart
Alan Dinehart

ADVENTURES OF RUSTY

(Released: July 23, 1945)

Director: Paul Burnford
Producer: Rudolph C. Flothow
Editor: Reg Browne
Story: Al Martin
Screen Play: Aubrey Wieberg
Music Director:
  M. R. Bakaleinikoff
Director of Photography:
  L. W. O'Connell, A.S.C.
Sound Recording:
  Howard Fogetti

Cast:
Ted Donaldson
Margaret Lindsay
Conrad Nagel
Gloria Holden
Robert Williams

Addison Richards
Arno Frey
Eddie Parker
Ace (Wonder Dog)

JUNGLE JIM

(Released: December, 1948)

Director: William Berke
Producer: Sam Katzman
Editor: Aaron Stoll
Story and Screen Play:
  Carroll Young
Art Director:
  Paul Palmentola

Music Director:
  Mischa Bakeleinikoff
Set Decorations:
  Sidney Clifford
Director of Photography:
  Lester White, A.S.C.

Cast:
Johnny Weismuller
Virginia Grey
George Reeves
Lita Baron
Rick Vallin
Holmes Herbert

THE COLUMBIA CLIFF-HANGERS:
MULTIPLE EPISODE SERIALS

Title	Year of Release	Title	Year of Release
Adventures of Captain Africa, The	1955	Jungle Raiders	1946
Adventures of Sir Galahad, The	1950	King of the Congo	1952
Atom Man vs. Superman	1950	Lost Planet, The	1953
Batman	1943	Mandrake the Magician	1939
Batman and Robin	1949	Monster and the Ape, The	1944
Black Arrow	1944	Mysterious Island	1951
Blackhawk	1952	Mysterious Pilot, The	1938
Blazing the Overland Trail	1956	Overland with Kit Carson	1934
Brenda Starr Reporter	1944	Perils of the Royal Mounted	1942
Brick Bradford	1947	Perils of the Wilderness	1955
Bruce Gentry	1949	Phantom, The	1943
Captain Midnight	1942	Pirates of the High Seas	1950
Captain Video	1951	Riding with Buffalo Bill	1955
Chick Carter, Detective	1946	Roar of the Iron Horse	1951
Cody of the Pony Express	1950	Sea Hound, The	1947
Congo Bill	1949	Secret Code, The	1942
Deadwood Dick	1940	Secret of Treasure Island, The	1938
Desert Hawk, The	1944	Shadow, The	1938
Flying G-Men	1939	Son of Geronimo	1952
Great Adventures of Cap't. Kidd, The	1953	Son of the Guardsman	1946
Great Adventures of Wild Bill Hickok, The	1938	Spider Returns, The	1941
		Spider's Web, The	1939
Green Archer, The	1940	Superman	1948
Gunfighters of the Northwest	1954	Terry and the Pirates	1939
Holt of the Secret Service	1941	Tex Granger	1948
Hop Harrigan	1946	Valley of Vanishing Men, The	1942
Iron Claw, The	1941	Vigilante, The	1947
Jack Armstrong	1947	White Eagle	1941
Jungle Menace	1938	Who's Guilty?	1946

In *Caine Mutiny*, Humphrey Bogart gave one of the top performances of his life as Captain Queeg (1954)

9 | Great Movies, Movie Greats

BECAUSE COLUMBIA HAD NO REGULAR STOCK COMPANY OF top stars during most of its history, when a particular vehicle was bought for production, the availability of suitable stars was not limited to the Gower Street lot. Thus, at one time or another (and in many cases, it *was* just one time) almost every major Hollywood star worked at Columbia.

Many unknowns were also used, due to budgetary or other considerations. But because of the extreme care with which many of the company's directors, like Capra, and other executives, like Sidney Buchman, handled the performers, they didn't stay unknown after their Gower Street visits. When Capra directed a romantic comedy in 1931, he drew attention away from the nominal stars* by titling the film for the "other woman" in the story. The title was *Platinum Blonde* and the woman was Jean Harlow. She had walked into the studio a pin-up queen, but she walked out a star.

---

*Loretta Young and Robert Williams.

The two ladies, Harlow and Young, co-starred for the studio again in a trifle called *Three Wise Girls*. It was the last appearance on Gower Street for Jean Harlow. She had become a top attraction for MGM and was never lent out again anywhere.

Miss Young was soon back to co-star with Spencer Tracy in an unusual drama directed by Frank Borzage called *Man's Castle*. Tracy was just at the point where his career was to take that big upward swing and it was to be another twenty-five years before he returned to Columbia. That was for *The Last Hurrah*, a grand role for Tracy as the old Bostonian politician. His next Columbia role was as a priest in *The Devil at 4 O'Clock* in 1961, with Frank Sinatra.

He came back for his very last film, Stanley Kramer's *Guess Who's Coming to Dinner?*, reunited at last with Katharine Hepburn after too long a hiatus—ten years since the screen's all-time favorite team had appeared together. (She had made *Suddenly, Last Summer* with Elizabeth Taylor at the studio in 1959.) It was a warmly involving story about an interracial marriage between their daughter, Katharine Houghton (in real life, Hepburn's niece), and Sidney Poitier. Much of the lingering charm of the film was outside of the actual story line, though. It was in the genuine regard that Tracy and Hepburn had for each other that shone through the faces of the two senior stars. Tracy was dying (his death occurred only a short while after shooting was completed) and they seemed to be enjoying their last great fling together with the whole world watching. That her great tenderness radiated throughout was duly noted by her peers when they awarded her the Best Actress Oscar.

At least part of the $35,000,000 that the film earned must be credited to the third star, Sidney Poitier. By 1967, he had become the third most popular star in the country. (In 1968, he would be first.) Among his best films were two others he had made at Columbia—*A Raisin in the Sun* and *To Sir with Love*, the first early in his film career, the second after he had extended his film career into other areas. *Guess* came while his career was peaking.

In the 70s, as had so many other superior performers, Poitier turned his attention to the other side of the camera—to directing other actors. His first effort was an excellent, although critically underrated, western. Poitier costarred with Harry Belafonte, who contributed a bravura performance in this saga about blacks in the old west. Staying closer to the truth of that experi-

Loretta Young tends to Spencer Tracy in this scene from *Man's Castle* (1933) ▶

In *The Last Hurrah*, Tracy was surrounded by as strong a brace of supporting players as has been assembled in one place: Pat O'Brien, Ricardo Cortez, James Gleason, and Edward Brophy. Basil Rathbone, John Carradine, and Donald Crisp were also featured (1958)

Tracy's last film, *Guess Who's Coming to Dinner?* with Sidney Poitier, Katharine Houghton, and Katharine Hepburn (1968)

320

Poitier's great breakthrough part

Sidney Poitier with Ruby Dee . . . and with Claudia McNeil in *A Raisin in the Sun* (1961)

To Sir With Love made an enormous amount of money; dancing with Sidney Poitier is England's Judy Geeson (1967)

Buck and the Preacher were Sidney Poitier and Harry Belafonte gunning down the bad guys in this rousing post-Civil-War western (1972)

Rosalind Russell and John Boles during a lighter moment in the travails of *Craig's Wife* (1936)

Mae West encounters William Gaxton and Victor Moore in *The Heat's On*—the boys seem impressed, to say the least

The Heat's On featured Mae West and all the chorus boys the studio could muster in 1943

ence than any film of the past had bothered to, the movie had more to say than most westerns, and said it in a fast-paced shoot-'em-up that should have pleased most viewers of the genre. Released as it was a few years before the major onslaught of black films, *Buck and the Preacher* got less audience attention than many of the decidedly inferior films that rode the crest of "blaxploitation" in the 70s.

Another star who worked for Columbia at all points in her long and legendary film career is Rosalind Russell. Now very much the Hollywood *grande dame*, she epitomizes much of what is wonderful in the movies. She made a dramatic statement in 1936, in her first film for the studio, *Craig's Wife*, a classic of the early "women's picture." Actually, it was directed by a woman, Dorothy Arzner, the only successful female directing during that period. Harry Cohn was convinced that a woman's hand was needed for this genre. The screenplay was by Mary McCall and even the editing scissors were in a woman's hands: Viola Lawrence.

And female players predominated in the story of a house-proud woman—Billie Burke and Jane Darwell among others. But most of all, it was Roz Russell's big moment. Playing the part of a woman actually older than she really was at the time, she made the most of the opportunity. As it had happened for so many others, she walked away a star. But unlike so many one-shots, she was to return to Columbia time and time again for some of the juiciest parts in her long career. Her very next role was a totally different part than that of the overly domesticated

Mrs. Craig—the untameable (except at the very end), wildly funny Hildy of *His Girl Friday*.

She did a number of less memorable comedies after that, until *My Sister Eileen*, one of the brightest comedies of the 40s.

There came another about-face to a dramatic role, the spinster in *Picnic*. This came in 1955, the midst of one of her busiest times, a decade when she swung from dramatic parts to comedy and musicals.

In the 60s, she would play a nun in a mild comedy, *The Trouble with Angels*, which was successful enough to warrant a sequel. All in all, hers was one of the most consistent connections with the studio.

A lot of other top Hollywood ladies made important movies for Columbia. Mae West met her match for once with William Gaxton in *The Heat's On*. A teenage Shirley Temple made her largest grossing film ever, *Kiss and Tell*, and got her first on-screen kiss, as the title promised. Bette Davis was featured in *Storm Center* and Kim Stanley was *The Goddess*. Marilyn Monroe made her second screen appearance ever in *Ladies of the Chorus* and Elizabeth Taylor not only took on Tennessee Williams, but even tackled the Bard in *Taming of the Shrew*. And an English lass, Lynn Redgrave, helped launch the British invasion of the 60s with *Georgy Girl*, one of the most popular imports ever. Jane Fonda left a mass of mediocre films behind her when she did *Cat Ballou*, proving that this best of the new actresses could handle comedy as well as anything else.

With Jane Fonda in *Cat Ballou* was the indomitable Lee Marvin. He had made a corralful of westerns at the studio before, as well as contributing memorable performances in *The Wild One* and *The Caine Mutiny*, but it was his double role in *Cat* that brought him his Oscar. And in 1966 he was with Burt Lancaster in a top-notch western, *The Professionals*.

A movie that was instrumental in bringing great public attention to one of the most popular entertainers of all time was *Pennies from Heaven*. It was an unusual role for the young Bing Crosby, who had been primarily viewed in frothy musicals before that. But this rather sad story won Crosby raves for his acting as well as his vocalizing. Another notable in the cast of *Pennies:* Louis Armstrong.

That other blonde bombshell, Marilyn Monroe, made her solo appearance for the ▶ studio with these *Ladies of the Chorus* (1948)

327

Jerome Courtland courted an almost grownup Shirley Temple, the Corliss Archer of *Kiss and Tell* (1945)

Kim Stanley had the title role in *The Goddess,* and that's Lloyd Bridges in *her* background (1958)

Bette Davis was a librarian fighting for civil liberties in *Storm Center;* that's Paul Kelly in the background (1956)

A confrontation between the greatest actress and the greatest star in movies: Katharine Hepburn and Elizabeth Taylor in *Suddenly, Last Summer* (1960)

Elizabeth Taylor and Richard Burton meet at yet another altar in the fittingly boisterous but unappreciated *Taming of the Shrew* (1967)

James Mason accompanies Lynn Redgrave to a contemporary ceremony in the pop-oriented and highly popular *Georgy Girl* (1966)

A drunken Lee Marvin and a frantic Jane Fonda in one of the best western spoofs ever made, *Cat Ballou* (1965)

Here in a first-rate dramatic western, *The Professionals*, Lee Marvin and Burt Lancaster detail their plans; Claudia Cardinale also starred (1966)

Another favorite from early on was James Stewart. His first chore was in 1938 and it was a winner—as the male lead opposite Jean Arthur in the Oscar-bearing *You Can't Take It with You*. After that, he was a natural choice for Capra's follow-up, *Mr. Smith Goes to Washington*, for which he was Oscar-nominated. The film was considered to have put him on a par with Gary Cooper as a box office attraction.

His war service and other commitments kept him from the studio until the 50s, when he returned to make a superior western, *The Man from Laramie*. Later, he did two of Columbia's important films of the 50s; *Bell, Book, and Candle*, from the Broadway stage hit, and *Anatomy of a Murder*, a screen translation of a best-selling novel. That performance earned him another nomination from the Academy.

Cary Grant came to Columbia after several years of kicking around in other studios' movies to make *When You're in Love* with Grace Moore, one of her later efforts. He had been considered the usual leading-man type, but his next film at Columbia proved he could handle comedy as well as anyone around,

Bing Crosby in 1936 in one of his best roles, in *Pennies From Heaven*

Joining Bing Crosby in *Pennies From Heaven* is Madge Evans

James Stewart in a tense scene from *The Man From Laramie* (1955)

In the courtroom drama, *Anatomy of a Murder,* James Stewart is defending Ben Gazzara; Lee Remick is Gazzara's wife (1959)

and it opened a whole new area for him and for his leading lady, Irene Dunne. Neither of them had done real comedy before, but Leo McCarey got marvelous performances from both of them in *The Awful Truth*, one of the most stylish of the old screwballs. He repeated his triumph in *Holiday*, with Hepburn, and *His Girl Friday,* with Russell. Then he switched gears for *Only Angels Have Wings*, and once more with *The Howards of Virginia*, a costume drama. *Penny Serenade* re-teamed him in a tender tearjerker with Irene Dunne. By this time, Grant had established not only surprising versatility, but the eternal grace and charm that was to become his hallmark. He played a murder suspect in *Talk of the Town*, another serious-sided screwball, and a lovable con artist in *Once Upon a Time*. (That's the one with the dancing caterpillar.)

It would seem as though he had exhausted all the possibilities at Columbia. He stayed away for twenty-two years, and when he came back, it was to make his final movie, *Walk, Don't Run*, an unfortunately forgettable picture that hardly seems the worthy capping of an unparalleled career. Perhaps he'll return to do another some day. He still looks like the Cary Grant he miraculously has always been, for as long as anyone can remember.

Cary Grant woos Martha Scott in the Revolutionary War story, *The Howards of Virginia* (1940)

Like Spencer Tracy, Humphrey Bogart's last film before his death was for Columbia. *The Harder They Fall* co-starred Rod Steiger and was based on Budd Schulberg's novel about the boxing racket. He had made a brief appearance on the lot in 1932 in a short feature called *Love Affair*. He wasn't to return until 1943, when he made one of the best of all the desert-set war movies, *Sahara*. He did *Dead Reckoning* with Lizabeth Scott in 1947; *Knock on Any Door* in 1949, along with another war film, *Tokyo Joe; In a Lonely Place*, with Gloria Grahame, an intriguing 1950 mystery set in Hollywood; and *Sirocco* the next year, 1951.

Bogey's big film for Columbia came in 1954 in a part that was completely different for him—the deranged captain of *The Caine Mutiny*. Surrounded by an all-star cast, he gave the part a depth of authority that made it completely believable.

Bogart was one actor who never had any problems with Harry Cohn. Cohn loved him as he did few other performers (Al Jolson was one of the others), and the four films Bogart made prior to *The Caine Mutiny* were made by his own production company, which he brought to Columbia. When Bogart was dying, Cohn issued constant announcements about the next film they

As tough as the tank he stands beside is the grizzled Bogart of *Sahara* (1944)

337

◄ In *Penny Serenade,* Irene Dunne and Cary Grant will experience heartbreak not hinted at in this early scene in Japan (1947)

would be making together—all to keep the failing star's spirits up. It worked . . . for a while.

Other Columbia films of the 50s, 60s, and 70s were, along with the Oscar winners already discussed, important and engaging features whose story lines were at least as compelling as their casts; Stanley Kubrick's *Dr. Strangelove* certainly had more than its share of both. Peter Sellers, George C. Scott, Sterling Hayden, and Keenan Wynn romped through this 1964 black comedy that had more to say about the condition of the world than any film had in years. It marked Kubrick as *the* new American director to watch.

The most inspired film actor of the 70s was unquestionably George C. Scott. His portrait of General Buck Turgidson in *Dr. Strangelove* had exposed everything about the quirkiness we had all been fearing in the hitherto sacrosanct military establishment. He played almost equally fearsome types in two later Columbia pieces, a cop in *The New Centurions,* and an oil prospector fighting Faye Dunaway in *Oklahoma Crude.*

But many other top-rated actors were also very much in evidence in almost all of the company's films. Fredric March appeared in an ill-fated *Death of a Salesman*, based on the Arthur Miller play, and in Paddy Chayefsky's *Middle of the Night.* Burt Lancaster starred in *The Swimmer* and *Castle Keep,* the latter a World War II thriller that didn't quite come off. One that did however, both for its array of stars and box office business was *The Guns of Navarone.* Gregory Peck, David Niven, and Anthony Quinn headed up the predominantly male cast of this relentless suspense story set in wartime Greece.

The tremendous success of *The Guns of Navarone* sparked off yet another round of imitative films: the new-style war epic with the plot tightly focused on a single, seemingly impossible mission—be it the taking of an enemy arsenal, the destruction of an enemy officers' headquarters, or a mass escape from prison camp. And as in *Navarone*, the regular army fighting unit was banished, replaced by a specially selected team of men, each with his own particular craft to enlist for the mission, and each a fairly well-defined character. This sort of special-team approach also became the theme for several non-war caper films. As a movie format, it was basically sound, for it could showcase a pantheon of male stars—and often employed foreign film-stars, which boosted the international ticket sales. The special-mission action film—an interesting approach to movie-making —unfortunately has long since been done to death.

◀ Bogart with Lizabeth Scott in *Dead Reckoning* (1947)

Stanley Kubrick's landmark comedy

The war room set from *Dr. Strangelove* (1964)

George C. Scott is caught between Peter Bull and Peter Sellers in *Dr. Strangelove*

A very different sort of thriller is *The Odessa File*, based on Frederick Forsyth's mammoth seller. The action is postwar, the protagonist neither soldier nor spy but a journalist, the obsessed amateur whose very displacement into the netherworld of chase and danger is more immediate to us than that of the trained, professional killer. Our man here is Jon Voight, and he is not part of a star pack, but most definitely on his own.

A great actor who played many great parts in his life was Paul Muni. Early in the war, he starred in what were two of the finer efforts of the more conventional genre film, *Commandos Strike at Dawn* and *Counter-Attack*. Then, in a totally different framework, he was to make his last film. Muni was perfectly cast as the involved, caring, gruff old doctor of *The Last Angry Man*. It was set in the poor, lower-class milieu of Brooklyn, a place and condition that Muni knew well. The film and the role were both properly fitting to cap one of the most distinguished acting careers in America.

Not every movie concentrated on humankind. As the first alarms were sounded in the media warning against mankind's potential for destroying the planet itself, people began seeing the human condition not in terms of individual survival, but in terms of the maintenance of the entire ecology. Nature films became important theatrical features, with perhaps greatest public interest in this type of film centered on wildlife. In this area, Columbia had a stand-out film which has become a perennial favorite, engendering not only movie sequels, but even a television series.

Born Free had as its major character a lioness. Elsa had been the heroine of a best-selling book and she was an enormous success on the screen as well. The film had two good elements going for it: the East African jungle location—as well photographed as any nature special—and a story that involved the audience in the fate of the big cats as inexorably as if they had been a human family.

The Owl and the Pussycat, on the other hand starred a tiger— Barbra Streisand, again, in a Broadway transplant, proving she shines just as brightly without an orchestra behind her. Another stage play, *Cactus Flower*, was flimsy whimsy at best, but it served a very important purpose—bringing the screen its newest not-so-dumb blonde, Goldie Hawn. In her initial appearance, she was duly accepted by the film world—and proof was the Oscar for Best Supporting Actress.

Bob & Carol & Ted & Alice were Robert Culp and Natalie Wood

343

The Guns of Navarone: the deadly target to be destroyed by an international stellar cast

and Elliot Gould and Dyan Cannon in one of the most explicit films released by a top studio with name players. It all seems a little tame now, but it brought a new degree of frankness with glossy production values to neighborhood theaters.

The Way We Were brought Robert Redford together with *the* super-star, Streisand, and provided the last occasion on which the word charisma would be legitimately appropriate.

With the release in 1971 of *The Last Picture Show*, Peter Bogdanovitch became another new American director to watch. And names like Cloris Leachman and Timothy Bottoms were on the way to becoming household words.

When *Fat City* was released, John Huston convinced the movie-goers that *he* was still the American director to watch—after almost forty years.

With *I Never Sang for My Father,* Melvyn Douglas returned to the studio after a long absence. After his run of screwballs in Columbia's golden comedy years, there had been only the indifferent *Guilt of Janet Ames* with Roz Russell. But this new film established him once again among the most talented and effective film actors ever.

344

Anthony Quinn is a Greek partisan and Gregory Peck an out-of-uniform officer in ▶
The Guns of Navarone (1961)

Among the newer actors, the most interesting seems to be Jack Nicholson, who scored so well in *Easy Rider* and *Five Easy Pieces*. In what is not the brightest of movie eras, when most actors play themselves over and over (and out), his is a talent of the versatility and range that marked the stars of better days. How easily he can slip in and out of comedy, for example, was exemplified by his masterful interpretation in a roaring good story about three sailors, *The Last Detail*.

But even if these aren't the best of times for movies, it isn't all that bad when stars like Streisand and Scott and Nicholson still appear regularly. The movies are something like love: Even when things are pretty bad, it's still pretty wonderful. Maybe that's why we love them so.

Paul Muni in *Commandos Strike at Dawn,* a gripping film of the war years (1943)

◀ Jon Voight and the object of his search—*The Odessa File* (1974)

Paul Muni again, in *Counter-Attack* (1945)

As the doctor who won't leave his slum patients, Paul Muni talks to David Wayne in
The Last Angry Man (1959)

Virginia McKenna, Bill Travers, and the little lions of *Born Free*

Virginia McKenna and Elsa of *Born Free* (1966)

Barbra Streisand and George Segal cavorted through *The Owl and the Pussycat* (1970)

Goldie Hawn is one of the shiniest newcomers to movie stardom

Barbra Streisand is a bag woman for the mafia in an episode from *For Pete's Sake* (1974)

Hail Columbia. When movies were movies, they made those Capras and screwballs and innumerable other sagas that are part of our national inheritance. When innovation and courage were called for, the studio was ready. Individual talent was nurtured (albeit sometimes painfully!) but artists grew and matured and bloomed without being smothered by committeeism.

In making the great leap from Poverty Row to major studio status, Columbia produced quality and quantity far beyond what could be expected from the company's frequently limited funds and physical resources. Its freshness and originality provided entertainment for audiences and leads for imitators.

Movies are an art and a business and the best films succeed at both. The vision, the ideas, the tenacity, and the skills of the filmmaker are embodied in the best of the Columbia movies. From mogul to make-up artist, the unmistakable stamp of excellence has been its enduring hallmark.

The way stardom was spelled in the seventies: Robert Redford and Barbra Streisand in *The Way We Were* (1973)

Natalie Wood, Dyan Cannon, Elliot Gould, and Robert Culp toast the new marital "freedom" in *Bob & Carol & Ted & Alice* (1969)

Timothy Bottoms and Cloris Leachman share an unhappy moment in *The Last Picture Show* (1971)

With Gene Hackman in *I Never Sang for My Father*, Melvyn Douglas gave a towering performance (1970)

After years as a successful light comedian in many films, Melvyn Douglas turned to dramatic roles. Here he is with Rosalind Russell in *The Guilt of Janet Ames* (1947)

Jack Nicholson as the rambunctious sailor of *The Last Detail* (1974)

LOVE AFFAIR

(Released: March 17, 1932)

Director: Thornton Freeland
Editor: Jack Dennis
From a Story by: Ursula Parrot
Adaptation and Dialogue:
  Jo Swerling
Continuity: Dorothy Howell
Director of Photography:
  Ted Tetzlaff

Footage: 6299 ft.

Cast:

Dorothy MacKaill	Jack Kennedy
Humphrey Bogart	Bradley Page
Halliwell Hobbes	Barbara Leonard
Astrid Alwyn	Harold Minjer

MAN'S CASTLE

(Released: November 20, 1933)

Director: Frank Borzage
Editor: Viola Lawrence
Story: Lawrence Hazard
Screen Play: Jo Swerling
Cameraman: Joseph August
Engineer: Wilbur Brown

Footage: 7018 ft.

Cast:

Spencer Tracy	Arthur Hohl
Loretta Young	Marjorie Rambeau
Glenda Farrell	Dickie Moore
Walter Connolly	Helen Jerome Eddy

CRAIG'S WIFE

(Released: September 1, 1936)

Director: Dorothy Arzner
Associate Producer:
  Edward Chodorov
Editor: Viola Lawrence
From the Pulitzer Prize Play by:
  George Kelly
Screen Play:
  Mary C. McCall, Jr.
Art Director:
  Stephen Goosson
Music Director:
  M. W. Stoloff

Costumes: Len Anthony
Director of Photography:
  Lucien Ballard, A.S.C.

Footage: 6952 ft.

Cast:
Rosalind Russell
John Boles
Billie Burke
Jane Darwell
Dorothy Wilson
Alma Kruger
Thomas Mitchell
Elisabeth Risdon
Raymond Walburn
Robert Allen
Nydia Westman
Kathleen Burke

PENNIES FROM HEAVEN

(Released: November 17, 1936)

Director: Norman Z. McLeod
Editor: John Rawlins

Music Director:
  George Stoll

Cast:
Bing Crosby

Story: William Rankin
Screen Play: Jo Swerling
Music: Arthur Johnson
Lyrics: John Burke
Song Arranger:
  John Scott Trotter
Art Director:
  Stephen Goosson

Director of Photography:
  Robert Pittack, A.S.C.

Footage: 7437 ft.

Madge Evans
Louis Armstrong
Donald Meek
John Gallaudet
William Stack
Nana Bryant
Tommy Dugan
Nydia Westman

THE HOWARDS OF VIRGINIA

(Released: September 19, 1940)

Director: Frank Lloyd
Assistant Director:
  William Tummell
Producer: Frank Lloyd
Associate Producer:
  Jack H. Skirball
Editor: Paul Weatherwax
From the Novel, *The Tree of
  Liberty* by: Elizabeth Page
Screen Play: Sidney Buchman
Music: Richard Hageman
Art Director: John Goddman
Interior Decoration:
  Howard Bristol
Montage Effects:
  Slavko Vorkapick

Gowns: Irene Saltern
Director of Photography:
  Bert Glennon, A.S.C.
Technical Adviser:
  Waldo Twitchell
Sound Recording:
  William H. Wilmarth

Footage: 10,620 ft.

Cast:
Cary Grant
Martha Scott
Sir Cedric Hardwicke
Alan Marshall
Richard Carlson
Paul Kelly
Irving Bacon
Elizabeth Risdon
Ann Revere
Richard Alden
Phil Taylor
Rita Quigley
Lobby Taylor
Richard Gaines
George Houston
Ralph Byrd
Dickie Jones
Buster Phelps
Wade Boteler
Mary Field
R. Wells Gordon
Charles Francis

PENNY SERENADE

(Released: April 24, 1941)

Director: George Stevens
Assistant Director:
  Gene Anderson
Producer: George Stevens
Associate Producer:
  Fred Guiol
Editor: Otto Meyer
Story: Martha Cheavens
Screen Play: Morrie Ryskind
Music: W. Franke Harling
Art Director: Lionel Banks

Music Director:
  M. W. Stoloff
Director of Photography:
  Joseph Walker, A.S.C.

Cast:
Irene Dunne
Cary Grant
Beulah Bondi
Edgar Buchanan
Ann Doren
Eva Lee Kuney
Leonard Willey
Wallis Clark
Walter Sederling
Baby Biffle

COMMANDOS STRIKE AT DAWN

(Released: December 27, 1942)

Director: John Farrow
Producer: Lester Cowan
Editor: Ann Bauchens
Story: C. S. Forester
Screen Play: Irwin Shaw
Music: Louis Gruenberg
Art Director: Edward Jewell
Music Director: M. W. Stoloff
Director of Photography:
    William C. Meldor, A.S.C.
Sound Recording: John Goodrich

Footage: 6581 ft.

Cast:
Paul Muni
Anna Lee
Lillian Gish
Sir Cedric Hardwicke
Ray Collins
Robert Coot
Rosemary DeCamp
Alexander Knox
Elisabeth Fraser
Richard Derr

Erville Alderson
Barbara Everest
Rod Cameron
Louis Jean Heydt
George Macready
Arthur Margetson

THE HEAT'S ON

(Released: October 29, 1943)

Director: Gregory Ratoff
Assistant Director:
    Robert Saunders
Editor: Otto Meyer
Dialogue Director:
    Serge Bertensson
Music: John Leipold
Art Director: Lionel Banks
Associate: Walter Holscher
Music Director: Yasha Bunschuk
Set Decorations: Joseph Kich
Costumes: Walter Plunkett
Director of Photography:
    Franz F. Planer, A.S.C.

Music Recording:
    Phillip Faulkner
Sound Recording:
    Lodge Cunningham

Footage: 6581 ft.

Cast:
Mae West
Victor Moore
William Gaxton
Lester Allen
Allen Dinehart
Mary Roche
Lloyd Bridges
Almira Sessions
Sam Asch
David Lichine
Leonard Sues

ONCE UPON A TIME

(Released: March, 1944)

Director: Alexander Hall
Assistant Director: William Mull
Producer: Louis F. Edelman
Editor: Gene Havlick
Story:
    Norman Corwin
    Lucille Fletcher Hermann
Screen Play:
    Lewis Meltzer
    Oscar Saul
Music: Frederick Hollander

Art Director:
    Lionel Banks
    Edward Jewell
Music Director:
    M. W. Stoloff
Set Decorations:
    Robert Priestley
Director of Photography:
    Franz F. Planer, A.S.C.

Cast:
Cary Grant
Janet Blair
James Gleason
Ted Donaldson
William Demarest

COUNTER-ATTACK

(Released: April, 1945)

Director: Zoltan Korda
Assistant Director:
Earl Bellamy
Editors:
Charles Nelson
Al Clark
Based on the Play by:
Illya Vershinin
Mikhail Buderman
Adaptation:
Janet and Philip Stevenson
Screen Play:
John Howard Lawson
Musical Score: Louise Gruenberg
Art Directors:
Stephen Goosso1
Edward Jewell

Set Direction:
Robert Priestly
Special Effects:
Lawrence W. Butler
Director of Photography:
James Wong Howe,
A.S.C.
Special Effects
Photography: Ray Cory

Footage: 8253 ft.

Cast:
Paul Muni
Marguerite Chapman
Harro Meller
Roman Bohmen
George Macready
Eric Rolf
Ludwig Donath
Rudolph Anders
Philip Van Zandt
Frederick Giermann
Paul Ander
Ivan Triesault

KISS AND TELL

(Released: July 12, 1945)

Director: Richard Wallace
Assistant Director:
Earl Bellamy
Producer: Sol C. Siegal
Assistant Producer: William Mull
Editor: Charles Nelson
Play and Screen Play:
F. Hugh Herbert
Music: Werner R. Heymann
Art Directors:
Stephen Goosson
Van Nest Polglase
Music Director: M. W. Stoloff
Set Decorations: Joseph Kish
Gowns: Jean Louis
Director of Photography:
Charles Lawton, Jr., A.S.C.

Sound Recording:
Jack Goodrich

Footage: 8267 ft.

Cast:
Shirley Temple (by
arrangement with
David O. Selznick)
Jerome Courtland
Walter Abel
Katherine Alexander
Robert Benchley
Porter Hall
Virginia Welles
Tom Tully
Darryl Hickman
Mary Philips
Scott McKay
Scott Elliott
Kathryn Card
Edna Holland

DEAD RECKONING

(Released: December, 1946)

Director: John Cromwell
Assistant Director:
Seymour Friedman
Producer: Sidney Biddel
Editor: Gene Havlick

Music Director:
M. W. Stoloff
Set Decorations:
Louis Diage
Gowns: Jean Louis

Cast:
Humphrey Bogart
Lizabeth Scott
Morris Carnovsky
Charles Cane

Story:
  Gerald Adams
  Sidney Bidwell
Adaptation: Allen Rivkin
Screen Play:
  Oliver H. P. Garrett
  Steve Fisher
Music: Marlin Skiles
Song: "Either It's Love or It Isn't," by:
  Allan Roberts
  Doris Fisher
Art Directors:
  Stephen Goosson
  Rudolph Sternad

Make-up: Clay Campbell
Hairstyles: Helen Hunt
Director of Photography:
  Leo Tover, A.S.C.
Sound Recording:
  Jack Goodrich

William Prince
Marvin Miller
Wallace Ford
James Bell
George Chandler

KNOCK ON ANY DOOR

(Released: January, 1949)

Director: Nicholas Ray
Assistant Director:
  Arthur S. Black
Editor: Viola Lawrence
From the Novel by:
  Willard Motley
Screen Play by:
  Daniel Taradash
  John Monks, Jr.
Art Director: Robert Peterson
Set Decorations:
  William Kiernan

Gowns: Jean Louis
Director of Photography:
  Burnett Guffey, A.S.C.

Cast:
Humphrey Bogart
George Macready
Allen Roberts
Susan Perry
Mickey Knox
Barry Kelley
John Derek
Cara Williams
Jimmy Conlin
Sumner Williams
Sid Melton

TOKYO JOE

(Released: July, 1949)

Director: Stuart Heisler
Assistant Director:
  Wilbur McGaugh
Producer: Robert Lord
Associate Producer:
  Henry S. Kesler
Editor: Viola Lawrence
From a Story by: Steve Fisher
Adaptation: Walter Doniger
Screen Play:
  Cyril Hume
  Bertram Millhauser
Music: George Antheil
Art Director: Robert Peterson
Music Director: M. W. Stoloff
Set Decorations: James Crowe

Dialogue Director:
  Jason Lindsey
Gowns: Jean Louis
Make-up: Clay Campbell
Hairstyles: Helen Hunt
Director of Photography:
  Charles Lawton, Jr.,
  A.S.C.
Sound Engineer:
  Russell Malmgren

Footage: 8124 ft.

Cast:
Humphrey Bogart
Alexander Knox
Florence Marly
Sessue Hayakawa
Jerome Courtland
Gordon Jones
Teru Shimada
Hideo Mori
Charles Meredith
Thys Williams
Lora Lee Michel

IN A LONELY PLACE

(Released: March, 1950)

Director: Nicholas Ray
Assistant Director:
  Earl Bellamy
Producer: Robert Lord
Associate Producer:
  Henry S. Kesler
Editor: Viola Lawrence
From a Story by:
  Dorothy B. Hughes
Adaptation: Edmund H. North
Screen Play: Andrew Slot
Music: George Antheil
Art Director: Robert Peterson
Music Director: M. W. Stoloff
Set Decorations:
  William Kiernan
Gowns: Jean Louis
Make-up: Clay Campbell
Hairstyles: Helen Hunt

Director of Photography:
  Burnett Guffey,
  A.S.C.
Technical Adviser:
  Rodney Amateau
Sound Engineer:
  Howard Fogetti

Cast:
Humphrey Bogart
Gloria Grahame
Frank Lovejoy
Carl Brenton Reid
Art Smith
Jeff Donnell
Martha Stewart
Robert Warwick
Morris Ankrum
William Ching
Steven Geray
Hadda Brooks
Alice Talton
Jack Reynolds
Ruth Warren
Ruth Gillette
Guy Beach
Lewis Howard

DEATH OF A SALESMAN

(Released: December, 1951)

Director: Laslo Benedek
Assistant Director:
  Frederick Briskin
Producer: Stanley Kramer
Associate Producer:
  George Glass
Editor: William Lyon
Editorial Supervision:
  Harry Gerstad
Based on the Play by:
  Arthur Miller
Screen Play: Stanley Roberts
Music: Alex North
Art Director: Cary Odell
Music Director: M. W. Stoloff
Set Decorations: William Kiernan

Production Design:
  Rudolph Sternadt
Make-up: Clay Campbell
Hairstyles: Helen Hunt
Production Manager:
  Clem Beauchamp
Director of Photography:
  Frank Planer, A.S.C.
Sound Engineer:
  George Cooper

Cast:
Fredric March
Mildred Dunnock
Kevin McCarthy
Cameron Mitchell
Howard Smith
Don Keefer
Jesse White
Claire Carleton
David Alpert

SIROCCO

(Released: March, 1952)

Director: Curtis Bernhardt
Assistant Director:
  Earl Bellamy
Producer: Robert Lord
Associate Producer:
  Henry S. Kesler

Set Decorations:
  Robert Priestley
Make-up: Clay Campbell
Hairstyles: Helen Hunt
Director of Photography:
  Burnett Guffey, A.S.C.

Cast:
Humphrey Bogart
Martha Toren
Lee J. Cobb
Everett Sloan
Gerald Mohr

Editor: Viola Lawrence
Based on the Novel, *Coup de Grace,* **by:** Joseph Kessel
Screen Play:
 A. I. Bezzerides
 Hans Jacoby
Music: George Autheil
Art Director: Robert Peterson
Music Director: M. W. Stoloff

Sound Engineer:
 Lodge Cunningham

Zero Mostel
Nick Dennis
Onslow Stevens
Ludwig Donath
David Bond

THE CAINE MUTINY

(Released: February 5, 1954)

Director: Edward Dmytryk
Assistant Director:
 Carter DeHaven, Jr.
Producer: Stanley Kramer
Editors:
 William Lyon
 Henry Batista
Based on the Novel by:
 Herman Wouk
Screen Play: Stanley Roberts
Additional Dialogue:
 Michael Blankfort
Music: Max Steiner
Art Director: Cary Odell
Set Decorations: Frank Tuttle
Production Design:
 Rudolph Sternad
Special Effects:
 Lawrence W. Butler

Gowns: Jean Louis
Make-up: Clay Campbell
Hairstyles: Helen Hunt
Director of Photography:
 Frank Planer, A.S.C.
2nd Unit Photography:
 Ray Cory, A.S.C.
Technical Adviser:
 Comdr. James C.
 Shaw, U.S.N.
Color Consultant:
 Francis Cugat
Sound Engineer:
 Lambert Day

Cast:
Humphrey Bogart
Jose Ferrer
Van Johnson
Fred MacMurray
Robert Francis
May Wynn
Tom Tully
E. G. Marshall
Lee Marvin
Warner Anderson
Claude Akins
Katharine Warren
Jerry Paris
Steve Brodie

THE MAN FROM LARAMIE

(Released: March, 1955)

Director: Anthony Mann
Assistant Director:
 William Holland
Producer: William Goetz
Editor: William Lyon
Based on the Story by:
 Thomas T. Flynn
Screen Play:
 Philip Yordan
 Frank Burt
Music: George Duning
Orchestrations: Arthur Morton
**Song, "The Man from
 Laramie," by:** Lester Lee
 Ned Washington

Art Director: Cary Odell
Music Director:
 M. W. Stoloff
Set Decorations:
 James Crowe
Make-up: Clay Campbell
Hairstyles: Helen Hunt
Director of Photography:
 Charles Lang, A.S.C.
Color Consultant:
 Henri Jaffa
Recording Supervisor:
 John Livadary
Sound: George Cooper

Cast:
James Stewart
Arthur Kennedy
Donald Crisp
Cathy O'Donnell
Alex Nicol
Aline MacMahon

364

THE HARDER THEY FALL

(Released: February 1956)

Director: Mark Robson
Producer: Philip Yordan
Based on the Novel by:
Budd Schulberg
Screen Play: Philip Yordan
Editor: Jerome Thomas
Art Editor: William Flannery

Set Decorations:
William Kiernan
Alfred Spencer
Director of Photography:
Burnett Guffey, A.S.C.

Cast:
Humphrey Bogart
Rod Steiger
Jan Sterling
Mike Lane
Max Baer
Jersey Joe Walcott

STORM CENTER

(Released: May, 1956)

Director: Daniel Taradash
Assistant Director:
Carter DeHaven, Jr.
Producer: Julian Blaustein
Editor: William A. Lyon
Story and Screen Play:
Daniel Taradash
Wlick Moll
Music: George Duning
Orchestrations: Arthur Morton

Art Director:
Cary Odell
Set Decorations:
Frank Tuttle
Make-up: Clay Campbell
Hairstyles: Helen Hunt
Director of Photography:
Burnett Guffey, A.S.C.

Cast:
Bette Davis
Brian Keith
Paul Kelly
Joe Mantell
Kevin Coughlin

THE GODDESS

(Released: June, 1958)

Director: John Cromwell
Assistant Director:
Charles H. Maguire
Producer: Milton Perlman
Editor: Carl Lerner
Special Supervision:
George Justin
Story and Screen Play:
Paddy Chayevsky
Music: Virgil Thompson
Art Director: Edward Haworth
Set Decorations:
Richard Meyerhoff
Tom Oliphant

Costumes:
Frank L. Thompson
Make-up: Robert Jiras
Hairstyles:
Willis Hanschett
Director of Photography:
Arthur J. Ornitz
Cameramen:
Dick Vorisek
Saul Midwall
Sound:
Ernest Zatorsky

Cast:
Kim Stanley
Lloyd Bridges
Steve Hill
Betty Lou Holland
Burt Brinkerhoff
Gerald Hiken
Joan Copeland
Bert Freed
Joyce Van Patten
Patty Duke

THE LAST HURRAH

(Released: October, 1958)

Director: John Ford
Assistant Directors:
Wingate Smith
Sam Nelson
Producer: John Ford
Editor: Jack Murray

Hairstyles: Helen Hunt
Director of Photography:
Charles Lawton, Jr.,
A.S.C.
Recording Supervisor:
John Livadary

Cast:
Spencer Tracy
Jeffrey Hunter
Dianne Foster
Pat O'Brien
Basil Rathbone

Based on the Novel by:
Edwin O'Connor
Screen Play: Frank Nugent
Art Director: Robert Peterson
Set Decorations: William Kiernan

Sound: Harry Mills

Donald Crisp
James Gleason

ANATOMY OF A MURDER

(Released: June, 1959)

Director: Otto Preminger
Assistant Director: David Silver
Producer: Otto Preminger
Assistant Producer: Max Slater
Editor: Louis R. Loeffler
Based on the Novel by:
Robert Traver
Screen Play: Wendell Mayes
Music: Duke Ellington
Music Editor: Richard Carruth
Set Decorations: Howard Bristol
Production Design: Boris Leven
Costume Coordinator:
Hope Bryce
Wardrobe:
Michael Harte
Van Lee Giokaris
Make-up:
Del Armstrong
Harry Ray

Hairstyles: Myrl Staltz
Script Supervisor:
Kathleen Fagan
Production Manager:
Henry Weinberger
Title Design: Saul Bass
Director of Photography:
Sam Leavitt, A.S.C.
Cameraman:
Irving Rosenberg
Lighting Technician:
James Almond
Sound: Jack Solomon

Cast:
James Stewart
Lee Remick
Ben Gazzara
Arthur O'Connell
Eve Arden
Kathryn Grant
George C. Scott
Orson Bean
Murray Hamilton

SUDDENLY, LAST SUMMER

(Released: 1959)

Producer: Sam Spiegel
Director: Joseph L. Mankiewicz
Screen Play: Gore Vidal and
Tennessee Williams
Based on the One-Act Play by:
Tennessee Williams
Photography: Jack Hildyard
Music Composed by:
Buxton Orr
Malcolm Arnold
Conducted by: Buxton Orr
Production Designed by:
Oliver Messel
Art Direction:
William Kellner

Set Decorations:
Scot Slimon
Production Supervisor:
Bill Kirby
Editors:
William W. Hornbeck
Thomas G. Stanford
Sound:
Peter Thornton
A. G. Ambler
John Cox

Cast:
Elizabeth Taylor
Katharine Hepburn
Montgomery Clift
Albert Dekker
Mercedes McCambridge
Gary Raymond
Mavis Villiers
Patricia Marmont
Joan Young
Maria Britneva
Sheila Robbins
David Cameron

366

THE LAST ANGRY MAN

(Released: August, 1959)

Director: Daniel Mann
Assistant Director:
Irving Moore
Producer: Fred Kohlmar
Editor: Charles Nelson
Based on the Novel by:
Gerald Green
Adaptation: Richard Murphy
Screen Play: Gerald Green
Music: George Duning
Orchestration: Arthur Morton
Art Director: Carl Anderson
Set Decorations: William Kiernan
Music Director: M. W. Stoloff

Gowns: Jean Louis
Make-up:
Clay Campbell, S.M.A.
Hairstyles: Helen Hunt
Director of Photography:
James Wong Howe,
A.S.C.
Recording Supervisor:
John Livadary
Sound: Harry Mills

Cast:
Paul Muni
David Wayne
Betsy Palmer
Luther Adler
Claudia McNeil
Joby Baker
Joanna Moore
Nancy R. Pollock
Billy Dee Williams
Robert F. Simon
Dan Tobin

A RAISIN IN THE SUN

(Released: February, 1961)

Director: Daniel Petrie
Assistant Director:
Sam Nelson
Producers:
David Susskind
Philip Rose
Editors:
William A. Lyon, A.C.E.
Paul Weatherwax, A.C.E.
Based on the Play by:
Lorraine Hansberry
Screen Play:
Lorraine Hansberry
Music: Laurence Rosenthal
Orchestrations: Arthur Norton

Art Director:
Carl Anderson
Set Decorations:
Louis Diage
Make-up: Ben Lane
Hairstyles: Helen Hunt
Director of Photography:
Charles Lawton, Jr.,
A.S.C.
Sound Supervision:
Charles J. Rice
Sound: George Cooper

Cast:
Sidney Poitier
Claudia McNeil
Ruby Dee
Diana Sands
Ivan Dixon
John Fielder
Louis Gossett
Stephen Perry
Joel Fluellen
Louis Terkel
Roy Glenn

THE GUNS OF NAVARONE

(Released: July, 1961)

Director: J. Lee Thompson
Assistant Director: Peter Yates
Producer: Carl Foreman
Associate Producers:
Cecil F. Ford
Leon Becker
Editor: Alan Osbiston
1st Assistant Editor:
Joan Morduch
Associate Editors:
John Victor Smith

Make-up: George Frost
Wally Schneiderman
Maps: Halas & Batchelor
Director of Photography:
Oswald Morris, B.S.C.
Additional Photography:
John Wilcox, B.S.C.
Cameraman: Denys Coop
Sound Recording:
John Cox
George Stephenson

Cast:
Gregory Peck
David Niven
Anthony Quinn
Stanley Baker
Anthony Quayle
James Darren
Irene Papas
Gia Scala
James Robertson
Justice

Raymond Poulton
O. Hafenrichter
Screen Play: Carl Foreman
Continuity: Pamela Davies
Music: Dimitri Tiomkin
Lyrics:
Paul Francis Webster
Alfred Perry
　Sung by: Elga Anderson
Production Designer:
Geoffrey Drake
Special Effects:
Bill Harrington
Wally Veevers
Production Manager:
　Harold Buck
Production Secretary:
Golda Offenheim
Wardrobe: Monty Berman
Wardrobe Design: Olga Lehman

Sound Editor:
Chris Greenham
Technical Advisors:
Lt. General Fritz
Bayerlein
Brig. General
D. S. T. Turnbull
Lt. Col. P. F.
Kertemilidis
Lt. Col. P. J. Hands
Comdr. John Theologitis
Major N. Lazaridis
Major W. D. Mangham

Richard Harris
Bryan Forbes
Allan Cuthbertson
Michael Trubshawe
Percy Herbert
George Mikell
Walter Gotell
Tutte Lemkow
Albert Lieven
Norman Wooland
Cleo Scouloudi
Nicholas
　Papakonstantinov
Christopher Rhodes

THE DEVIL AT 4 O'CLOCK

(Released: August, 1961)

Director: Mervyn LeRoy
Assistant Directors:
Carter DeHaven, Jr.
Floyd Joyer
Producer: Fred Kohlmar
Editor: Charles Nelson
Production Assistant:
Milton Feldman
Based on the Novel by:
Max Catto
Screen Play: Liam O'Brien
Music: George Duning
Orchestration: Arthur Morton
Art Director: Jack Beckman
Set Decorations: Louis Diage

Make-up: Ben Lane
Director of Photography:
Joseph Dirce
Sound:
Joseph Westmoreland
Sound Supervisor:
Charles J. Rice

Cast:
Spencer Tracy
Frank Sinatra
Kevin Mathews
Jean Pierre Aumont
Gregoire Aslan
Barbara Luna
Cathy Lewis
Martin Brandt
Marcel Dalio
Ann Duggan
Bernie Hamilton
Lou Merrill
Tom Middleton
Louis Mercier
Michel Montau

ADVISE AND CONSENT

(Released: 1962)

Producer: Otto Preminger
Director: Otto Preminger
Screenplay: Wendell Mayes
Based on the Novel by: Allen Drury
Music: Jerry Fielding
Production Designer: Lyle Wheeler
Film Editor: Louis R. Loeffler

Stills:
Al St. Hilaire
Josh Weiner
Music Editor: Lee Osborne
Music Recording: Murray Spivack
Sound Effects Editor: Leon Birnbaum
Script Supervisor: Kathleen Fagan

Director of Photography:
Sam Leavitt, A.S.C.
Camera Operators:
Saul Midwall
Emil Oster, Jr.
Sound:
Harold Lewis
William Hamilton
Electrical Supervisor: James Almond
Construction Manager: Arnold Pine
Key Grip: Morris Rosen
Make-up:
Del Armstrong
Robert Jiras
Hairdressing: Myrl Stoltz
Wardrobe:
Joe King
Adele Parmenter
Property Master:
Meyer Gordon

Set Decorator: Eli Benneche
Costume Coordinator: Hope Bryce
Miss Tierney's Clothes Designed by:
Bill Blass
Assistant to the Producer: Max Slater
Production Manager: Jack McEdward
Unit Manager: Henry Weinberger
Production Assistant: David De Silva
Production Secretary:
Florence Nerlinger
Technical Advisor: Allen Drury
First Assistant Director:
L. V. McCardle, Jr.
Assistant Director: Don Kranze
Assistant Director: Larry Powell
Assistant Director: Charles Bohart
Lyrics for "The Song from Advise and Consent" by: Ned Washington
Filmed in: Panavision
Titles Designed by: Saul Bass

Cast:

Franchot Tone
Lew Ayres
Henry Fonda
Walter Pidgeon
Charles Laughton
Don Murray
Peter Lawford
Gene Tierney
Burgess Meredith
Eddie Hodges
Paul Ford
George Grizzard
Inga Swenson
Paul McGrath
Will Geer
Edward Andrews
Betty White
Malcolm Atterbury
J. Edward McKinley
William Quinn
Tiki Santos
Raoul De Leon
Tom Helmore

Hilary Eaves
Rene Paul
Michele Montau
Raj Mallick
Paul Stevens
Russ Brown
Janet Jane Carty
Chet Stratton
Larry Tucker
John Granger
Sid Gould
Bettie Johnson
Cay Forester
William H. Y. Knighton, Jr.
Hon. Henry Fountain
    Ashurst
Hon. Guy M. Gillette
Irv Kupcinet
Robert C. Wilson
Alan Emory
Jessie Stearns Buscher
Milton Berliner
Allen W. Cromley

Bruce Zortman
Wayne Tucker
Al McGranary
Joe Baird
Harry Denny
Leon Alton
George Denormand
Ed Haskett
Virgil Johannsen
Paul Power
Maxwell Reed
Mario Cimino
Edwin K. Baker
Clive L. Halliday
Roger Clark
Robert Malcolm
Dick Ryan
Gene Mathews
Leoda Richards
Bernard Sell
Brandon Beach
Hal Taggart

THE L-SHAPED ROOM

(Released: 1962)

Directed and Written by:
Bryan Forbes
Based on the Novel by:
Lynne Reid Banks

Cast:
Leslie Caron
Tom Bell
Brock Peters

Verity Emmett
Patricia Phoenix
Jennifer White

Photography: Douglas Slocombe
Jazz Sequences: John Barry
Conducted by: Muir Mathieson
Editor: Anthony Harvey

Cicely Courtneidge
Avis Bunnage
Emlyn Williams

Bernard Lee
Nanette Newman

REQUIEM FOR A HEAVYWEIGHT
(Released: 1962)

Director: Ralph Nelson
Screen Play by: Rod Serling, as adapted from his teleplay
Camera: Arthur J. Ornitz
Editor: Carl Lerner
Music: Laurence Rosenthal

Cast:
Anthony Quinn
Jackie Gleason
Mickey Rooney
Julie Harris
Stan Adams
Madame Spivy
Herbie Faye

Jack Dempsey
Cassius Clay
  (Mohammed Ali)
Steve Belloise
Lou Gilbert
Arthur Mercante

DR. STRANGELOVE: OR HOW I LEARNED TO STOP WORRYING AND LOVE THE BOMB
(Released: January, 1964)

Director: Stanley Kubrick
Assistant Director: Eric Rattray
Producer: Stanley Kubrick
Associate Producer:
  Victor Lyndon
Editor: Anthony Harvey
Assistant Editor: Ray Lovejoy
Based on the Novel, *Red Alert,*
  by: Peter George
Screen Play:
  Stanley Kubrick
  Terry Southern
  Peter George
Continuity: Pamela Carlton
Music: Laurie Johnson
Art Director: Peter Murton
Production Design: Ken Adams
Special Effects: Wally Veevers
Production Manager:
  Clifton Brandon
Traveling Matte: Vic Margutti
Assembly Editor: Geoffrey Fry
Make-up: Stewart Freeborn

Hairstyles:
  Barbara Ritchie
Wardrobe:
  Bridget Sellers
Director of Photography:
  Gilbert Taylor, B.S.C.
Cameraman:
  Melvin Pike
Camera Assistant:
  Bernard Ford
Dubbing Mixer:
  John Alfred
Aviation Advisor:
  Capt. John Crewdson
Sound Editor:
  Leslie Hodgson
Sound Supervisor:
  John Cox

Cast:
Peter Sellers
George C. Scott
Sterling Hayden
Keenan Wynn
Slim Pickens
Peter Bull
Tracy Reed
James Earl Jones
Jack Creley
Frank Berry
Robert O'Neil
Glen Beck
Roy Stephens
Shane Rimmer
Hal Galili
Paul Tamarin
Lawrence Herder
Gordon Tanner
Joan McCarthy

FAIL-SAFE
(Released: May, 1964)

Director: Sidney Lumet
Assistant Director:
  Harry Falk, Jr.
Producer: Max E. Youngstein

Cameraman:
  Al Taffett
Sound Editor:
  Jack Fitzstephens

Cast:
Henry Fonda
Dan O'Herlihy
Walter Matthau

Associate Producer:
Charles H. McGuire
Editor: Ralph Rosenblum
From the Novel by:
Eugene Burdick
Harvey Wheeler
Screen Play: Walter Bernstein
Continuity: Marguerite James
Art Director: Albert Brenner
Set Decorations: J. C. Delaney
Special and Animated Effects:
Storyboard, Inc.
Costumes: Anna Hill Johnstone
Make-up: Harry Buchman
Titles: F. Hillsberg, Inc.
Director of Photography:
Gerald Hirschfield, A.S.C.

Sound Mixer:
William Swift
Chief Electrician:
Howard Fortune

Frank Overton
Edward Binns
Fritz Weaver
Larry Hagman
William Hansen
Russell Hardie
Russell Collins
Sorrell Booke
Nancy Berg
John Connell
Frank Simpson
Hildy Parks
Janet Ward
Dom DeLouise
Dana Elcar
Stuart Germain
Louise Larabee
Frieda Altman

CAT BALLOU

(Released: February, 1965)

Producer: Harold Hecht
Associate Producer:
Mitch Lindemann
Director: Elliot Silverstein
Based on a Novel by:
Roy Chanslor
Screenplay by:
Walter Newman
Frank R. Pierson
Film Editor:
Charles Nelson, A.C.E.
Songs by:
Mack David
Jerry Livingston
Director of Photography:
Jack Marta
Art Director: Malcolm Brown
Choreographer: Miriam Nelson
2nd Unit Director: Yakima Canutt

Assistant Directors:
Lee Lukather
Ray Gosnell
Set Decorator:
Richard Mansfield
Sound Supervisor:
Charles J. Rice
Hair Styles by:
Virginia Jones, C.H.S.
Make-up Supervision:
Ben Lane, S.M.A.
**Miss Fonda's Gown
Designed by:**
Bill Thomas
Eastman Color by: Pathé

Cast:
Jane Fonda
Lee Marvin
Michael Callan
Dwayne Hickman
Nat King Cole
Stubby Kaye
Tom Nardini
John Marley
Reginald Denny
Jay C. Flippen
Arthur Honnicutt

BORN FREE

(Released: 1966)

Director: James Hill
Screen Play: Gerald L. C. Copley
Based on the books by:
Joy Adamson
Camera (Technicolor):
Kenneth Talbot
Editor: Don Deacon

Cast:
Virginia McKenna
Bill Travers
Geoffrey Keen
Peter Lukoye
Omar Chambati
Bill Godden

Bryan Epsom
Robert Cheetham
Robert Young
Geoffrey Best
Surya Patel

Music: John Barry
Song: John Barry, Don Black
Technical Advisor: George Adamson
Assistant Director:
William P. Carlidge

GEORGY GIRL

(Released: 1966)

Director: Silvio Arrizano
Screen Play: Margaret Forster
and Peter Nichols
Based on the Novel by:
Margaret Forster
Photography: Ken Higgins
**Music Composed and Conducted
by:** Alexander Faris
Title Song—Music by:
Tom Springfield
Sung by: The Seekers

Cast:
James Mason
Alan Bates
Lynn Redgrave
Charlotte Rampling
Bill Owen
Rachel Kempson

Denise Coffey
Dorothy Alison
Peggy Thorpe-Bates
Dandy Nichols
Terence Soall
Jolyan Booth

IN COLD BLOOD

(Released: 1967)

Director: Richard Brooks
Written by: Richard Brooks
Based on the book by:
Truman Capote
Photography: Conrad Hall
Music: Quincy Jones
Editor: Peter Zinner
Art Direction: Robert Boyle

Cast:
Robert Blake
Scott Wilson
John Forsythe
Paul Stewart
Gerald S. O'Loughlin
Jeff Corey
John Gallaudet
James Flavin

Charles McGraw
James Lantz
Will Geer
John McLiam
Ruth Storey
Brenda C. Currin
Paul Hough

TO SIR WITH LOVE

(Released: June, 1967)

Director: James Clavell
Assistant Director: Ted Sturgis
Producer: James Clavell
Executive Producer: John R. Sloan
Editor: Peter Thornton
From the Novel by:
E. R. Braithwaite
Screen Play: James Clavell
Continuity: Yvonne Richards
Music: Ron Grainer
Art Director: Tony Woollard
Music Director: Philip Martell
Set Decorations: Ian Whittaker
Production Manager: Basil Rayburn
Casting: Harvey Woods

Cast:
Sidney Poitier
Christian Roberts
Judy Geeson
Suzy Kendall
The "Mindbenders"
Barbara Pegg
Ann Bell
Faith Brook
Christopher Chittell
Geoffrey Bayldon
Patricia Routledge
Adrienne Posta
Edward Burnham
Rita Webb

Grahame Charles
Albert Lampert
Chitra Neogy
Elna Pearl
Stewart Bevan
Carla Challoner
Joseph Cuby
Lynn Sue Moon
Jane Peach
Gareth Robinson
Stephen Whittaker
Anthony Villaroel
Michael Des Barres
Margaret Heald

372

Montage: George White
Montage Stills:
 Laurie Ridley
 Dennis C. Stone
Wardrobe Supervisor:
 John Wilson Apperson
Make-up: Jill Carpenter
Hairstyles: Betty Glasow
Director of Photography:
 Paul Beeson, B.S.C.
Cameraman: Harry Gillam
Sound Recording:
 Bert Ross
 Ted Karnon
Sound Editor: Dino DiCampo

Fiona Duncan
Fred Griffiths
Mona Bruce
Marianne Stone
Dervis Ward
Peter Attard
Sally Cann

Ellison Kemp
Donita Shawe
Richard Willson
Sally Gosselin
Kevin Hubbard
Howard Knight
Roger Shepard

GUESS WHO'S COMING TO DINNER

(Released: December, 1968)

Director: Stanley Kramer
Assistant Director: Ray Gosnell
Producer: Stanley Kramer
Associate Producer:
 George Glass
Editor: Robert C. Jones
Screen Play: William Rose
Music: DeVol
Song, "Glory of Love," by:
 Billy Hill
  Sung by: Jacqueline Fontaine
Set Decorations: Frank Tuttle
Production Design:
 Robert Clatworthy
Production Supervisor:
 Ivan Volkman
Script Supervisor:
 Marshall Sclom
Special Effects: Gesa Gaspar
Wardrobe Supervisor: Jean Louis

Costumes: Joe King
Make-up:
 Ben Lane
 Joseph Di Bella
Hairstyles: Helen Hunt
Property Master:
 Clarence Peet
Director of Photography:
 Sam Leavitt, A.S.C.
Process Photography:
 Larry Butler
Cameraman:
 William Gossman
Chief Electrician:
 Les Everson
Sound:
 Charles J. Rice
 Robert Martin
Re-recording:
 Clem Portman

Cast:
Spencer Tracy
Sidney Poitier
Katharine Hepburn
Katharine Houghton
Cecil Kellaway
Beah Richards
Roy E. Glenn, Sr.
Isabell Sanford
Virginia Christine
Alexander Hay
Barbara Rudolph
D'Urville Martin
Tom Heaton
Grace Gaynor
Skip Martin
John Hudkins

BOB & CAROL & TED & ALICE

(Released: October, 1969)

Director: Paul Mazursky
Assistant Director: Anthony Ray
Producer: Larry Tucker
Executive Producer:
 M. J. Frankovich
Editor: Stuart H. Pappe
Screen Play:
 Paul Mazursky
 Larry Tucker

Cast:
Natalie Wood
Robert Culp
Elliott Gould
Dyan Cannon
Horst Ebersberg
Lee Bergere
Donald F. Muhich
Noble Lee

Alida Ihle
Constance Eagan
John Brent
Gary Goodrow
Carol O'Leary

Music: Quincy Jones
Art Director: Pato Guzman
Set Decorations: Frank Tuttle
Choreography: Miriam Nelson
Costumes: Moss Mabry
Make-up: Ben Lane
Hairstyles: Virginia Jones
Production Manager:
   William O'Sullivan
Property Master: Max Frankel
Director of Photography:
   Charles E. Lang, A.S.C.
Sound Supervisor: Charles J. Rice
Sound:
   Dean Thomas
   Arthur Piantadosi

Holderread, Jr.
K. T. Stevens
Celeste Yarnall
Lynn Bordon
Linda Burton
Greg Mullavey
Andre Phillippe
Diane Berghoff
John Halloran
Susan Merin
Jeffrey Walker
Vicki Thal
Joyce Easton
Howard Dayton

CACTUS FLOWER

(Released: December, 1969)

Director: Gene Saks
Assistant Director: Anthony Ray
Producer: M. J. Frankovitch
Editor: Maury Winetrobe
From the Play by: Abe Burrows
Based on a French Play by:
   Barillet and Grady
Screen Play: I. A. L. Diamond
Music: Quincy Jones
Set Decorations: Ed Boyle
Production Design:
   Robert Clatworthy
Choreography: Miriam Nelson
Costumes: Moss Mabry

Make-up:
   John O'Gorman
Men's Wardrobe:
   Guy Verhill
Production Manager:
   William O'Sullivan
Property Master:
   Max Frankel
Director of Photography:
   Charles E. Lang,
   A.S.C.
Sound:
   Whitey Ford
   Arthur Piantadosi

Cast:
Walter Matthau
Ingrid Bergman
Goldie Hawn
Jack Weston
Rick Lenz
Vito Scotti
Irene Hervey
Eve Bruce
Irwin Charone
Matthew Saks

THE OWL AND THE PUSSYCAT

(Released: November, 1970)

Director: Herbert Ross
Assistant Director:
   William C. Gerrity
Producer: Ray Stark
Editor: John F. Burnett
Supervising Editor:
   Margaret Booth
Based on the Play *The Owl and*
   the Pussycat **by:** Bill Manhoff
Screen Play: Buck Henry
Music: Richard Halligan
Lyrics: Blood, Sweat and Tears
Music Performed by:
   Blood, Sweat and Tears

Casting:
   Marion Dougherty
Costumes: Ann Roth
Wardrobe:
   Shirlee Strahm
   George Newman
Make-up: Joe Cranzano
Hairstyles:
   Robert Grimaldi
Title Design:
   Wayne Fitzgerald
Directors of Photography:
   Harry Stradling, A.S.C.
   Andrew Laszlo, A.S.C.

Cast:
Barbra Streisand
George Segal
Robert Klein
Allen Garfield
Roz Kelly
Jacques Sandulescu
Jack Manning
Grace Carney
Barbara Anson
Kim Chan
Stan Gottlieb
Joe Madden
Fay Sappington

Music Editor: William Saracino
Art Directors:
  Robert Wightman
  Philip Rosenberg
Production Design:
  John Robert Lloyd
Design Supervision: Ken Adam
Set Decorations: Leif Pedersen
Script Supervisor:
  Marguerite James
Production Manager:
  Robert Greenhut
Production Assistant: Leo Garen

Production Sound:
  Arthur Piantadosi
  Dennis Maitland
Gaffer: Richard Quinlan

Marilyn Briggs
Marshall Ward
Tom Atkins
Stan Bryant

THE LAST PICTURE SHOW

(Released: October, 1971)

Director: Peter Bogdanovich
Assistant Director:
  Robert Rubin
Assistant to the Director:
  Gary Chason
2nd Assistant Director:
  William Morrison
Producer: Stephen J. Friedman
Executive Producer:
  Bert Schneider
Associate Producer:
  Harold Schneider
Editor: Donn Cambern
Based on the Novel by:
  Larry McMurtry
Screen Play:
  Larry McMurtry
  Peter Bogdanovich
Art Director:
  Walter Scott Herndon
Production Design: Polly Platt
Design Assistant:
  Vincent Cresciman
Production Coordinator:
  Marilyn Lasalandra
Script Supervisor:
  Marshall Sculom
Casting: Ross Brown
Location Manager:
  Frank Marshall
Production Manager: Don Guest
Construction Supervisor:
  Ed Shanley
Construction Coordinator:
  Al Litteken

Boom Man: Dean Salmon
Painter: George Lillie
Production Secretary:
  Elly Mitchell
Production Assistant:
  Mae Woods
Director of Photography:
  Robert Surtees, A.S.C.
Cameraman:
  Terry Meade
Sound Effects:
  Edit-Rite, Inc.
Re-recording:
  Producers Sound
  Service, Inc.
Gaffer: Alan Goldenhar
Mixer: Tom Overton

Cast:
Timothy Bottoms
Jeff Bridges
Cybill Sheperd
Ben Johnson
Cloris Leachman
Ellen Burstyn
Eileen Brennan
Clu Gulager
Sam Bottoms
Randy Quaid
Bill Thurman
Barc Doyle
Gary Brockette
Helena Humann
Lloyd Catlett
Robert Glenn
John Hillerman
Janice O'Malley
Floyd Mahaney
Kimberly Hyde
Noble Willingham
Marjory Jay
Joye Hash
Pamela Keller
Gordon Hurst
Mike Hosford
Faye Jordon
Charlie Seybert
Grover Lewis
Rebecca Ulrick
Merrill Shepherd
Buddy Wood
Kenny Wood
Leon Brown

375

Wardrobe:
 Nancy McArdle
 Mickey Sherrard
Props:
 Walter Starkey
 Louis Donelan

Bobby McGriff
Jack Mueller
Robert Arnold
Frank Marshall
Otis Elmore
Charles Salmon
George Gaulden
Will Morris Hannis
The Leon Miller Band

BUCK AND THE PREACHER

(Released: April, 1972)

Director: Sidney Poitier
Assistant Director:
 Jesus Marin
 Sheldon Schrager
Producer: Joel Glickman
Associate Producer:
 Herb Wallerstein
Editor: Pembroke J. Herring
Story:
 Ernest Kinoy
 Drake Walker
Screen Play: Ernest Kinoy
Music: Benny Carter
Performed by: Sonny Terry
 and Brownie McGhee
Set Decorations:
 Ernest Carrasco
Production Design:
 Sydney Z. Litwack
2nd Unit Director:
 Chuck Haywood
Costumes: Guy Verhille
Wardrobe:
 Adolph Ramirez, Jr.
 Erman Sessions
Make-up: Rosa Guerrero
Hairstyles: Harold Melvin
Special Effects: Leon Ortega
Script Supervisor: Malcolm Atterbury, Jr.
Production Consultant:
 Alfonso Sanchez Tello
Casting: Billy Gordon
Dialogue: Alice Spivak
Props: Antonio Mata
Gaffer: Luis Garcia
Director of Photography:
 Alex Phillips, Jr.

Special Photography:
 Gilbert-Waugh
 Productions
Cameraman:
 Manuel Santaella
Sound Mixer:
 Tom Overton
Dubbing Mixer:
 Richard Portman
Sound Effects:
 Edit International, Ltd.

Cast:
Sidney Poitier
Harry Belafonte
Ruby Dee
Cameron Mitchell
Denny Miller
Nita Talbot
John Kelly
Tony Brubaker
Bobby Johnson
James McEachin
Clarence Muse
Lynn Hamilton
Doug Johnson
Errol John
Ken Menard
Pamela Jones
Drake Walker
Dennis Hines
Fred Waugh
Bill Shannon
Phil Adams
Walter Scott
John Howard
Shirleena Manchur
La Markova
Hannelore Richter
Valerie Heckman
Stephanie Lower
Enrique Lucero
Julie Robinson
Jose Carlo Ruis
Jerry Gatlin
Ivan Scott
Bill Cook
John Kennedy

THE WAY WE WERE

(Released: October, 1973)

Director: Sydney Pollack
Assistant Director:
Howard Koch, Jr.
2nd Assistant Director:
Jerry Zeismer
Producer: Ray Stark
Associate Producer:
Richard Roth
Editor: Margaret Booth
Based on the Novel by:
Arthur Laurents
Screen Play: Arthur Laurents
Music: Marvin Hamlisch
Song: "The Way We Were,"
Marvin Hamlisch
Lyrics: Marilyn and
Alan Bergman
Set Decorations:
William Kiernan
Production Design:
Stephen Grimes
Costumes:
Dorothy Jenkins
Moss Mabry
Make-up:
Donald Cash, Jr.
Gary Liddiard
Hairstyles: Kaye Pownall
Script Supervisor: Betty Crosby

Production Manager:
Russ Saunders
Props: Richard M. Rubin
Titles: Phill Norman
Director of Photography:
Harry Stradling, Jr.,
A.S.C.
Sound: Jack Solomon
Sound Effects:
Kay Rose
Re-recording:
Richard Portman

Cast:
Barbra Streisand
Robert Redford
Bradford Dillman
Lois Chiles
Patrick O'Neal
Viveca Lindfors
Allyn Ann McLerie
Murray Hamilton
Herb Edelman
Diana Ewing
Sally Kirkland
Marcia Mae Jones
Don Keefer
George Ganes
Eric Boles
Barbara Peterson
Roy Jenson
Brendan Kelly
James Woods
Connie Forslund
Robert Gerringer
Susie Blakely
Ed Power
Suzanne Zenor
Dan Seymour

THE LAST DETAIL

(Released: 1973)

Producer: Gerald Ayres
Director: Hal Ashby
Screenplay by: Robert Towne
Based on the Novel by:
Darryl Ponicsan
Director of Photography:
Michael Chapman
Film Editor:
Robert C. Jones
Sound: Tom Overton
Re-Recording:
Richard Portman
Sound Effects Editing:
Edit-International, Ltd.
Assistant Film Editor:
Robert Barrere

Production Designer:
Michael Haller
Unit Production Manager:
Marvin Miller
Dan McCauley
Assistant Director:
Wes McAfee
Second Assistant Directors:
Gordon Robinson
Al Hopkins
Production Secretaries:
Sheila Woodland
Velda Reimer

Cast:
Jack Nicholson
Otis Young
Randy Quaid
Clifton James
Carol Kane
Michael Moriarty
Luana Anders
Kathleen Miller
Nancy Allen
Gerry Salsberg
Don McGovern
Pat Hamilton
Michael Chapman
Jim Henshaw

Music Editor: George Brand
Music: Johnny Mandel
Associate Producer:
  Charles Mulvehill
Assistant to the Producer:
  Nicholas Kudla II
Casting by: Lynn Stalmaster
Make-up: Maureen Sweeney
Costumes: Ted Parvin
Properties: Sid Greenwood
Scenic: George Dunkel
Script Supervisor: Bob Forrest

Appendix A

Columbia Pictures Feature Films From 1922

The *New York Herald-Tribune,* in its obituary of Harry Cohn, quoted him thus: "We believe here . . . that writers are more important than either stars or director, because the story is the foundation of the film. A weak story with the greatest cast ever assembled cannot produce a great picture."

The following list of all Columbia feature films gives the year of release of each title and the names of the men and women responsible for the stories—the writers.* In those cases where the screen play is based on another source, both the screen writer and the original writer are named.

*Despite his oft mentioned respect for his writers, Cohn frequently placed severe restrictions on them. At a time when Sam Briskin was in charge of production and Bob Riskin was writing important screenplays, Cohn decreed that the writers couldn't use the company phones. This bit of verse made the studio rounds:

> "Oh Columbia, the gem of commotion
> Where writers may not use the phone,
> Where Riskin speaks only to Briskin
> And Briskin speaks only to Cohn!"

Probably not many of the writers heard it—they were usually off the lot, using pay phones.

TITLE	WRITER	YEAR OF RELEASE
Abandon Ship	Richard Sale	1957
Abdul the Damned	Robert Neumann, Ashley Dukes, Robert Burford, W. Chetham-Strode	1936
Above the Clouds	George B. Seitz, Albert DeMond	1933
Abused Confidence	Henry Decoin, Jean Beyer	1939
Acquitted	Mary Roberts Rinehart, Dorothy Howell	1929
Across the Badlands	Barry Shipman	1950
Across the Border	Owen Francis, Edgar Edwards	1922
Across the Sierras	Paul Franklin	1941
Adam Had Four Sons	Charles Bonner, William Hurlburt, Michael Blankfort	1941
Address Unknown	Kressman Taylor, Herbert Dalmas	1944
Adventure in Manhattan	May Edington, Sidney Buchman, Harry Sauber, Jack Kirkland	1936
Adventure in Sahara	Sam Fuller, Maxwell Shane	1938
Adventure in Washington	Jeanne Spencer, Albert Benham, Lewis R. Foster, Arthur Caesar	1941
Adventures in Silverado	Robert Louis Stevenson, Kenneth Gamet, Tom Kilpatrick, Jo Pagano	1948
Adventures of Martin Eden	Jack London, W. L. River	1942
Adventures of Rusty	Al Martin, Aubrey Wisberg	1945
Advise and Consent	Allen Drury, Wendell Mayes	1962
Affair in Trinidad	Oscar Saul, James Gunn	1952
Affairs of a Rogue, The	Norman Ginsbury, Nicholas Phipps, Reginald Long, Wilfred Pettit	1948
Affairs of Messalina, The	Carmine Gallone	1954
Africa Speaks	Walter Futter, Lowell Thomas	1930
After Business Hours	Douglas Z. Doty	1925
After Midnight with Boston	Jack Boyle, Aubrey Wisberg, Howard J. Green	1943
After the Dance	Harrison Jacobs, Harold Shumate, Bruce Manning	1935
After the Storm	Harold Shumate, Elmer Harris, Will Ritchie	1928
Against the Law	Harold Shumate	1934
Age of Consent	Norman Lindsay, Peter Yeldham	1969
Air Hawks	Griffin Jay, Grace Neville	1935
Air Hostess	Grace Perkins, Milton Raison, Keene Thompson	1933
Air Hostess	Louise Rousseau, Robert Libott, Frank Burt	1949
Al Jennings of Oklahoma	Al Jennings, Will Irwin, George Bricker	1950
Alias Boston Blackie	Jack Boyle, Paul Yawitz	1942
Alias Mr. Twilight	Arthur E. Orloff, Brenda Weisberg, Malcolm Stuart Boylan	1947
Alias the Lone Wolf	Louis Joseph Vance, Dorothy Howell, Edward H. Griffith	1927
Alibi for Murder	Theodore Tinsley, Tom Van Dycke	1936
All American Sweetheart	Robert E. Kent, Grace Neville, Fred Niblo, Michael L. Simmons	1937
All Ashore	Blake Edwards, Robert Wells, Richard Quine	1953
All the King's Men	Robert Penn Warren, Robert Rossen	1949
All the Young Men	Hall Bartlett	1960

TITLE	WRITER	YEAR OF RELEASE
Alvarez Kelly	Franklin Coen	1953
Amazing Mr. Williams, The	Sy Bartlett, Dwight Taylor, Richard Maibaum	1939
Ambush at Tomahawk Gap	David Lang	1953
Ambushers, The	Donald Hamilton, Herbert Baker	1968
American Madness	Robert Riskin	1932
Among the Missing	Florence Wagner, Fred Niblo Jr., Herbert Asbury	1934
Anatomy of a Murder	Robert Travers and Wendell Mayes	1959
And Baby Makes Three	Lou Breslow, Joseph Hoffman	1949
And So They Were Married	Sarah Addington, Doris Anderson, Joseph Anthony, A. Laurie Brazee	1936
And Suddenly It's Murder	Rodolfo Sonego, Giorgio Arlono, Stefano Strucchi, Luciano Vincenzoni	1964
Anderson Tapes, The	Lawrence Sanders, Frank R. Pierson	1971
Angels over Broadway	Ben Hecht	1940
Ann Carver's Profession	Robert Riskin	1933
Anna Lucasta	Phillip Yordan, Arthur Laurents	1949
Anzio	Wynford Vaughn-Thomas, Harry Craig, Frank De Felitta, Duilio Coletti, Giuseppe Mangione	1968
Apache	Ramon Romero, Harriet Hinsdale	1929
Apache Ambush	David Lang	1955
Apache Country	Norman S. Hall	1952
Apache Gold	Karl May, H. G. Petersson	1965
Apache Territory	Louis L'Amour, Charles R. Marion, Geo. W. George, Frank Moss	1958
Appointment in Berlin	B. P. Fineman, B. F. Manien, Horace McCoy, Michael Hogan	1943
Arizona	Augustus Thomas, Dorothy Howell, Robert Riskin	1931
Arizona	Clarence Budington Kelland, Claude Binyon	1941
Arizona Raiders	Frank Gruber, Richard Schayer, Alex Gottlieb, Mary and Willard Willingham	1965
Arkansas Swing, The	Barry Shipman	1948
Around the Corner	Jo Swerling	1930
Assignment K	Hartley Howard, Val Guest, Bill Strutton, Maurice Foster	1968
Assignment—Paris	Pauline Gallico, Paul Gallico, William Bowers, Walter Goetz, Jack Palmer White	1952
As the Devil Commands	Keene Thompson, Jo Swerling	1933
As the Sea Rages	Werner Helwig, Jeffrey Dell, Jo Eisinger	1960
Atlantic Adventure	Diana Bourbon, John T. Neville, Nat N. Dorfman	1935
Atlantic Convoy	Robert Lee Johnson	1942
Attorney for the Defense	J. K. McGuinness, Jo Swerling	1932
Autumn Leaves	Jack Jevne, Lewis Meltzer, Robert Blees	1956
Avenger, The	Jack Townley, George Morgan	1931
Avenging Waters	Nate Gatzert	1936
Awakening of Jim Burke	Michael Simmons	1935

TITLE	WRITER	YEAR OF RELEASE
Awful Truth, The	Arthur Richman, Vina Delmar	1937
Babette Goes to War	Raoul Levy, Gerard Oury, Jacques Emmanuel, Michel Audiard	1960
Babies for Sale	Robert Frayne Chapin, Robert D. Andrews	1940
Baby, the Rain Must Fall	Horton Foote	1965
Bachelor's Baby	Garrett Elsden Fort, Julien Sands	1927
Bachelor Girl	Jack Townley	1929
Backfire	Clet Coroner, Didier Goulard, Maurice Fabre, Jean Becker	1956
Bad for Each Other	Irving Wallace, Horace McCoy	1953
Bad Men of the Hills	Luci Ward	1942
Bait	Samuel W. Taylor, Hugo Haas	1954
Bambole	Rodolfo Sonega, Tullio Pinelli, Luigi Magni, Leo Benvenuti, Pierode Bernardi	1965
Bamboo Prison, The	Jack DeWitt, Edwin Blum	1955
Band of Outsiders	Dolores Hitchens, Jean Luc-Godard	1966
Bandit of Sherwood Forest, The	Paul A. Castleton, Wilfrid H. Pettit, Melvin Levy	1946
Bandit of Zhobe, The	Richard Maibaum, John Gilling	1959
Bandits of Eldorado	Barry Shipman	1949
Barabbas	Pär Lagerkvist, Christopher Fry	1962
Barbary Pirate	Robert Libott, Frank Burt	1949
Barbed Wire	Gerald Geraghty	1952
Barefoot Boy, The	David Kirland	1923
Barefoot Mailman, The	Theodore Pratt, James Gunn, Francis Swann	1951
Battle in Outer Space	Jotaro Okami, Shinichi Sekizawa	1960
Battle of Rogue River	Douglas Heyes, Manny Seff	1954
Battle of the Coral Sea	Stephen Kandel, Daniel Ullman	1959
Battle Stations	Ben Finney, Crane Wilbur	1956
Battling Fool, The	W. S. Van Dyke	1924
Beat the Devil	James Helvick, John Huston, Truman Capote	1964
Beautiful But Broke	Arthur Housman, Monte Brice, Manny Seff	1944
Beautiful Sinner	Wilfrid Lucas	1924
Beauty on Parade	Arthur E. Orloff, George Bricker	1950
Because They're Young	John Farris, James Gunn	1960
Bed and Board	Francois Truffaut, Claude de Givray, Bernard Revon	1971
Bedford Incident, The	Mark Rascovich	1965
Bedtime Story	Horace Jackson, Grant Garrett, Richard Flournoy	1941
Before I Hang	Karl Brown, Robert D. Andrews	1941
Before Midnight	Robert Quigley	1933
Before Winter Comes	Frederick L. Keefe, Andrew Sinclair	1969
Behind Closed Doors	Lilian Ducey, H. Milner Kitchen, Howard J. Green	1929
Behind Prison Gates	Leslie T. White, Arthur T. Horman	1939
Behind the Evidence	Harold Shumate	1935
Behind the Mask	Jo Swerling, Dorothy Howell	1932
Behold a Pale Horse	Emeric Pressburger, J. P. Miller	1964
Bell, Book and Candle	John Van Druten, Daniel Taradash	1958

TITLE	WRITER	YEAR OF RELEASE
Belle of Broadway	J. Grubb Alexander, Jean Peary	1926
Belle Sommers	Richard Alan Simmons	1961
Beloved Vagabond, The	W. J. Locke, Hugh Mills, Walter Creighton, Arthur Wimperis	1937
Below the Sea	Jo Swerling	1933
Berserk	Aben Kendal, Herman Cohen	1967
Best Man Wins, The	Ben G. Kohn, Bruce Manning, Ethel Hill	1935
Best Man Wins	Mark Twain, Edward Huebsch	1948
Best of Enemies, The	Luciano Vincenzoni, Jack Pulman	1962
Better Way, The	William Hamilton Osborne, Dorothy Howell	1926
Betty Co-ed	Arthur Dreifuss, George H. Plympton	1946
Between Midnight and Dawn	Gerald Drayson Adams, Leo Katcher, Eugene Ling	1950
Beware of Blondes	George Hull, Harvey Thew, Peter Milne	1928
Beware of Blondie	Chic Young, Jack Henley	1950
Beware Spooks	Richard F. Flournoy, Al Duffy, Brian Marlow	1939
Beyond Mombasa	James Eastwood, Richard English, Gene Levitt	1956
Beyond the Law	Harold Shumate	1934
Beyond the Purple Hills	Norman S. Hall	1950
Beyond the Sacramento	Luci Ward	1940
Big Boss, The	Howard J. Green	1941
Big Gundown, The	Sergio Donati, Sergio Sellima, Franco Solinas, Fernando Morand	1968
Big Gusher, The	Harold R. Greene, Daniel Ullman	1951
Big Heat, The	William P. McGivern, Sydney Boehm	1953
Big Mouth, The	Bill Richmond, Jerry Lewis	1967
Big Sombrero, The	Olive Cooper	1948
Big Timer, The	Robert Riskin, Dorothy Howell	1932
Birds Do It	Leonard Kaufman, Arnie Kogen, Art Arthur	1966
Birds Do It, Bees Do It	Nicholas Noxon	1975
Birds of Prey	George Bronson Howard, Dorothy Howell	1927
Bite the Bullet	Richard Brooks	1975
Bitter Tea of General Yen, The	Grace Zaring Stone, Edward E. Paramore	1933
Bitter Victory	Rene Hardy, Nicholas Ray, Gavin Lambert	1958
Black Arrow, The	Robert Louis Stevenson, Richard Schayer, David P. Sheppard, Thomas Seller	1948
Black Dakotas, The	Ray Buffum, DeVallon Scott	1954
Black Eagle, The Story of a Horse	O. Henry, Edward Heubsch, Hal Smith	1948
Black Gunn	Franklin Coen	1973
Black Knight, The	Alec Coppel, Dennis O'Keefe, Bryan Forbes	1954
Black Moon	Clements Ripley, Wells Root	1934
Black Parachute, The	Paul Gangelin, Clarence Upson Young	1944
Black Room	Arthur Strawn, Henry Myers	1935
Blackbird, The or *The Maltese Falcon Flies Again*	Dashiell Hammett, David Giles	1975

383

TITLE	WRITER	YEAR OF RELEASE
Blackjack Ketchum, Desperado	Louis L'Amour, Luci Ward, Jack Natteford	1956
Blackmailer, The	Lee Loeb, Harold Buchman, Joe Krumgold	1936
Blazing Across the Pecos	Norman S. Hall	1948
Blazing Six Shooters	Paul Franklin	1940
Blazing Sun	Jack Townley	1950
Blazing the Western Trail	J. Benton Cheney	1945
Blazing Trail, The	Barry Shipman	1949
Bless the Beasts & Children	Glendon Swarthout, Mac Benoff	1971
Blind Alley	James Warwick, Philip MacDonald, Michael Blankfort, Albert Duffy	1939
Blind Date	Vida Hurst, Ethel Hill	1934
Blind Spot	Barry Perowne, Martin Goldsmith	1947
Blond Captive	Lowell Thomas	1932
Blonde from Brooklyn	Erna Lazarus	1945
Blonde from Singapore, The	Houston Branch, George Bricker	1941
Blondie	Murat B. (Chic) Young, Richard Flournoy	1938
Blondie's Anniversary	Murat B. (Chic) Young, Jack Henley	1948
Blondie's Big Deal	Murat B. (Chic) Young, Lucile Watson Henley	1949
Blondie's Big Moment	Murat B. (Chic) Young, Connie Lee	1947
Blondie's Blessed Event	Murat B. (Chic) Young, Connie Lee Karen DeWolf, Richard Flournoy	1942
Blondie Brings Up Baby	Murat B. (Chic) Young, Karen DeWolf, Robert Chapin, Gladys Lehman, Richard Flournoy	1939
Blondie for Victory	Murat B. (Chic) Young, Fay Kanin, Karen DeWolf, Connie Lee	1942
Blondie Goes Latin	Murat B. (Chic) Young, Quinn Martin, Richard Flournoy, Karen DeWolf	1941
Blondie Goes to College	Murat B. (Chic) Young, Warren Wilson, Clyde Bruckman, Lou Breslow	1942
Blondie Has Servant Trouble	Murat B. (Chic) Young, Albert Duffy, Richard Flournoy	1940
Blondie's Hero	Murat B. (Chic) Young, Jack Henley	1949
Blondie Hits the Jackpot	Murat B.. (Chic) Young, Jack Henley	1949
Blondie in Society	Murat B. (Chic) Young, Eleanore Griffin, Karen DeWolf	1941
Blondie in the Dough	Murat B. (Chic) Young, Arthur Max, Jack Henley	1947
Blondie Knows Best	Murat B. (Chic) Young, Edward Bernds, Al Martin	1946
Blondie Meets the Boss	Murat B. (Chic) Young, Kay Van Riper, Richard Flournoy	1939
Blondie on a Budget	Murat B. (Chic) Young, Charles Molyneux Brown, Richard Flournoy	1940
Blondie Plays Cupid	Murat B. (Chic) Young, Richard Flournoy, Karen DeWolf	1940
Blondie Takes a Vacation	Murat B. (Chic) Young, Karen DeWolf, Robert Chapin, Richard Flournoy	1939
Blondie's Holiday	Murat B. (Chic) Young, Connie Lee	1947
Blondie's Lucky Day	Murat B. (Chic) Young, Connie Lee	1946

TITLE	WRITER	YEAR OF RELEASE
Blondie's Reward	Murat B. (Chic) Young, Edward Bernds	1948
Blondie's Secret	Murat B. (Chic) Young, Jack Henley	1948
Blood Ship, The	Norman Springer, Fred Myton	1927
Blue Canadian Rockies	Gerald Geraghty	1952
Bob & Carole & Ted & Alice	Paul Mazursky, Larry Tucker	1969
Bodyhold	George Bricker	1949
Bonanza Town	Barry Shipman, Bert Horswell	1951
Bonjour Tristesse	Francoise Sagan, Arthur Laurents	1958
Boogie Man Will Get You, The	Hal Fimberg, Robert B. Hunt, Edwin Blum, Paul Gangelin	1942
Boots Malone	Milton Holmes	1952
Border Law	Stuart Anthony	1931
Born Free	Joy Adamson, Gerald L. C. Copley	1966
Born Yesterday	Garson Kanin, Albert Mannheimer	1950
Boston Blackie and the Law	Jack Boyle, Harry J. Essex, Malcolm Stuart Boylan	1946
Boston Blackie Booked on Suspicion	Jack Boyle, Malcolm Stuart Boylan, Paul Yawitz	1945
Boston Blackie Goes Hollywood	Jack Boyle, Paul Yawitz	1942
Boston Blackie's Chinese Venture	Jack Boyle, Maurice Tombragel	1948
Boston Blackie's Rendezvous	Jack Boyle, Fred Schiller, Edward Dein	1945
Both Barrels Blazing	William Lively	1944
Boy from Stalingrad, The	Robert Arden, Robert Lee Johnson, Ferdinand Reyher	1943
Boys' School	Pierre Very, J. H. Blanchon	1939
Branded	Randall Faye	1931
Brave Bulls, The	Tom Lea, John Bright	1951
Brave Warrior	Robert E. Kent	1952
Brian's Song	William Blinn	1972
Bridge on the River Kwai, The	Pierre Boulle	1957
Brief Moment	S. N. Behrman, Brian Marlow, Edith Fitzgerald	1933
Brief Season	Renato Castellani, Adriano Baracco	1970
Brigand, The	George Bruce, Jesse Lasky, Jr.	1952
Brigand of Kandahar, The	John Gilling	1965
Bring Your Smile Along	Richard Quine, Blake Edwards	1955
Broadway Bill	Mark Hellinger, Robert Riskin	1934
Broadway Daddies	Victoria Moore, Anthony Coldeway	1928
Broadway Hoofer	Gladys Lehman	1930
Broadway Scandals	Howard Green, Gladys Lehman, Norman Houston	1929
Brother John	Ernest Kinoy	1971
Brotherhood of Satan, The	Sean McGregor, William Welch	1971
Brothers	Herbert Ashton, Jr., Dorothy Howell, John Thomas Neville, Charles R. Condon	1930
Brothers Rico, The	Georges Simenon, Lewis Meltzer, Ben Perry	1957
Buchanan Rides Alone	Jonas Ward, Charles Lang	1958
Buck and the Preacher	Ernest Kinoy, Drake Walker	1972
Buckaroo from Powder River	Norman S. Hall	1947
Bulldog Drummond at Bay	Herman Cyril McNeile (Sapper), Frank Gruber	1947
Bulldog Drummond Strikes Again	Herman Cyril McNeile (Sapper), Edna and Edward Anhalt, Lawrence Edmund Taylor	1947

Bullet is Waiting, A	Thames Williamson, Casey Robinson	1954
Bullets for Bandits	Robert Lee Johnson	1940
Bullets for Rustlers	John Rathmell	1940
Bunny Lake is Missing	Evelyn Piper, John and Penelope Mortimer	1965
Burglar, The	David Goodis	1957
Burglars, The	Henri Verneuil, Vahe Katcha	1972
Buster and Billie	Ron Turbeville	1974
Buttercup Chain, The	Janice Elliot, Peter Draper	1971
Butterflies Are Free	Leonard Gershe	1972
Bye Bye Birdie	Michael Stewart, Charles Strouse, Lee Adams, Irving Brecher	1963
By Whose Hand?	Marion Orth	1927
By Whose Hand?	Harry Adler, Isadore Bernstein, Stephen Roe	1932
Cactus Flower	Barillet and Gredy, Abe Burrows, I. A. L. Diamond	1969
Cadets on Parade	Frank Fenton, Martha Barnett, Howard J. Green	1942
Cafe Hostess	Tay Garnett, Tom Buckingham, Harold Shumate	1939
Caine Mutiny, The	Herman Wouk, Stanley Roberts, Michael Blankfort	1954
California Conquest	Robert E. Kent	1952
California Frontier	Monroe Shaff, Arthur Hoerl	1938
California Split	Joseph Walsh	1974
California Trail, The	Jack Natteford, Lambert Hillyer	1933
Call of the Rockies	J. Benton Cheney, Ed Earl Repp	1938
Call of the West	Florence Ryerson, Colin Clements	1930
Calling of Dan Matthews	Harold Bell Wright, Dan Jarrett, Don Swift, Karl Brown	1936
Calypso Heat Wave	Orville H. Hampton, David Chandler	1957
Camp on Blood Island, The	Jon Manchip White, Val Guest	1958
Canal Zone	Blaine Miller, Jean DuPont Miller, Robert Lee Johnson	1942
Cangaceiro	Lima Barreto	1954
Cannibal Attack	Carroll Young	1954
Captain Hates the Sea, The	Wallace Smith	1934
Captain Pirate	Rafael Sabatini, Robert Libott, Frank Burt, John Meredyth Lucas	1952
Captive Girl	Carroll Young	1950
Cardinal, The	Henry Morton Robinson, Robert Dozier	1963
Cargo to Capetown	Lionel Houser	1950
Carnet De Bal, Un	Julien Duvivier	1939
Carnival	Robert Riskin	1935
Carolina Blues	M. M Musselman, Kenneth Earl, Joseph Hoffman, Al Martin	1944
Carthage in Flames	Emilio Salgari, Carmine Gallone, Ennio de Concini, Duccio Tessari	1961
Case against Brooklyn, The	Ed Reid, Daniel B. Ullman, Raymond T. Marcus	1958
Case of the Missing Man, The	Lee Loeb, Harold Buchman	1935
Cash on Demand	Jacques Gillies, David T. Chantler, Lewis Greifer	1961

Title	Writer	Year of Release
Casino Royale	Ian Fleming, Wolf Mankowitz, John Law, Michael Sayers	1967
Castle Keep	William Eastlake, Daniel Taradash, David Rayfiel	1969
Cat Ballou	Roy Chanslor, Walter Newman, Frank R. Pierson	1965
Cattle Raiders	Folmer Blangsted, Joseph Poland, Ed Earl Repp	1938
Cattle Thief, The	J. A. Duffy, Nate Gatzert	1936
Cell 2455, Death Row	Caryl Chessman, Jack DeWitt	1955
Cha-Cha-Cha Boom!	James B. Gordon	1956
Chain Gang	Howard J. Green	1950
Chain of Circumstances	David Long	1951
Challenge of the Range	Ed Earl Repp	1948
Champagne for Breakfast	E. Morton Hough, George Waggner	1935
Chance of a Lifetime, The	Jack Boyle, Paul Yawitz	1943
Charge of the Lancers	Robert E. Kent	1953
Charley's Aunt	Brandon Thomas, F. McGrew Willis	1931
Chase, The	Horton Foote, Lillian Hellman	1966
Chicago Syndicate	William Sackheim, Joseph Hoffman	1955
Child of Manhattan	Preston Sturges, Gertrude Purcell	1933
China Corsair	Harold R. Greene	1951
China is Near	Marco Bellocchio, Elda Tattoli	1968
China Venture	Anson Bond, George Worthing Yates, Richard Collins	1953
Chinatown at Midnight	Robert Libott, Frank Burt	1949
Chloe in the Afternoon	Eric Rohmer	1972
Chosen Survivors	H. B. Cross, Joe Reb Moffley	1974
Cigarette Girl	Edward Huebsch, Henry K. Moritz	1947
Circus Queen Murder, The	Anthony Abbot (Fulton Oursler), Milton Raison, Lou Breslow	1933
Cisco Pike	Bill L. Norton	1972
City of Fear	Steven Ritch, Robert Dillon	1958
City Streets	I. Bernstein, Fred Niblo, Jr. Lou Breslow	1938
City Without Men	Budd Schulberg, Martin Berkeley, W. L. River, George Sklar, Donald Davis	1943
Claire's Knee	Eric Rohmer	1971
Close Call for Boston Blackie, A	Jack Boyle, Ben Markson, Malcolm Stuart Boylan	1946
Close Call for Ellery Queen, A	Ellery Queen (Frederic Dannay and Manfred B. Lee), Eric Taylor, Gertrude Purcell	1942
Clouded Yellow, The	Janet Green	1951
Clouds over Europe	Brock Williams, Jack Whittingham, Arthur Wimperis	1939
Clown, The	Dorothy Howell, Harry O. Hoyt	1927
Coast Guard	Albert Duffy, Richard Maibaum, Harry Segall	1939
Cockleshell Heroes	George Kent, Bryan Forbes, Richard Maibaum	1956
Cocktail Hour	James K. McGuinness, Richard Schayer, Gertrude Purcell	1933

387

Code of the Range	Peter B. Kyne, Ford Beebe	1936
Code 7 Victim 5!	Peter Welbeck, Peter Yeldham	1965
Collector, The	John Fowles, Stanley Mann, John Kohn	1965
College Coquette, The	Ralph Graves, Norman Houston	1929
College Hero, The	Henry R. Symonds, Dorothy Howell	1927
Colorado Trail, The	Charles Francis Royal	1938
Comanche Station	Burt Kennedy	1960
Combat Squad	Wyott Ordung	1953
Come Closer, Folks	Aben Kandel, Lee Loeb, Harold Buchman	1936
Comic, The	Carl Reiner, Aaron Ruben	1969
Commandos Strike at Dawn, The	C. S. Forester, Irwin Shaw	1943
Confessions of a Window Cleaner	Christopher Wood, Val Guest	1975
Confessions of Boston Blackie, The	Jack Boyle, Paul Yawitz, Jay Dratler	1941
Conquest of Cochise	DeVallon Scott, Arthur Lewis	1953
Convicted	Cornell Woolrich, Edgar Edwards	1938
Convicted	Martin Flavin, William Bowers, Fred Niblo, Jr. Seton I. Miller	1950
Convicted Woman	Martin Mooney, Alex Gottlieb, Joseph Carole	1940
Corky of Gasoline Alley	Frank O. King, Edward Bernds	1951
Cornered	William Colt MacDonald, Ruth Todd	1932
Coroner Creek	Luke Short (Frederick Dilley Glidden), Kenneth Gamet	1948
Corpse Came C. O. D., The	Jimmie Starr, George Bricker, Dwight Babcock	1947
Corruption	Donald and Derek Ford	1968
Counsel for Crime	Harold Shumate, Fred Niblo, Jr., Lee Loeb, Harold Buchman, Grace Neville	1937
Count Three and Pray	Herb Meadow	1955
Counter Attack	Janet and Philip Stevenson, Ilya Vershinin, Mikhail Ruderman, John Howard Lawson	1945
Counter-Espionage	Louis Joseph Vance, Aubrey Wisberg	1942
Counterfeit	William Rankin, Bruce Manning	1936
Counterfeit Lady	Harold Shumate, Tom Van Dycke	1936
Counterspy Meets Scotland Yard	Phillips H. Lord, Harold R. Greene	1950
Court Martial	Elmer Harris, Anthony Coldeway	1928
Cover Girl	Erwin Gelsey, Virginia Van Upp, Marion Parsonnet, Paul Gangelin	1944
Cow Town	Gerald Geraghty	1949
Cowboy	Frank Harris, Edmund H. North	1958
Cowboy and the Indians, The	Dwight Cummins, Dorothy Yost	1949
Cowboy Blues	J. Benton Cheney	1946
Cowboy Canteen	Paul Gangelin, Felix Adler	1943
Cowboy from Lonesome River	Luci Ward	1944
Cowboy in the Clouds	Elizabeth Beecher	1943
Cowboy Star	Frank Melford, Frances Guihan	1936
Craig's Wife	George Kelly, Mary McCall, Jr.	1936
Crash Landing	Fred Freiberger	1958
Crazy Joe	Nicholas Gage	1974
Creature with the Atom Brain	Curt Siodmak	1955
Creatures the World Forgot	Michael Carreras	1971
Creeping Flesh, The	Peter Spenceley, Jonathan Rumbold	1972

TITLE	WRITER	YEAR OF RELEASE
Crime and Punishment	Fyodor Dostoevsky, Constance Garnett, S. K. Lauren, Joseph Anthony	1935
Crime Doctor	Max Marcin, Graham Baker, Louis Lantz, Jerome Odlum	1943
Crime Doctor's Courage, The	Max Marcin, Eric Taylor	1945
Crime Doctor's Diary, The	Max Marcin, David Dressler, Edward Anhalt	1949
Crime Doctor's Gamble, The	Max Marcin, Raymond L. Schrock, Jerry Warner, Edward Bock	1947
Crime Doctor's Manhunt, The	Max Marcin, Eric Taylor, Leigh Brackett	1946
Crime Doctor's Strangest Case, The	Max Marcin, Eric Taylor	1943
Crime Doctor's Warning, The	Max Marcin, Eric Taylor	1945
Crime of Helen Stanley	Charles R. Condon, Harold Shumate	1934
Crime Takes a Holiday	Henry Altimus, Jefferson Parker, Charles Logue	1938
Criminal Cargo	Eric Taylor, Albert DeMond	1939
Criminal Code, The	Martin Flavin, Seton I. Miller, Fred Niblo, Jr.	1931
Criminal Lawyer	Harold R. Greene	1951
Criminals of the Air	Jack Cooper, Owen Francis	1937
Crimson Blade, The	John Gilling	1964
Crimson Kimono, The	Samuel Fuller	1959
Cripple Creek	Richard Schayer	1952
Cromwell	Ken Hughes	1970
Crooked Web, The	Lou Breslow	1955
Cruisin' Down the River	Blake Edwards, Richard Quine	1953
Cry for Happy	George Campbell, Irving Brecher	1961
Cry of the Werewolf	Griffin Jay, Charles O'Neal	1944
Curse of the Demon	Montague R. James, Charles Bennett, Hal E. Chester	1957
Curse of the Mummy's Tomb, The	Henry Younger	1964
Customs Agent	Hal Smith, Russell S. Hughes, Malcolm Stuart Boylan	1950
Cyclone Fury	Barry Shipman, Ed Earl Repp	1951
Cyclone Prairie Rangers	Elizabeth Beecher	1943
Damn the Defiant!	Frank Tilsley, Nigel Kneale, Edmund H. North	1961
Dancing in Manhattan	Erna Lazarus	1944
Dandy in Aspic, A	Derek Marlowe	1968
Danger Signal, The	Douglas Z. Doty	1925
Dangerous Adventure, A	Owen Francis, John Rathmell	1937
Dangerous Affair, A	Howard J. Green	1931
Dangerous Blondes	Kelly Roos, Richard Flournoy, Jack Henley	1943
Dangerous Business	Harry Essex, Hal Smith	1946
Dangerous Crossroads	Charles Condon, Horace McCoy	1933
Dangerous Intrigue	Harold Shumate, Grace Neville	1936
Dangerous Paradise	(Unknown)	1925
Daring Danger	William Colt MacDonald, Michael Trevelyan	1932
Daring Young Man, The	Karen DeWolf, Connie Lee	1942

TITLE	WRITER	YEAR OF RELEASE
Dark Past, The	James Warwick, Malvin Wald, Oscar Saul, Philip MacDonald, Michael Blankfort, Albert Duffy	1949
David Harding, Counterspy	Phillips H. Lord, Clint Johnston, Tom Reed	1950
Dawn Trail, The	Forrest Sheldon, John Thomas Neville	1930
Day in the Death of Joe Egg, A	Peter Nichols	1972
Dead Heat on a Merry-Go-Round	Bernard Girard	1966
Dead or Alive	Albert Band, Ugo Liberatore, Louis Garfinkle	1968
Dead Reckoning	Gerald Adams, Sidney Biddell, Oliver H. P. Garrett, Steve Fisher, Allen Rivkin	1947
Deadline, The	Lambert Hillyer	1931
Deadly Affair, The	John LeCarre, Paul Dehn	1967
Death Flies East	Philip Wylie, Albert DeMond, Fred Niblo, Jr.	1935
Death Goes North	Edward R. Austin	1939
Death of a Salesman	Arthur Miller, Stanley Roberts	1931
Deceiver, The	Bella Muni, Abem Finkel, Jo Swerling, Jack Cunningham, Charles Logue	1931
Deception	Nat Pendleton, Harold Tarshis	1932
Decision at Sundown	Vernon L. Flaharty, Charles Lang, Jr.	1958
Defense Rests, The	Jo Swerling	1934
Delayed Flight	Dail Ambler	1964
Desert Bride, The	Elmer Harris, Ewart Adamson	1928
Desert Horseman, The	Sherman Lowe	1946
Desert Vengeance	Stuart Anthony	1931
Desert Vigilante	Earle Snell	1949
Desperadoes, The	Max Brand (Frederick Faust), Robert Carson	1943
Desperadoes, The	Clarke Reynolds, Walter Brough	1969
Desperate Chance for Ellery Queen, A	Ellery Queen (Frederick Dannay and Manfred B. Lee), Eric Taylor	1942
Destroyer	Frank Wead, Lewis Meltzer, Borden Chase	1943
Detective, The	G. K. Chesterton, Thelma Schnee and Robert Hamer	1954
Devil at 4 O'Clock, The	Max Catto and Liam O'Brien	1961
Devil Commands, The	William Sloane, Robert D. Andrews and Milton Gunzberg	1941
Devil Goddess	Dwight Babcock, George Plympton	1955
Devil is Driving, The	Lee Loeb, Harold Buchman, Joe Milward, Richard Blake	1937
Devil Ship	Lawrence Edmund Taylor	1947
Devil's Henchmen, The	Eric Taylor	1949
Devil's Imposter, The	John Briley	1972
Devil's Mask, The	Carlton E. Morse, Charles O'Neal, Dwight Babcock	1946
Devil's Playground	Norman Springer, Liam O'Flaherty, Jerome Chodorov, Dalton Trumbo	1937
Devil's Squadron	Richard V. Grace, Howard J. Green, Bruce Manning, Lionel Houser	1936

390

TITLE	WRITER	YEAR OF RELEASE
Devil's Trail, The	Phillip Ketchum, Robert Lee Johnson	1942
Devil-Ship Pirates, The	Jimmy Sangster	1963
Diamond Head	Peter Gilman, Marguerite Roberts	1962
Discontented Husbands	Evelyn Campbell, Jack Sturmwasser	1924
Die! Die! My Darling	Anna Blaisdell, Richard Matheson	1965
Dirigible	Frank Wead, James Warner Bellah, Jo Swerling, Dorothy Howell	1931
Dirty Little Billy	Charles Moss, Stan Dragoti	1972
Divorce American Style	Robert Kaufman, Norman Lear	1967
Do You Know This Voice?	Evelyn Berckman, Neil McCallum	1965
Doctor Takes a Wife, The	Aleen Wetstein, George Seaton, Ken Englund	1940
Dr. Faustus	Christopher Marlowe, Nevill Coghill	1968
Dr. Strangelove: Or How I Learned to Stop Worrying and Love the Bomb	Peter George, Stanley Kubrick, Terry Southern	1964
Doctors' Wives	Frank G. Slaughter, Daniel Taradash	1971
Dodge City Trail	Vernon Smith, Harold Shumate	1936
$ (Dollars)	Richard Brooks	1971
Domino Kid, The	Rory Calhoun, Kenneth Gamet, Hal Biller	1957
Donovan Affair, The	Owen Davis, Dorothy Howell, Howard J. Green	1929
Don't Gamble with Love	Lee Loeb, Harold Buchman	1936
Don't Knock the Rock	Robert E. Kent, James Gordon	1957
Don't Knock the Twist	James Gordon	1962
Don't Raise the Bridge, Lower the River	Max Wilk	1968
Doughboys in Ireland	Howard J. Green, Monte Brice	1943
Down Rio Grande Way	Paul Franklin	1942
Down to Earth	Harry Segall, Edwin Blum, Don Hartman	1947
Driftwood	Richard Harding Davis, Lillie Hayward	1928
Drive A Crooked Road	James Benson Nablo, Blake Edwards, Richard Quine	1954
Drive, He Said	Jeremy Larner, Jack Nicholson	1971
Drums of Tahiti	Robert E. Kent, Douglas Heyes	1953
Duel on the Mississippi	Gerald Drayson Adams	1955
Duffy	Donald Cammell, Harry Joe Brown, Jr., Pierre de la Salle	1968
Durango Kid, The	Paul Franklin	1940
Eadie Was a Lady	Monte Brice	1944
Earth vs. the Flying Saucers	Donald E. Keyhoe, George Worthing Yates, Raymond T. Marcus	1956
East of Fifth Avenue	Lew Levenson, Jo Swerling	1933
East of Sudan	Jud Kinberg	1964
Easy Rider	Peter Fonda, Dennis Hopper, Terry Southern	1969
Eavesdropper	Beatriz Guido, Edmundo Eichelbaum, Mabel Itzcovich, Joe Goldberg, Leopoldo Torre Nillson	1965
Eddy Duchin Story, The	Leo Katchen, Samuel Taylor	1956
Edge of Eternity	Ben Markson, Knute Swenson, Richard Collins	1959

TITLE	WRITER	YEAR OF RELEASE
Eight Bells	Percy G. Mandley, Ethel Hill, Bruce Manning	1935
Eight Iron Men	Harry Brown	1952
El Alamein	Herbert Purdum, George Worthing Yates	1953
El Dorado Pass	Earle Snell	1948
Electronic Monster, The	Charles Eric Maine, J. MacLaren-Ross	1960
Ellery Queen and the Murder Ring	Ellery Queen (Frederic Dannay and and Manfred B. Lee), Eric Taylor, Gertrude Purcell	1941
Ellery Queen and the Perfect Crime	Ellery Queen (Frederic Dannay and Manfred B. Lee), Eric Taylor	1941
Ellery Queen, Master Detective	Ellery Queen (Frederic Dannay and Manfred B. Lee), Eric Taylor	1940
Ellery Queen's Penthouse Mystery	Ellery Queen (Frederic Dannay and Manfred B. Lee), Eric Taylor	1941
Emergency Wedding	Dalton Trumbo, Nat Perrin, Claude Binyon	1950
End of the Affair, The	Graham Greene, Leonore Coffee	1955
End of the Trail	Stuart Anthony	1933
End of the Trail	Zane Grey, Harold Shumate	1936
Endless Summer, The	Bruce Brown	1967
Enemy Agents Meet Ellery Queen	Ellery Queen (Frederic Dannay and Manfred B. Lee), Eric Taylor	1942
Enemy General, The	Dan Pepper, Burt Picard	1960
Enemy of Men, An	Douglas Brenston	1926
Enter Laughing	Joseph Stein, Carl Reiner	1967
Escape From Devil's Island	Fred de Gresac, Earle Snell, Fred Niblo, Jr.	1935
Escape From San Quentin	Raymond T. Marcus	1957
Escape in the Fog	Aubrey Wisberg	1945
Escape to Glory	Sidney Biddell, Frederic Frank, P. J. Wolfson	1940
Eternal Woman, The	Wellyn Totman	1928
Eve Knew Her Apples	Rian James, E. Edwin Moran	1944
Ever Since Venus	McElbert Moore, Arthur Dreifuss, Victor McLeod, Connie Lee	1944
Every Day is a Holiday	Mel Ferrer, Jose Maria Palacio	1966
Every Man's Woman	Glaucio Gill, Eduardo Borras, Ernio de Concini, Franco Rosi	1968
Everything's Ducky	John Fenton Murray, Benedict Freedman	1961
Experiment in Terror	Gordon and Mildred Gordon	1962
Executioner, The	Gordon McDonell	1970
Extortion	Earl Felton	1938
Face Behind the Mask, The	Thomas Edward O'Connell, Arthur Levinson, Allen Vincent, Paul Jarrico	1941
Face of a Fugitive	Peter Dawson, David T. Chantler, Daniel B. Ullman	1959
Fail Safe	Eugene Burdick, Harvey Wheeler, Walter Bernstein	1964
Faker, The	Howard J. Green	1929

TITLE	WRITER	YEAR OF RELEASE
Fall of Eve, The	Gladys Lehman, Frederick and Fanny Hatton	1929
False Alarm, The	Leah Baird, W. H. Clifford	1926
Family Secret, The	Marie Baumer, James Cavanagh, Francis Cockrell, Andrew Sold	1951
Fan Club, The	Irving Wallace	1975
Fashion Madness	Victoria Moore, Olga Printzlau	1927
Fast and Sexy	E. M. Margadonna, Dino Risi, Luciano Corda, Joseph Stefano	1960
Fat City	Leonard Gardner	1972
Fatal Mistake	Walter Anthony	1924
Father and Son	Elmer Harris, Jack Townley	1929
Father is a Bachelor	James Edward Grant, Aleen Leslie	1950
Faust and the Devil	Charles Gounod, Leopold Marchard, Herman G. Weinberg	1940
Fearless Lover, The	Scott Dunlap	1925
Feather in Her Hat, A	I. A. R. Wylie, Lawrence Hazard	1935
Feudin' Rhythm	Barry Shipman	1949
Fifty Fathoms Deep	Harvey Gates, R. Chanslor, Dorothy Howell	1931
Fight for Honor	H. W. George	1924
Fight for Life	Paul De Kruif, Pare Lorentz	1940
Fight to the Finish, A	Harold Shumate	1937
Fighting Buckaroo	Luci Ward	1942
Fighting Code, The	Lambert Hillyer	1933
Fighting Fool, The	Frank Howard Clark	1932
Fighting for Justice	Gladwell Richardson, Robert Quigley	1932
Fighting Frontiersman, The	Ed Earl Repp	1946
Fighting Guardsman, The	Alexandre Dumas, Franz Spencer, Edward Dein	1945
Fighting Marshal, The	Frank Howard Clark	1931
Fighting Ranger, The	Warren Battle, Harry O. Hoyt	1934
Fighting Shadows	Ford Beebe	1935
Fighting Sheriff, The	Stuart Anthony	1931
Fighting the Flames	Douglas Z. Doty	1925
Fighting Youth	Paul Archer, Dorothy Howell	1925
Final Edition	Roy Chanslor, Dorothy Howell	1932
Final Hour, The	Harold Shumate	1936
Find the Witness	Richard B. Sale, Grace Neville, Fred Niblo, Jr.	1937
Finest Hours, The	Winston K. Churchill, Victor Wolfson	1964
Fire Down Below	Max Catto, Irwin Shaw	1957
Fire over Africa	Robert Westerby	1954
First Comes Courage	Elliott Arnold, Lewis Meltzer, Melvin Levy, George Sklar	1943
First Deadly Sin, The	Lawrence Sanders, Steve Shagan	1975
First Men in the Moon	H. G. Wells, Nigel Kneale, Jan Read	1964
First Offenders	J. Edward Slavin, Walter Wise	1939
First Time, The	Jean Rouverol, Hugo Butler, Frank Tashlin, Dane Lussier	1951
Five	Arch Oboler	1951
Five Against the House	Jack Finney, Stirling Silliphant, William Bowers, John Barnwell	1955

TITLE	WRITER	YEAR OF RELEASE
Five Angles on Murder	John Cresswell	1953
Five Easy Pieces	Bob Rafelson, Adrian Joyce	1970
Five Finger Exercise	Peter Shaffer, Frances Goodrich, Albert Hackett	1962
Five Golden Hours	Hans Wilhelm	1961
Five Little Peppers and How They Grew	Margaret Sidney (Harriet Mulford Stone Lothrup), Nathalie Bucknall	1939
Five Little Peppers at Home	Margaret Sidney (Harriet Mulford Stone Lothrup), Harry Sauber	1940
Five Little Peppers in Trouble	Margaret Sidney (Harriet Mulford Stone Lothrup), Harry Rebuas (Harry Sauber)	1940
5000 Fingers of Dr. T., The	Dr. Seuss, Allen Scott	1953
Flame of Calcutta	Sol Shor, Robert E. Kent	1953
Flame of Stamboul	Daniel B. Ullman	1951
Flight	Ralph Graves	1929
Flight into Nowhere	William Bloom, Clarence Jay, Schneider, Jefferson Parker, Gordon Rigby	1938
Flight Lieutenant	Richard Carroll, Betty Hopkins, Michael Blankfort	1942
Flight of the Doves	Frank Gabrielson, Ralph Nelson	1971
Flight to Fame	Michael L. Simmons	1938
Flood, The	John Thomas Neville, Fred Niblo, Jr.	1931
Flying Fontaines, The	Don Mullally, Lee Erwin	1959
Flying Marine, The	Jack Natteford, Norman Houston	1929
Flying Missile, The	Harvey S. Haislip, N. Richard Nash, Richard English, James Gunn	1950
Fog	Valentine Williams, Dorothy Rice Sims, Ethel Hill, Dore Schary	1933
Fool and His Money, A	George Barra McCutcheon, Douglas Z. Doty	1925
Foolish Virgin	Lois Zellner	1924
Footlight Glamour	Chic Young, Karen DeWolf, Connie Lee	1943
Footsteps in the Fog	W. W. Jacobs, Dorothy Reid, Lenore Coffee, Arthur Pierson	1955
For Ladies Only	George F. Worts, Robert Lord	1927
For Pete's Sake	Stanley Shapiro, Maurice Rachlin	1974
For Singles Only	Arthur Hoerl, Albert Derr, Hal Collins, Arthur Dreifuss	1968
For The Love o' Lil	J. Leslie Thrasher, Gladys Lehman, Dorothy Howell, Bella Cohen	1930
For The Love of Rusty	Al Martin, Malcolm Stuart Boylan	1947
Forbidden	Frank Capra, Jo Swerling	1932
Forbidden Island	Charles B. Griffith	1958
Forbidden Trail	Milton Krims	1932
Forgive and Forget	Charles Furthman, Jack Sturmwasser	1923
Fort Savage Raiders	Barry Shipman	1951
Fort Ti	Robert E. Kent	1953
Fortune, The	Carol Eastman	1975
Fortunes of Captain Blood	Rafael Sabatini, Michael Hogan, Robert Libott, Frank Burt	1950
40 Carats	Barillet and Gredy, Jay Allen, Leonard Gershe	1973

TITLE	WRITER	YEAR OF RELEASE
40 Guns to Apache Pass	Willard and Mary Willingham	1966
49th Man, The	Ivan Tors, Harry Essex	1953
Four Poster, The	Jan de Hartog, Allan Scott	1953
Fragment of Fear	Paul Dehn	1971
Framed	Jack Patrick, Ben Maddow	1947
Frameup, The	Richard Wormser, Harold Shumate	1937
From Here to Eternity	James Jones, Daniel Taradash	1953
Frontier Fury	Betty Burbridge	1943
Frontier Gunlaw	Victor McLeod, Bennett Cohen	1946
Frontier Outpost	Barry Shipman	1949
Frontiers of '49	Nate Gatzert	1939
Fugitive at Large	Eric Taylor, Harvey Gates	1939
Fugitive from a Prison Camp	Albert Demond	1940
Fugitive Lady	Herbert Ashbury, Fred Niblo, Jr.	1934
Fugitive Sheriff	Nate Gatzert	1936
Full of Life	John Fante	1957
Fuller Brush Girl, The	Frank Tashlin	1950
Fuller Brush Man, The	Roy Huggins, Frank Tashlin, Devery Freeman	1948
Funny Girl	Isobel Lennart, Jule Styne, Bob Bob Merrill	1968
Funny Lady	Jay Presson Allen	1975
Further up the Creek	Val Guest, John Warren, Len Heath	1959
Fury at Gunsight Pass	David Lang	1956
Fury of the Congo	Carroll Young	1951
Fury of the Jungle	Horace McCoy, Ethel Hill, Dore Schary	1933
Fury of the Pagan	Gino Mangini, Umberto Scarpelli	1962
Gallant Blade, The	Ted Thomas, Edward Dein, Walter Ferris, Morton Grant, Wilfrid Pettit	1948
Gallant Defender	Peter B. Kyne, Ford Beebe	1936
Gallant Journey	Byron Morgan, William A. Wellman	1946
Galloping Thunder	Ed Earl Repp	1946
Game is Over, The	Emile Zola, Jean Cau, Roger Vadim	1967
Game that Kills, The	J. Benton Cheney, Grace Neville, Fred Niblo, Jr.	1937
Gamma People, The	Louis Pollock, John Gilling, John Gossage	1956
Gang o' Mine	(Unknown)	1924
Garment Jungle	Lester Velie, Harry Kleiner	1957
Gasoline Alley	Frank O. King, Edward Bernds	1950
Gay Senorita, The	Edward Eliscu, J. Robert Bren	1945
Gene Autry and the Mounties	Norman S. Hall	1950
Gene Krupa Story, The	Orin Jannings	1960
Genghis Khan	Berkely Mather, Clarke Reynolds, Beverley Cross	1965
Gentleman from Nowhere, The	Edward Anhalt	1948
Gentleman Misbehaves, The	Robert Wyler, John B. Clymer, Richard Weil	1946
Georgy Girl	Margaret Forster, Peter Nichols	1966
Getting Straight	Ken Kolb, Robert Kaufmann	1970
Ghost of the China Sea	Charles B. Griffith	1958
Ghost that Walks Alone, The	Doris Shattuck (Richard Shattuck), Clarence Upson Young	1944

TITLE	WRITER	YEAR OF RELEASE
Giant Claw, The	Samuel Newman, Paul Gangelin	1957
Gideon of Scotland Yard	J. J. Marric, T. E. B. Clarke	1958
Gidget	Frederick Kohner, Gabrielle Upton	1959
Gidget Goes Hawaaian	Frederick Kohner, Ruth Brooks Flippen	1961
Gidget Goes to Rome	Frederick Kohner, Ruth Brooks Flippen, Katherine and Dale Eunson	1963
Gilda	A. E. Ellington, Marion Parsonnet, Jo Eisinger	1946
Girl Friend, The	Gene Towne, Graham Baker, Gertrude Purcell, Benny Rubin	1935
Girl in Danger	Harold Shumate	1934
Girl in the Case	Pierre Couderc (Charles F. Royal), Joseph Hoffman, Dorcas Cochran	1944
Girl of the Limberlost, The	Gene Stratton Porter, Erna Lazarus	1945
Girls' School	Tess Slesinger, Richard Sherman	1938
Girls' School	Jack Henley, Brenda Weisberg	1950
Girls Can Play	Albert Demond, Lambert Hillyer	1937
Girls of the Road	R. D. Andrews	1940
Girls Under 21	Fanya Foss, Jay Dratler	1940
Gladiator, The	Philip Wylie, Charles Melson, Arthur Sheekman	1938
Glamour For Sale	John Bright	1940
Glamour Girl	Lee Gold, M. Coates Webster	1948
Glass Houses	Alexander Singer, Judith Singer	1971
Glass Wall, The	Ivan Tors, Maxwell Shane	1953
Go West, Young Lady	Karen DeWolf, Richard Flournoy	1941
Goal!	Brian Granville	1967
Go-Between, The	Harold Pinter	1971
Goddess, The	Paddy Chayefsky	1958
Godspell	John-Michael Tegelak, David Greene	1973
Going Steady	Budd Grossman, Sumner A. Long	1958
Gold Widows	Scott Darling	1928
Golden Boy	Clifford Odets, Louis Meltzer, Daniel Taradash, Sarah Y. Mason, Victor Heeman	1939
Golden Hawk, The	Frank Yerby, Robert E. Kent	1952
Golden Virgin, The	Nicholas Monserrat, Charles Kaufman	1953
Golden Voyage of Sinbad, The	Brian Clemens	1974
Goldtown Ghost Riders	Gerald Geraghty	1953
Good Bad Girl, The	Winifred Van Duzer, Jo Swerling	1931
Good Day For a Hanging	John Reese, Daniel B. Ullman, Maurice Zimm	1959
Good Girls Go to Paris	William Cowen, Lenore Coffee, Gladys Lehman, Ken Englund	1939
Good Humor Man, The	Roy Huggins, Frank Tashlin	1950
Good Luck, Mr. Yates	Hal Smith, Sam Rudd, Lou Breslow, Adele Comandini	1943
Good Neighbor Sam	Jack Finney, James Fritzell, Everett Greenbaum, David Swift	1964
Good Times	Tony Barrett	1967
Gorgon, The	J. Llewellyn Devine, John Gilling	1964
Grand Exit	Gene Towne, Graham Baker, Bruce Manning, Lionel Hauser	1935

TITLE	WRITER	YEAR OF RELEASE
Gravy Train, The	Bill Kerby, David Whitney	1974
Great Manhunt, The	Sidney Gilliat	1950
Great Plane Robbery, The	Harold Green, Albert Demond	1940
Great Sioux Massacre, The	Fred C. Dobbs	1965
Great Swindle, The	Eric Taylor, Albert Demond	1941
Guard that Girl	Lambert Hillyer	1935
Guess Who's Coming to Dinner	William Rose	1968
Guilt of Janet Ames, The	Lenore Coffee, Louella MacFarlane, Allen Rivkin, Devery Freeman	1947
Guilty	Dorothy Howell	1930
Guilty Generation, The	Jo Milward, James Kerby Hawkes, Jack Cunningham	1931
Gumshoe	Neville Smith	1972
Gun Fury	Kathleen B. Granger, George Granger, Robert A. Granger, Irving Wallace, Roy Huggins	1953
Gun that Won the West, The	James B. Gordon	1955
Gunfighters, The	Zane Grey, Alan LeMay	1947
Gunman's Walk	Ric Hardman, Frank Nugent	1958
Gunmen from Laredo	Clarke E. Reynolds	1958
Gunning for Vengeance	Louise Rousseau, Ed Earl Repp	1945
Guns of Fort Petticoat, The	C. William Harrison, Walter Doniger	1957
Guns of Navarone	Alistair MacLean, Carl Foreman	1961
Guy, a Gal and a Pal, A	Gerald Drayson Adams, Monte Brice	1945
Hail to the Rangers	Gerald Geraghty	1943
Hamlet	William Shakespeare	1970
Hammerhead	James Mayo, William Best, Herbert Baker, John Briley	1968
Hand in Hand	Sidney Harmon, Diana Morgan, Leopold Atlas	1960
Hands across the Rockies	Norbert Davis, Paul Franklin	1941
Hangman's Knot	Roy Huggins	1952
Happening, The	James D. Buchanan, Ronald Austi, Frank R. Pierson	1967
Happy Birthday, Wanda June	Kurt Vonnegut, Jr.	1971
Happy Time, The	Samuel A. Taylor, Robert Fontaine, Earl Felton	1952
Hard Man, The	Leo Katcher	1957
Hard Times for the Prince	Ruggero Maccari, Ettore Scola	1966
Harder They Fall, The	Budd Schulberg, Philip Yordan	1956
Harem Girl	Edward Bernds, Elwood Ullman	1952
Harlem Globetrotters	Alfred Palca	1951
Harmon of Michigan	Richard Goldstone, Stanley Rauh, Frederic Frank, Howard J. Green	1941
Harriet Craig	George Kelly, Anne Froelick, James Gunn	1950
Harvard, Here I Come	Karl Brown, Albert Duffy	1942
Harvey Middleman, Fireman	Ernest Pintoff	1965
Have Rocket, Will Travel	Raphael Hayes	1959
Hawk of Wild River, The	Howard J. Green	1951
He Laughed Last	Richard Quine, Blake Edwards	1956
He Stayed for Breakfast	Sidney Howard, Michel Duran, P. J. Wolfson, Michael Fessier, Ernst Vajda	1940

TITLE	WRITER	YEAR OF RELEASE
Head	Bob Rafelson, Jack Nicholson	1968
Headin' East	Joseph Hoffman, Monroe Shaff, Ethel LaBlanche, Paul Franklin	1937
Heading West	Ed Earl Repp	1946
Heart of Show Business, The	Larry Rhing	1957
Heat's On, The	Fitzroy Davis, George S. George, Fred Schiller	1943
Heir to Trouble	Ken Maynard, Nate Gatzert	1935
He's a Cockeyed Wonder	Jack Henley	1950
Hell Below Zero	Hammond Innes, Alex Coppel, Max Trell	1954
Hell Bent For Love	Harold Shumate	1934
Hell Cat, The	Adele Buffington, Fred Niblo, Jr.	1934
Hell Cats of the Navy	Charles A. Lockwood, Hans Christian Adamson, David Lang, Raymond Marcus	1957
Hellions, The	Harold Swanton, Patrick Kirwan, Harold Huth	1961
Hell is a City	Maurice Procter, Val Guest	1960
Hell's Horizon	Tom Gries	1955
Hell's Island	Tom Buckingham, Jo Swerling	1930
Hello Annapolis	Tom Reed, Donald Davis	1942
Hello Trouble	Lambert Hillyer	1932
Hell-Ship Morgan	Harold Shumate	1936
Her Accidental Husband	Lois Zellner	1923
Her First Beau	Florence Ryerson, Colin Clements, Gladys Lehman, Karen DeWolf	1941
Her First Romance	Herman Wouk, Albert Mannheimer	1951
Her Husband's Affairs	Ben Hecht, Charles Lederer	1947
Her Wonderful Lie	Ernst Marischka, Gustave Holm, Hamilton Benz, Rowland Leigh	1949
Here Comes Mr. Jordan	Henry Segall, Sidney Buchman	1941
Heroes of Telemark	Ivan Moffat, Ben Marzman	1961
Heroes of the Alamo	Rob Wenty	1938
Heroes of the Range	Nate Gatzert	1936
Hey Boy! Hey Girl!	Raphael Hayes, James West	1959
Hey Rookie	E. B. (Zeke) Colvan, Doris Colvan, Henry Myers, Edward Eliscu, Jay Gorney	1944
Hey There, It's Yogi Bear	Joseph Barbera, Warren Foster, William Hanna	1964
Hidden Power	Gordon Rigby	1939
High Flight	Jack Davies, Joseph Landon, Kenneth Hughes	1957
High Speed	Harold Shumate, Adele Buffington	1932
Highway Patrol	Lambert Hillyer, Robert E. Kent, Stuart Anthony	1938
Hills of Utah	Les Savage, Jr., Gerald Geraghty	1951
Hireling, The	Wolf Mankowitz	1973
His Girl Friday	Ben Hecht, Charles MacArthur, Charles Lederer	1940
Hit the Hay	Richard Weil, Charles R. Marion, Fred L. Fox, Henry Hoople	1945
H-Man	Hideo Kaijo, Takeshi Kimura	1959
Hoedown	Barry Shipman	1950

398

Title	Writer	Year of Release
Hold the Press	Horace McCoy	1933
Holiday	Philip Barry, Donald Ogden Stewart, Sidney Buchman	1938
Holiday in Havana	Morton Grant, Robert Lees, Frederick I. Rinaldo, Karen DeWolf	1949
Hollywood Roundup	Monroe Shaff, Joseph Hoffman, Ethel LaBlanche	1937
Hollywood Speaks	Jo Swerling, Norman Krasna	1932
Home in San Antone	Barry Shipman	1949
Homicidal	Robb White	1961
Homicide Bureau	Earle Snell	1938
Honolulu Lu	Eliot Gibbons, Paul Yawitz, Ned Dandy	1941
Hook, Line and Sinker	Rod Amateau, David Davis	1969
Horsemen, The	Joseph Kessel, Dalton Trumbo	1971
Horsemen of the Sierras	Barry Shipman	1949
Hot Blood	Jean Evans, Jesse Lasky, Jr.	1956
Hot Dog	(Unknown)	1923
Householder, The	R. Prawer Jhabvla	1963
Houston Story, The	James B. Gordon	1955
Howards of Virginia, The	Elizabeth Page, Sidney Buchman	1940
How to Murder a Rich Uncle	Didier Daix, John Paxton	1957
How to Save a Marriage and Ruin Your Life	Stanley Shapiro, Nate Monaster	1968
How, When and With Whom	Maurice Martin, Tullio Pinelli, Antonio Pietrangeli	1969
Human Desire	Emile Zola, Alfred Hayes	1954
Hunchback of Rome, The	Carmine Bologna	1963
Hurricane	Norman Springer, Evelyn Campbell, Enid Hibbard	1927
Hurricane Island	David Mathews	1951
Husbands	John Cassavetes	1971
I Aim at the Stars	George Froeschel, U. Wolter, H. W. John, Jay Dratler	1960
I Am the Law	Fred Allhoff, Jo Swerling	1938
I Love a Bandleader	John Grey, Paul Yawitz	1945
I Love a Mystery	Carlton E. Morse, Charles O'Neal	1945
I Love Trouble	Roy Huggins	1947
I Love You Love	Allessandro Blassetti, Luigi Chiarini, Carlo Romano, Antonio Savignano	1963
I Married Adventure	Osa Johnson, Donald Clark, Albert Duffy	1940
I Never Sang for my Father	Robert Anderson	1970
I Only Asked	Sid Colin, Jack Davies	1958
I Promise to Pay	Lionel Houser, Mary McCall	1937
I Surrender Dear	M. Coates Webster, Hal Collins	1948
I Walk the Line	Madison Jones, Alvin Sargent	1970
I Was a Prisoner on Devil's Island	Otto and Edgar Van Eyss, Karl Brown	1941
Idol on Parade	William Camp, John Antrobus	1959
If You Could Only Cook	F. Hugh Herbert, Gertrude Purcell, Howard J. Green	1935
I'll Fix It	Leonard Spigelgass, Ethel Hill, Dorothy Howell	1934
I'll Love You Always	Lawrence Hazard, Vera Caspary, Sidney Buchman	1935

TITLE	WRITER	YEAR OF RELEASE
I'll Take Romance	Stephen Morehouse Avery, George Oppenheimer, Jane Murfin	1937
I'm All Right Jack	Alan Hackney, Frank Harvey, John Boulting	1960
Images	Robert Altman	1973
Impatient Years, The	Virginia Van Upp	1944
In a Lonely Place	Dorothy B. Hughes, Andrew Solt, Edmund H. North	1950
In Cold Blood	Truman Capote, Richard Brooks	1968
In Early Arizona	Nate Gatzert	1939
In Spite of Danger	Anthony Coldeway	1935
In the French Style	Irwin Shaw	1963
Indiscretion of an American Wife	Cesare Zavattini, Luigi Chiarini, Giorgio Prosperi, Truman Capote	1954
Indian Territory	Norman S. Hall	1950
Indian Uprising	Richard Schayer, Kenneth Gamet	1951
Innocence	Lewis Allen Brown, Jack Sturmwasser	1923
Inside Detroit	Robert E. Kent, James B. Gordon	1955
Interlude	David Deutsch, Lee Langley, Hugh Leonard	1968
Interns, The	Richard Frede, Walter Newman, David Swift	1962
Invaders, The	Emeric Pressburger, Rodney Ackland	1942
Invasion U.S.A.	Robert Smith, Franz Spencer	1952
Investigation of a Citizen Above Suspicion	Ugo Perro, Elio Petri	1971
Iron Glove, The	Robert E. Kent, Samuel J. Jacoby, Jesse L. Lasky, Jr., DeVallon Scott, Douglas Heyes	1954
Is Everybody Happy?	Monte Brice	1943
Island of Doomed Men	Robert D. Andrews	1940
Isle of Forgotten Women	Louella Parsons, Norman Springer	1927
It Came from Beneath the Sea	George Worthing Yates, Harold J. Smith	1955
It Can't Last Forever	Lee Loeb, Harold Buchman	1937
It Had to be You	Don Hartman, Allen Boretz, Norman Panama, Melvin Frank	1947
It Happened in Hollywood	Myles Connolly, Ethel Hill, Harvey Ferguson, Sam Fuller	1937
It Happened One Night	Samuel Hopkins Adams, Robert Riskin	1934
It Happened to Jane	Norman Katkov, Max Wilk	1959
It Should Happen to You	Garson Kanin	1954
It's a Great Life	Chic Young, Connie Lee, Karen DeWolf	1943
It's All Yours	Adelaide Heilbron, Mary C. McCall, Jr.	1937
It's Great to be Young	Karen DeWolf, Jack Henley	1946
Jack McCall, Desperado	David Chandler, John O' Dea	1953
Jam Session	Harlan Ware, Patterson McNutt, Manny Seff	1944
Jason and the Argonauts	Jan Read, Beverley Cross	1963
Jazz Boat	Rex Rienits, Ken Hughes, John Antrobus	1960
Jealousy	Argyll Campbell, Kubec Glasmon, Joseph Moncure March	1934

TITLE	WRITER	YEAR OF RELEASE
Jeanne Eagels	Daniel Fuchs, Sonya Levien, John Fante	1957
Jesse James vs The Daltons	Edwin Westrate, Robert E. Kent, Samuel Newman	1954
Joe Macbeth	Philip Yordan	1956
Johnny Allegro	James Edward Grant, Karen DeWolf, Guy Endore	1949
Johnny O'Clock	Milton Holmes, Robert Rossen	1947
Jolson Sings Again	Sidney Buchman	1949
Jolson Story, The	Harry Chandlee, Andrew Solt, Stephen Longstreet	1946
Jubal	Paul I. Wellman, Russell S. Hughes, Delmer Daves	1956
Juggler, The	Michael Blankfort	1953
Juke Box Rhythm	Lou Morheim, Mary C. McCall Jr., Earl Baldwin	1959
Junction City	Barry Shipman	1952
Jungle Jim	Carroll Young	1949
Jungle Jim in the Forbidden Land	Carroll Young, Samuel Newman	1951
Jungle Man-Eaters	Carroll Young, Samuel Newman	1954
Jungle Manhunt	Carroll Young, Samuel Newman	1951
Jungle Moon Men	Jo Pagano, Dwight V. Babcock	1954
Junior Army	Albert Bein, Paul Gangelin	1942
Just before Dawn	Max Marcin, Eric Taylor, Aubrey Wisberg	1946
Just before Nightfall	Claude Chabrol	1971
Just for Fun	Milton Subotsky	1963
Justice of the Far North	Norman Dawn	1925
Justice of the Range	Ford Beebe	1935
Juvenile Court	Robert E. Kent, Henry Taylor, Michael L. Simmons	1938
Kansas City Kitty	Manny Seff, Monte Brice	1944
Kazan	James Oliver Curwood, Arthur A. Ross	1949
Keeper of the Bees	Gene Stratton Porter, Lawrence E. Watkin, Malcolm Stuart Boylan, Ralph Rose, Jr.	1947
Key, The	Jan De Hartog, Carl Foreman	1958
Key Witness	J. Donald Wilson, Edward Bock, Raymond L. Shrock	1947
Kid from Amarillo, The	Barry Shipman	1951
Kid from Broken Gun, The	Barry Shipman, Ed Earl Repp	1952
Kid Sister, The	Dorothy Howell, Harry O. Hoyt	1927
Kill Her Gently	Paul Erickson	1958
Kill Me Quick—I'm Cold	Francesca Maselli	1967
Kill the Umpire	Frank Tashlin	1950
Killer Ape	Carroll Young, Arthur Hoerl	1953
Killer at Large	Carl Clausen, Harold Shumate	1936
Killer that Stalked New York, The	Milton Lehman, Harry Essex	1950
Killers of Kilimanjaro	J. A. Hunter, Dan P. Mannix, Richard Maibaum, Cyril Hume, John Gilling	1960
King of Dodge City, The	Gerald Geraghty	1941
King of Marvin Gardens, The	Bob Rafelson, Jacob Brackman	1972

Title	Writer	Year
King of the Wild Horses	Early Haley, Fred Myton	1933
King of the Wild Horses	Ted Thomas, Brenda Weisberg	1947
King Rat	James Clavell, Bryan Forbes	1965
King Steps Out, The	Gustav Holm, Ernest Decsey, Hubert Marischa, Ernest Marischa	1936
Kiss and Tell	F. Hugh Herbert	1945
Kiss the Girls and Make Them Die	Dino Maiuri, Jack Pulman	1967
Klondike Kate	Houston Branch, M. Coates Webster	1943
Knock on any Door	Willard Motley, Daniel Taradash, John Monks, Jr.	1949
Konga, the Wild Stallion	Harold Shumate	1939
La Traviata	Giuseppe Verdi, F. M. Piavo	1967
La Verite	Henri-Georges Clouzot	1961
Ladies in Retirement	Reginald Denham, Edward Percy, Garrett Fort	1941
Ladies Must Play	Paul Hervey Fox, Dorothy Howell	1930
Ladies of Leisure	Milton Herbert Gropper, Jo Swerling	1930
Ladies of the Chorus	Harry Sauber, Joseph Carole	1948
Lady and the Bandit, The	Alfred Noyes, Jack DeWitt, Duncan Renaldo, Robert Libott, Frank Burt	1951
Lady and the Mob, The	George Bradshaw, Price Day, Richard Maibaum, Gertrude Purcell	1939
Lady by Choice	Jo Swerling, Dwight Taylor	1934
Lady for a Day	Damon Runyon, Robert Riskin	1933
Lady from Nowhere	Ben Grauman Kohn, Fred Niblo, Jr., Arthur Strawn, Joseph Krumgold	1936
Lady from Shanghai, The	Sherwood King, Orson Welles	1947
Lady in Question, The	Marcel Achard, Lewis Meltzer	1940
Lady in the Car, The	Sebastien Japrisot, Richard Harris, Eleanor Perry	1970
Lady is Willing, The	L. Vernueil, Guy Bolton	1934
Lady is Willing, The	James Edward Grant, Albert McCleery	1942
Lady Objects, The	Robert Riskin, Gladys Lehman, Charles Kenyon	1938
Lady of Secrets	Katherine Brush, Joseph Anthony, Zoe Akins	1936
Lady Raffles	Jack Jungmeyer, Fred Stanley, Dorothy Howell	1928
L'Alibi	Marcel Achard, J. Companeez, R. Juttke	1939
Lamp in the Desert	(Unknown)	1923
Landrush	Michael Simmons	1946
Laramie	Barry Shipman	1949
Laramie Mountains	Barry Shipman	1952
Last Angry Man, The	Gerald Green, Richard Murphy	1959
Last Blitzkreig, The	Lou Morheim	1959
Last Days of Boot Hill	Norman S. Hall	1947
Last Detail, The	Darryl Ponicsan, Robert Towne	1974
Last Frontier	Richard Emery Roberts, Philip Yordan, Russell S. Hughes	1955
Last Horseman, The	Ed Earl Repp	1943
Last Hurrah, The	Edwin O'Connor, Frank Nugent	1958
Last Man, The	Elliot Clawson, Francis Faragoh, Keene Thompson	1932

TITLE	WRITER	YEAR OF RELEASE
Last Man to Hang, The	Gerald Bullett, Maurice Elvey, Ivor Montagu, Max Trell	1956
Last of the Buccaneers	Robert E. Kent	1950
Last of the Comanches	Kenneth Gamet	1952
Last of the Lone Wolf	Louis Joseph Vance, Dorothy Howell	1930
Last of the Pony Riders	Ruth Woodman	1953
Last of the Redmen	James Fenimore Cooper, Herbert Dalmas, George H. Plympton	1947
Last Parade, The	Casey Robinson, Dorothy Howell, Jo Swerling	1931
Last Picture Show, The	Larry McMurtry, Peter Bogdanovich	1971
Last Posse, The	Seymour and Connie Lee, Bennett and Kenneth Gamet	1953
Last Rebel, The	Warren Kiefer	1971
Last Round-Up, The	Jack Townley, Earle Snell	1947
Last Train from Bombay	Robert Libott	1952
Laugh Your Blues Away	Harry Sauber, Ned Dandy	1942
Law and Disorder	Iran Passer, William Richert, Kenneth Harris Fishman	1974
Law Beyond the Range	Lambert Hillyer	1935
Law Comes to Texas, The	Nate Gatzert	1939
Law of the Barbary Coast	Robert Libott, Frank Burt	1948
Law of the Canyon	Eileen Gary	1947
Law of the Northwest	Luci Ward	1942
Law of the Plains	Maurice Geraghty	1938
Law of the Ranger	Jesse A. Duffy, Joseph Levering, Nate Gatzert	1937
Law of the Texan	Monroe Shaff, Arthur Hoerl	1939
Law vs Billy the Kid, The	John T. Williams	1954
Lawless Empire	Elizabeth Beecher, Bennett Cohen	1945
Lawless Plainsmen	Luci Ward	1942
Lawless Rider	Nate Gatzert	1936
Lawless Street, A	Brad Ward, Kenneth Gamet	1955
Lawrence of Arabia	T. E. Lawrence, Lowell Thomas, Robert Bolt	1962
League of Frightened Men, The	Rex Stout, Eugene Solow, Guy Endore	1937
Leather Gloves	Richard English, Brown Holmes	1948
Leave it to Blondie	Chic Young, Connie Lee	1945
Legend of Tom Dooley, The	Stan Shpetner	1959
Legion of Terror	Bert Granet	1936
Let No Man Write My Epitaph	Willard Motley, Robert Presnell, Jr.	1960
Let Us Live	Joseph F. Dinneen, Anthony Veiller, Allen Rivkin	1939
Let the Good Times Roll	(Unknown)	1973
Let's Do It Again	Arthur Richman, Mary Loos, Richard Sale	1953
Let's Fall In Love	Herbert Fields	1934
Let's Get Married	A. H. Z. Carr, Ethel Hill	1937
Let's Go Steady	William B. Sackheim, Erna Lazarus	1945
Let's Have Fun	Harry Sauber	1942
Let's Live Tonight	Bradley King, Gene Markey	1935
Let's Rock	Hal Hackady	1958
Liberation of L. B. Jones, The	Jesse Hill Ford, Stirling Silliphant	1970
Life at the Top	John Braine, Mordecai Richler	1966

TITLE	WRITER	YEAR OF RELEASE
Life Begins at 17	Richard Baer	1958
Life Begins with Love	Dorothy Bennett, Thomas Mitchell, Brown Holmes	1937
Life with Blondie	Chic Young, Connie Lee	1945
Light Fingers	Alfred Henry Lewis, John Francis Natteford	1929
Lightning Flyer, The	Barry Barringer	1931
Lightning Guns	William S. Milligan, Victor Arthur	1950
Lightning Swords of Death	Kazuo Koike, Goyu Kojema	1974
Lilith	J. R. Salamanca, Robert Rossen	1964
Line-Up, The	George Waggner	1934
Lineup, The	Stirling Silliphant	1958
Lion and the Lamb, The	E. Phillips Oppenheim, Matt Taylor	1931
Little Adventuress, The	Michael L. Simmons, Paul Jarrico	1938
Little Miss Broadway	Arthur Dreifuss, Victor McLeod, Betty Wright	1947
Little Miss Roughneck	Fred Niblo, Jr., Grace Neville, Michael Simmons	1938
Little Prince and the Eight-Headed Dragon, The	Hiroshi Okawa	1964
Living Free	Joy Adamson, Millard Kaufman	1972
Loaded Pistols	Dwight Cummins, Dorothy Yost	1948
Lock Up Your Daughters	Bernard Miles, Keith Waterhouse, Willis Hall	1969
Lone Hand Texan, The	Ed Earl Repp	1947
Lone Prairie, The	Ed Earl Repp, J. Benton Cheney, Fred Myton	1942
Lone Rider, The	Frank H. Clark, Forest Sheldon	1930
Lone Star Moonlight	Louise Rousseau, Ande Lamb	1946
Lone Star Pioneers	Nate Gatzert	1939
Lone Star Vigilantes	Luci Ward	1941
Lone Wolf and His Lady, The	Louis Joseph Vance, Edward Dein, Malcolm Stuart Boylan	1949
Lone Wolf in London, The	Louis Joseph Vance, Brenda Weisberg, Arthur E. Orloff	1947
Lone Wolf in Mexico, The	Louis Joseph Vance, Phil Magee, Maurice Tombragel, Martin Goldsmith	1947
Lone Wolf in Paris, The	Louis Joseph Vance, Arthur T. Horman	1938
Lone Wolf Keeps a Date, The	Louis Joseph Vance, Earl Felton, Sidney Salkow	1940
Lone Wolf Meets a Lady, The	Louis Joseph Vance, John Larkin, Sidney Salkow	1940
Lone Wolf Returns, The	Louis Joseph Vance, H. Grubb Alexander	1926
Lone Wolf Returns, The	Louis Joseph Vance, Joseph Krumgold, Bruce Manning, Lionel House	1936
Lone Wolf Spy Hunt, The	Louis Joseph Vance, Jonathan Latimer	1939
Lone Wolf Strikes, The	Louis Joseph Vance, Dalton Trumbo, Harry Segall, Albert Duffy	1940
Lone Wolf Takes a Chance, The	Louis Joseph Vance, Earl Felton, Sidney Salkow	1941
Lone Wolf's Daughter	Louis Joseph Vance, Seigfried Herzig	1929
Long Gray Line, The	Marty Maher, Nardi Reeder Campion, Edward Hope	1955

Title	Writer	Year
Long Haul, The	Mervyn Mills, Ken Hughes	1957
Long Ride Home, The	Nelson and Shirley Wolford, Halsted Welles	1967
Long Ships, The	Frans Bengtsson, Berkely Mather, Beverley Cross	1964
Looking Glass War, The	John Le Carre, Frank R. Pierson	1970
Lord Jim	Joseph Conrad, Richard Brooks	1965
Lords of Flatbush, The	Stephen F. Verona, Gayle Gleckler, Martin Davidson	1974
Lorna Doone	Richard D. Blackmore, Jesse L. Lasky, Jr., Richard Schayer, George Bruce	1951
Loss of Innocence	Rumer Godden, Howard Koch	1961
Lost Command, The	Jean Larteguy, Nelson Gidding	1966
Lost Horizon	James Hilton, Robert Riskin	1937
Lost Horizon	James Hilton, Larry Kramer	1973
Lost in the Desert	Jamie Hayes	1970
Lost One, The	Giuseppe Verdi, F. M. Piave, Hamilton Benz	1948
Lost Tribe, The	Arthur Hoerl, Don Martin	1949
Louisiana Hayride	Paul Yawitz, Manny Seff	1944
Love Affair	Ursula Parrott, Jo Swerling, Dorothy Howell	1932
Love and Pain and the Whole Damn Thing	Alvin Sargent	1973
Love Has Many Faces	Marguerite Roberts	1965
Love Machine, The	Jacqueline Susann, Samuel Taylor	1971
Love Me Forever	Victor Schertzinger, Jo Swerling, Sidney Buchman	1935
Love on a Pillow	Christiane Rochefort, Roger Vadim, Claude Choublier	1963
Love—Tahiti Style	Ennio de Concini, Franco Rossi	1963
Love-Ins, The	Hal Collins, Arthur Dreifuss	1967
Lover Come Back	Helen Topping Miller, Dorothy Howell	1931
Loves of Carmen, The	Prosper Merrimee, Helen Deutsch	1948
Lovin' Molly	Larry McMurtry, Stephen Friedman	1974
Loving	Don Devlin	1970
L-Shaped Room, The	Lynne Reid Banks, Bryan Forbes	1962
Lucky Legs	Stanley Rubin, Jack Hartfield	1942
Lulu Belle	Charles MacArthur, Edward Sheldon, Everett Freeman, Karl Kamb	1948
Lust for Gold	Barry Storm, Ted Sherdeman, Richard English	1949
Luv	Murray Schisgal, Elliott Baker	1967
M	Norman Reilly Raine, Leo Katcher, Waldo Salt	1951
Macbeth	William Shakespeare, Roman Polanski, Kenneth Tynan	1972
Machine Gun McCain	Mino Roli, Giuliano Montaldi	1970
Mackenna's Gold	Will Henry, Carl Foreman	1969
Mad Dog Coll	Leo Lieberman, Edward Schreiber	1961
Mad Magician, The	Crane Wilbur	1954
Mad Men of Europe	Guy Du Maurier, Ian Hay, Edward Knoblock, Dennis Wheatley	1940

405

TITLE	WRITER	YEAR OF RELEASE
Mad Room, The	Bernard Girard, A. C. Mantis	1969
Made in Italy	Ruggero Maccari, Ettore Scola	1967
Madonna of the Streets	W. B. Maxwell, Jo Swerling	1930
Magic Carpet, The	David Mathews	1951
Magic Face, The	Mort Briskin, Robert Smith	1951
Magic World of Topo Gigio, The	Mario Faustinelli, Guido Stagnaro, Maria Perego	1965
Maiden for a Prince, A	Pasquale Festa Campanile	1967
Main Event, The	Harold Shumate, Lee Loeb	1938
Major Dundee	Harry Julian Fink, Oscar Saul, Sam Peckinpah	1965
Make Believe Ballroom	Al Jarvis, Martin Block, Albert Duffy, Karen DeWolf	1949
Maker of Men	Howard J. Green, Edward Sedgwick	1932
Making the Headlines	Howard J. Green, Jefferson Parker	1938
Man against Woman	Keene Thompson, Jo Swerling	1932
Man Called Flintstone, The	R. S. Allen, Harvey Bullock	1966
Man Called Sledge, A	Vic Morrow	1971
Man for all Seasons, A	Robert Bolt	1966
Man from Colorado, The	Borden Chase, Robert D. Andrews, Ben Maddow	1948
Man from Laramie, The	Thomas T. Flynn, Philip Yordan, Frank Burt	1955
Man from Sundown, The	Paul Franklin	1939
Man from the Diner's Club	Bill Blatty, John Fenton Murray	1963
Man from Tumbleweeds, The	Charles F. Royal	1940
Man Inside, The	M. E. Chaber, David Shaw	1958
Man in the Dark	Tom Van Dycke, Henry Altimus, George Bricker, Jack Leonard	1953
Man in the Saddle	Ernest Haycox, Kenneth Gamet	1951
Man of Action	William Colt MacDonald, Robert Quigley	1933
Man on a String	Boris Morros, Charles Samuels, John Kafka, Virginia Shaler	1960
Man They Could Not Hang, The	George W. Sayre, Leslie White, Karl Brown	1939
Man Trailer, The	Lambert Hillyer	1934
Man Who Dared, The	Maxwell Shane, Alex Gottlieb, Edward Bock, Malcolm Stuart Boylan	1946
Man Who Lived Twice, The	Tom Van Dycke, Henry Altimus, Arthur Strawn, Fred Niblo, Jr.	1936
Man Who Returned to Life, The	Samuel W. Taylor, Gordon Rigby	1942
Man Who Turned to Stone, The	Raymond T. Marcus	1957
Man with Connections, The	Claude Berri	1971
Man with Nine Lives, The	Harold Shumate, Karl Brown	1940
Man's Castle	Lawrence Hazard, Jo Swerling	1933
Man's Game, A	Harold Shumate	1934
Man's World, A	Jack Roberts, George Bricker, Edward T. Love	1942
Manhattan Angel	George H. Plympton, Albert Derr	1948
Manhattan Shakedown	Theodore Tinsley, Edgar Edwards	1939
Maniac	Jimmy Sangster	1962
Mark of the Gorilla	Carroll Young	1950
Mark of the Whistler, The	Cornell Woolrich, George Bricker	1944

Marooned	Martin Caidin, Mayo Simon	1969
Marriage Came Tumbling Down, The	Catherine Payson, Albert Cossery, Jacques Poitrenaud	1968
Marriage Market, The	Evelyn Campbell, Jack Sturmwasser	1923
Married Woman, A	Jean-Luc Goddard	1965
Marrying Kind, The	Ruth Gordon, Garson Kanin	1952
Mary Lou	M. Coates Webster	1948
Mary of the Movies	Louis Lewyn	1923
Mary Ryan, Detective	Harry Fried, George Bricker	1949
Masculine Feminine	Guy de Maupassant, Jean-Luc Goddard	1966
Mask of the Avenger	George Bruce, Jesse Lasky, Jr., Ralph Bettinson, Philip MacDonald	1951
Massacre Canyon	David Lang	1954
Master of Men	Chester Erskin, Eugene Solow, Edward E. Paramore, Seton I. Miller	1933
Masterston of Kansas	Douglas Heyes	1955
Matinee Idol, The	Robert Lord, Ernest Pagano, Peter Milne	1928
Mating of Millie	Adele Comandini, Louella MacFarlane, St. Clair McKelway	1948
Matter of Days, A	Yves Ciampi	1969
Matter of Resistance, A	Jean-Paul Rapperea	1966
McKenna of the Mounted	Randall Faye, Stuart Anthony	1932
Me and the Colonel	Franz Werfel, S. N. Behrman, George Freoschel	1958
Medico of Painted Springs, The	James L. Ruble, Winston Miller, Wyndham Gittens	1941
Meet Boston Blackie	Jack Boyle, Jay Dratler	1941
Meet Me on Broadway	George Bricker, Jack Henley	1946
Meet Miss Bobby Socks	Muriel Roy Bolton	1944
Meet Nero Wolfe	Rex Stout, Howard J. Green, Bruce Manning, Joseph Anthony	1936
Meet the Stewarts	Elizabeth Dunn, Karen De Wolf	1942
Meet the Wife	Lynn Starling, F. McGrew Willis, Walter De Leon	1931
Mein Kampf	Adolph Hitler, Erwin Lester	1961
Melody Man, The	Howard J. Green, Herbert Fields, Richard Rodgers, Lorenz Hart	1930
Member of the Wedding	Carson McCullers, Edna and Edward Anhalt	1953
Menace, The	Edgar Wallace, Dorothy Howell, Roy Chanslor	1932
Men in Her Life	Warner Fabian, Robert Riskin, Dorothy Howell	1931
Men in Her Life, The	Lady Eleanor Smith, Frederick Kohner, Michael Wilson, Paul Trivers	1941
Men of the Hour	Anthony Coldeway	1935
Men of the Night	Lambert Hillyer	1934
Men without Law	Lew Seiler, Dorothy Howell	1930
Men without Souls	Harvey Gates, Robert D. Andrews, Joseph Carole	1940
Mexicali Rose	Gladys Lehman, Norman Houston	1930
Miami Expose	James B. Gordon	1956

TITLE	WRITER	YEAR OF RELEASE
Miami Story, The	Robert E. Kent	1954
Michael Kohlhaas	Edward Bond	1969
Mickey One	Alan Surgal	1961
Middle of the Night	Paddy Chayefsky	1959
Midnight Express, The	George W. Hill, Douglas Z. Doty	1924
Mi`itary Academy	Henry Taylor, Karl Brown, David Silverstein	1940
Military Academy with that 10th Ave. Gang	Howard J. Green	1950
Millerson Case, The	Gordon Rigby, Carlton Sand, Raymond L. Shrock	1947 1947
Millie's Daughter	Donald Henderson Clarke, Edward Huebsch	1947
Mills of the Gods	Melville Baker, John S. Kirkland, Garrett Fort	1935
Mind of Mr. Soames, The	John Hale, Edward Simpson	1970
Mine with the Iron Door, The	Harold Bell Wright, Don Swift, Daniel Jarrett	1936
Miracle Woman, The	Robert Riskin, John Meehan, Jo Swerling	1931
Miss Grant Takes Richmond	Everett Freeman, Nat Perrin, Devery Freeman, Frank Tashlin	1949
Miss Sadie Thompson	W. Somerset Maugham, Harry Kleiner	1953
Missing Daughters	Adele B. Buffington, Michael L. Simmons, George Bricker	1939
Missing Juror, The	Leon Abrams, Richard Hill Wilkinson, Charles O'Neal	1944
Missing Ten Days	Bruce Graeme, John Meehan, Jr., James Curtis	1941
Mission over Korea	Richard Tregaskis, Jesse L. Lasky, Jr., Eugene Ling, Martin M. Goldsmith	1953
Mr. Deeds Goes to Town	Clarence Budington Kelland, Robert Riskin	1936
Mr. District Attorney	Sidney Marshall, Ian McLellan Hunter, Ben Markson	1946
Mr. Sardonicus	Ray Russell	1961
Mr. Smith Goes to Washington	Lewis Ransom Foster, Sidney Buchman	1939
Mr. Soft Touch	Milton Holmes, Orin Jannings	1949
Mr. Winkle Goes to War	Theodore Pratt, Waldo Salt, George Corey, Louis Solomon	1944
Mob, The	Ferguson Findley, William Bowers	1951
Model Shop	Jacques Demy	1969
Modern Mothers	Peter Milne	1928
Montana Territory	Barry Shipman	1951
More than a Secretary	Matt Taylor, Dale Van Every, Lynn Starling	1937
More the Merrier, The	Robert Russell, Frank Ross, Richard Flournoy, Lewis R. Foster	1943
More to be Pitied than Scorned	Charles E. Blaney, Edward J. LeSaint	1923
Most Dangerous Man Alive	Phillip Rock, Michael Pate, James Leicester	1961
Most Precious Thing in Life	Travis Ingham, Ethel Hill, Dore Schary	1934
Mothra	Shinichuro Nakamura, Takehiko Fukunaga, Yoshie Hotta	1962

408

TITLE	WRITER	YEAR OF RELEASE
Motor Madness	Grace Neville, Fred Niblo, Jr.	1937
Mountain Road, The	Theodore White, Alfred Hayes	1960
Mouse that Roared, The	Leonard Wibberley, Roger McDougall, Stanley Mann	1959
Mule Train	Alan James, Gerald Geraghty	1950
Murder by Contract	Ben Simcoe	1958
Murder Czech Style	Jan Otcenasek, Jiri Weiss	1968
Murder in Greenwich Village	Robert T. Shannon, Michael L. Simmons	1937
Murder in Times Square	Stuart Palmer, Paul Gangelin	1943
Murder is News	Theodore A. Tinsley, Edgar Edwards	1939
Murder on the Roof	Edward Doherty, F. Hugh Herbert	1930
Murder Reported	Robert Chapman, Doreen Montgomery	1957
Murderers' Row	Donald Hamilton, Herbert Baker	1966
Music Goes Round, The	Sidney Buchman, Jo Swerling	1936
Music in My Heart	James Edward Grant	1940
Mussolini Speaks	Benito Mussolini, Lowell Thomas	1933
Mutations, The	Robert D. Weinbach, Edward Mann	1974
Mutineers, The	Don Gordon, Ben Bengal, Joseph Carole	1949
My Dog Buddy	Ray Kellogg	1960
My Dog Rusty	William Sackheim, Brenda Weisberg	1948
My Kingdom for a Cook	Lili Hatvany, Andrew Solt, Joseph Hoffman, Jack Henley, Harold Goldman	1943
My Name is Julia Ross	Anthony Gilbert, Muriel Roy Bolton	1945
My Sister Eileen	Ruth McKenney, Joseph Fields, Jerome Chodorov	1942
My Sister Eileen	Ruth McKenney, Joseph Fields, Jerome Chodorov, Blake Edwards, Richard Quine	1955
My Six Convicts	Donald Powell Wilson, Michael Blankfort	1952
My Son is a Criminal	Arthur T. Horman	1939
My Son is Guilty	Karl Brown, Harold Shumate, Joseph Carole	1940
My True Story	Margit Mantica, Howard J. Green, Brown Holmes	1951
My Woman	Brian Marlow	1933
Mysterious Avenger, The	Peter B. Kyne, Ford Beebe	1936
Mysterious Intruder	Eric Taylor	1946
Mysterious Island	Jules Verne, John Prebble, Daniel Ullman, Crane Wilbur	1962
Mysterious Witness	Eugene Manlove Rhodes	1923
Mystery of Thug Island	De Risi Arpad, Ottavio Poggi	1966
Mystery Ship	Alex Gottlieb, David Silverstein	1941
Name the Woman	Erle C. Kenton, Peter Milne	1928
Name the Woman	Frederick A. Thompson, Herbert Asbury, Fred Niblo, Jr.	1934
Naval Academy	Robert James Cosgriff, David Silverstein, Gordon Rigby	1941
Nebraskan, The	David Lang, Martin Berkeley	1953
Nevadan, The	George W. George George F. Slavin, Rowland Brown	1950

Title	Writer	Year of Release
Never Trust a Gambler	Jerome Odlum, Jesse L. Lasky, Jr.	1951
New Centurions, The	Joseph Wambaugh, Stirling Silliphant	1972
New Champion, The	Dorothy Howell	1925
New Interns, The	Richard Frede, Wilton Schiller	1964
New Orleans Uncensored	Orville H. Hampton, Lewis Meltzer	1955
Nicholas and Alexandra	Robert K. Massie, James Goldman	1972
Night Club Lady	Anthony Abbott, Robert Riskin	1932
Night Editor	Hal Burdick, Scott Littleton, Hal Smith	1946
Night Holds Terror, The	Andrew Stone	1955
Night Mayor, The	Sam Marx, Gertrude Purcell	1932
Night of Terror	Willard Mack, Beatrice Van, William Jacobs	1933
Night of the Generals, The	Hans Hellmut Kirst, Hadley Chase, Joseph Kessel, Paul Dehn	1967
Night Stage to Galveston	Norman S. Hall	1952
Night the World Exploded, The	Jack Netteford, Luci Ward	1957
Night to Remember, A	Kelley Roos, Richard Flournoy, Jack Henley	1942
Nights of Lucrezia Borgia, The	Mario Caino, Aldo Segri	1960
Nightfall	David Goodis, Stirling Silliphant	1956
Nine Girls	Wilfrid H. Petitt, Karen DeWolf, Connie Lee, Al Martin	1944
1984	George Orwell, William P. Templeton, Ralph Bettinson	1956
Ninth Guest, The	Gwen Bristow, Bruce Manning, Owen Davis, Garnett Weston	1934
No Greater Glory	Ferenc (Franz) Molnar, Jo Swerling	1934
No Greater Love	Isadore Bernstein	1932
No More Orchids	Grace Perkins, Gertrude Purcell, Keene Thompson	1932
No Place for a Lady	Eric Taylor	1942
No Sad Song for Me	Ruth Southard, Howard Koch	1950
No Time to be Young	John McPartland, Raphael Hayes	1957
No Time to Marry	Paul Gallico, Paul Jarrico	1938
No Sex, Please—We're British	Anthony Marriett, Alistair Foot, Johnny Mortimer, Brian Cooke	1975
Nobody's Children	Doris Malloy, Harry Sauber	1940
None Shall Escape	Alfred Neumann, Joseph Than, Lester Cole	1944
North from the Lone Star	Charles F. Royal	1941
North of Nome	Houston Branch, Albert Demond	1936
North of Shanghai	Harold Buchman, Maurice Rapf	1939
North of the Rockies	Herbert Dalmas	1942
North of the Yukon	Bennett R. Cohen	1939
Not a Ladies' Man	Robert Hyde, Rian James	1942
Nothing But the Best	Stanley Ellin, Frederic Raphael	1964
Nothing to Wear	Peter Milne	1928
Notorious Landlady, The	Margery Sharp, Larry Gelbart, Blake Edwards	1962
Notorious Lone Wolf, The	Louis Joseph Vance, William J. Bowers, Martin Berkeley, Edward Dein, Garrett Graham	1946

TITLE	WRITER	YEAR OF RELEASE
Obey the Law	Max Marcin	1926
Obey the Law	Harry Sauber, Arthur Caesar	1933
Object Alimony	Elmer Harris, Peter Milne	1929
Odessa File, The	Frederick Forsyth, Kenneth Ross, George Markstein	1974
Odongo	Islin Auster, John Gilling	1956
Officer and the Lady, The	Lambert Hillyer, Joseph Hoffman	1941
Okinawa	Arthur Ross, Jameson Brewer, Leonard Stern	1952
Oklahoma Crude	Marc Norman	1973
Old Dark House, The	J. B. Priestely, Robert Dillon	1963
Old West, The	Gerald Geraghty	1952
Old Wyoming Trail, The	J. Benton Cheney, Ed Earl Repp	1937
Oliver!	Charles Dickens, Lionel Bart	1968
Olympics in Mexico, The	(Unknown)	1969
On the Isle of Samoa	Joseph Santley, Brenda Weisberg, Harold Greene	1950
On Top of Old Smoky	Gerald Geraghty	1953
On The Waterfront	Budd Schulberg, Malcolm Johnson	1954
Once More, with Feeling	Harry Kurnitz	1960
Once to Every Woman	A. J. Cronin, Jo Swerling	1933
Once Upon A Time	Norman Corwin, Lucile Fletcher Herrmann, Lewis Meltzer, Oscar Saul	1944
One Dangerous Night	Louis Joseph Vance, Arnold Phillips, Max Nosseck, Donald Davis	1942
One Girl's Confession	Hugh Haas	1953
One Glorious Night	Harvey Gates, J. Grubb Alexander	1925
One is Guilty	Harold Shumate	1934
One Man Justice	William Colt MacDonald, Paul Perez	1937
One Man Law	Lambert Hillyer	1932
One Mysterious Night	Jack Boyle, Paul Yawitz	1944
One Night of Love	Dorothy Speare, Charles Beahan, Edmund North, James Gow, S. K. Lauren	1934
One Way Ticket	Ethel Turner, Vincent Lawrence, Joseph Anthony, Oliver H. P. Garrett, Grover Jones	1935
One Way to Love	Lester Lee, Larry Marks, Joseph Hoffman, Jack Henley	1945
One Way Trail, The	Claude Rister, George Plympton	1931
Only a Shop Girl	Charles E. Blaney, Edward J. LeSaint	1923
Only Angels Have Wings	Howard Hawks, Jules Furthman	1939
Only Two Can Play	Kingsley Amis, Bryan Forbes	1962
Open Season	David Osborne, Liz Charles Williams	1974
Opening Night, The	Albert Payson Terhune, Edward E. Griffith	1927
Operation Mad Ball	Arthur Carter, Jed Harris, Blake Edwards	1957
Operation X	Irene Nemirowsky, Robert Thoeren, William Rose	1950
Otley	Martin Waddell, Jan LeFranais, Dick Clement	1969

TITLE	WRITER	YEAR OF RELEASE
Our Man in Havana	Graham Greene	1960
Our Wife	Lillian Day, Lyon Mearson, P. J. Wolfson	1941
Out of the Depths	Aubrey Wisberg, Martin Berkeley, Ted Thomas	1946
Out West with the Peppers	Margaret Sidney, Harry Rebuas (Harry Sauber)	1940
Outcast of Black Mesa	Elmer Clifton, Barry Shipman	1950
Outlaw is Coming, The	Norman Maurer, Elwood Ullman	1965
Outlaw of the Orient	Ralph Graves, Charles Francis Royal, Paul Franklin	1937
Outlaws of the Panhandle	Paul Franklin	1941
Outlaws of the Prairie	Harry F. Olmstead, Ed Earl Repp	1938
Outlaws of the Rockies	J. Benton Cheney	1945
Outlaw Stallion, The	David Lang	1954
Outpost of the Mounties	Charles Francis Royal	1939
Outside These Walls	Ferdinand Reyher, Harold Buchman	1939
Outside the 3-Mile Limit	Eric Taylor, Albert Demond	1940
Over-Exposed	Richard Sale, Mary Loos, James Gunn, Gil Orlovitz	1956
Over the Santa Fe Trail	Eileen Gary, Louise Rousseau	1947
Over 21	Ruth Gordon Kanin, Sidney Buchman	1945
Overland Express	Monroe Shaff	1938
Overland to Deadwood	Paul Franklin	1942
Owl and the Pussycat, The	Bill Manhoff, Buck Henry	1970
Pacific Adventure	Ken G. Hall, Max Afford, John Chandler, Alex Coppel	1947
Pack Train	Norman S. Hall	1953
Pagan Lady	William DuBois, Benjamin Glazer	1931
Paid to Dance	Leslie T. White, Robert E. Cohen	1937
Pal Joey	John O'Hara, Richard Rodgers, Lorenz Hart, Dorothy Kingsley	1957
Pal O' Mine	Edith Kennedy, Jack Sturmwasser	1924
Palomino, The	Tom Kilpatrick	1950
Panic on the Air	Theodore Tinsley, Harold Shumate	1936
Parachute Nurse	Elizabeth Meehan, Rian James	1942
Paradise Lagoon	J. M. Barrie, Vernon Harris	1957
Paratrooper	Hillary St. George Saunders, Richard Maibaum, Frank Nugent	1953
Pardon My Gun	Wyndham Gittens	1942
Pardon My Past	Patterson McNutt, Harlan Ware, Earl Felton, Karl Kamb	1945
Parents on Trial	J. Robert Bren, Gladys Atwater, Lambert Hillyer	1939
Paris Model	Robert Smith	1953
Parole Girl	Norman Krasna	1933
Parole Racket	Barry Star, Harold Shumate, Owen Francis	1937
Parson and the Outlaw, The	Oliver Drake, John Mantley	1957
Party's Over, The	Daniel Kussell, S. K. Lauren	1934
Party Wire	Bruce Manning, John Howard Lawson, Ethel Hill	1935
Passion of the North	(Unknown)	1924
Passionate Friends	(Unknown)	1923

TITLE	WRITER	YEAR OF RELEASE
Passport to Alcatraz	Albert DeMond	1940
Passport to China	Gordon Wellesley	1961
Passport to Suez	Alden Nash, John Stone	1943
Pathfinder, The	James Fenimore Cooper, Robert E. Kent	1952
Paula	Larry Marcus, James Poe, William Sackheim	1952
Paying the Price	Leah Baird	1927
Payment in Blood	Tito Campi, E. G. Rowland	1968
Pecos River	Barry Shipman	1951
Pendulum	Stanley Niss	1969
Penitentiary	Martin Flavin, Seton I. Miller, Fred Niblo, Jr.	1938
Pennies from Heaven	Katherine Leslie Moore, William Rankin, Jo Swerling	1936
Penny Serenade	Martha Cheavena, Morrie Ryskind	1941
Pepe	L. Bush-Fekete, Dorothy Kingsley, Claude Binyon	1960
Perilous Holiday	Robert Carson, Roy Chanslor	1946
Personality	Gladys Lehman	1930
Personality Kid	Cromwell MacKechnie, Lewis Helmar Herman, William B. Sackheim	1946
Petty Girl, The	Mary McCarthy, Nat Perrin	1950
Phantom Gold	Nate Gatzert	1938
Phantom Stagecoach, The	David Lang	1957
Phantom Submarine, The	Augustus Muir, Joseph Krumgold	1941
Phantom Thief, The	Jack Boyle, G. A. Snow, Richard Wormser, Richard Weil, Malcolm Stuart Boylan	1946
Phantom Valley	J. Benton Cheney	1948
Phffft	George Axelrod	1955
Pickup	Joseph Kopta, Hugo Haas, Arnold Phillips	1951
Pickup Alley	A. J. Forrest, John Paxton	1957
Picnic	William Inge	1955
Pinto Kid, The	Fred Myton	1941
Pioneers of the Frontier	Fred Myton	1939
Pioneer Trail	Nate Gatzert	1938
Pirates of Blood River, The	Jimmy Sangster, John Hunter, John Gilling	1962
Pirates of Tripoli	Allen Marsh	1954
Platinum Blonde	Harry E. Chandlee, Douglas W. Churchill, Robert Riskin, Dorothy Howell, Jo Swerling	1931
Please Turn Over	Basil Thomas, Norman Hudis	1960
Pleasure before Business	William Branch, Earnest S. Pagano	1927
Police Car 17	Lambert Hillyer	1933
Poor Girls	Sophie Bogen, William Branch	1927
Porgy and Bess	Dubose Heyward, Dorothy Heyward, Ira Gershwin, N. Richard Nash	1959
Port Afrique	Bernard Victor Dryer, Frank Partos John Cresswell	1956
Port Said	Louis Pollock, Brenda Weisberg	1948

TITLE	WRITER	YEAR OF RELEASE
Power of the Press	Frederick A. Thompson, Sonya Levien	1928
Power of the Press	Sam Fuller, Robert D. Andrews	1943
Power of the Whistler, The	Aubrey Wisberg	1944
Prairie Gunsmoke	Jack Ganzhorn, Fred Myton	1942
Prairie Raiders	Ed Earl Repp	1947
Prairie Roundup	Joseph O'Donnell	1950
Prairie Schooners	George Cory Franklin, Robert Lee Johnson, Fred Myton	1940
Prairie Stranger	James Rubel, Winston Miller	1941
Prescott Kid, The	Claude Rister, Ford Beebe	1934
Price of Honor, The	Dorothy Howell	1927
Price She Paid, The	Lois Zellner	1924
Pride of the Marines	Gerald Beaumont, Harold Shumate	1936
Prince of Diamonds	Paul Hervey Fox, Gene Markey	1930
Prince of Pirates	William Copeland, Herbert Kline, John O'Dea, Samuel Newman	1952
Prince of Thieves, The	Alexandre Dumas, Maurice Tombragel, Charles H. Schneer	1947
Prison Ship	Joseph Mischel, Ben Markson	1945
Prison Warden	Eric Taylor	1949
Prisoner, The	Bridget Boland	1955
Prisoners of the Casbah	William Raynor, DeVallon Scott	1953
Prize of Gold, A	Max Catto, Robert Buckner, John Paxton	1955
Problem Girls	Aubrey Wisberg, Jack Pollexfen	1953
Professionals, The	Frank O'Rourke, Richard Brooks	1966
Psyche 59	Francoise des Ligneris, Julian Halevy	1964
Public Menace, The	Ethel Hill, Lionel Houser	1935
Pumpkin Eater, The	Penelope Mortimer, Harold Pinter	1964
Purple Heart Diary, The	Frances Langford, William Sackheim	1951
Pursuit of Happiness, The	Thomas Rogers, Jan Boothe, George L. Sherman	1971
Pushover	Thomas Walsh, William S. Ballinger, Roy Huggins	1954
Pygmy Island	Carroll Young	1950
Queen Bee	Edna Lee, Ranald MacDougall	1955
Queen of the Pirates	K. Nachman, R. Olsen, Nino Stresa	1961
Queens, The	Tenino Guerra, Giorgio Salveni, Rodolfo Senego, Ruggero Maccari, Luigi Magni	1967
Quick Gun, The	Steve Fisher, Robert E. Kent	1964
Quick on the Trigger	Elmer Clifton	1948
Quitter, The	Dorothy Howell	1929
R.P.M.	Erich Segal	1970
Racing for Life	Henry McRae	1924
Racing Luck	Joseph Carole, Al Martin, Harvey Gates	1948
Racket Man, The	Casey Robinson, Paul Yawitz, Howard J. Green	1944
Racketeers in Exile	Harry Sauber	1937
Rage	Jesus Velasquez, Guillermo Hernandez, Gilberto Gazcon, Teddi Sherman, Fernando Mendez	1966

414

Raiders of Tomahawk Creek	Robert Schaefer, Eric Freiwald, Barry Shipman	1950
Rain or Shine	James Gleason, Jo Swerling	1930
Rainbow 'Round My Shoulder	Blake Edwards, Richard Quine	1952
Raisin in the Sun, A	Lorraine Hansberry	1961
Range Feud, The	Milton Krims, George H. Plympton	1931
Ranger Courage	Nate Gatzert	1936
Rangers Step in, The	Joseph Levering, Nate Gatzert	1937
Ransom	George B. Seitz, Dorothy Howell	1928
Reach for Glory	John Rae, John Kohn, Jud Kinberg	1962
Reckless Moment, The	Elizabeth Sanxay Holding, Henry Garson, Robert W. Solderberg, Mel Dinelli, Robert E. Kent	1949
Reckless Ranger	Joseph Levering, J. A. Duffy Nate Gatzert	1937
Reckoning, The	John McGrath	1970
Red Lips	Giuseppe Bennati, Paola Levi	1963
Red Snow	Tom Hubbard, Orville Hampton, William Shaw	1952
Redhead from Manhattan	Rex Taylor, Joseph Hoffman	1943
Reflection of Fear, A	Edward Hume, Lewis John Carlino	1972
Reformatory	Gordon Rigby	1938
Relentless	Kenneth Perkins, Winston Miller	1948
Reluctant Saint, The	John Fante, Joseph Petracca	1962
Remember	Dorothy Perkins, J. Grubb Alexander	1926
Renegades, The	Harold Shumate, Melvin Levy, Francis Edward Faragoh	1946
Renegades of the Sage	Earle Snell	1949
Reprisal!	Arthur Gordon, David P. Harmon, Raphael Hayes, David Dortort	1956
Requiem for a Heavyweight	Rod Serling	1962
Restless Youth	Cosmo Hamilton, Howard J. Green	1929
Return of Daniel Boone, The	Paul Franklin, Joseph Hoffman	1941
Return of Monte Cristo, The	Alexandre Dumas, Curt Siodmak, Arnold Phillips, George Bruce, Alfred Neumann	1946
Return of October, The	Connie Lee, Karen DeWolf, Melvin Frank, Norman Panama	1948
Return of Rusty, The	Al Martin, Lewis Helmar Herman, William B. Sackheim	1946
Return of the Durango Kid, The	J. Benton Cheney	1944
Return of the Vampire	Kurt Neumann, Griffin Jay, Randall Faye	1943
Return of the Whistler, The	Cornell Woolrich, Edward Bock, Maurice Tombragel	1948
Return of Wild Bill, The	Walt Coburn, Robert Lee Johnson, Fred K. Myton	1940
Return to Warbow	Les Savage, Jr.	1958
Reveille with Beverly	Jean Ruth, Howard J. Green, Jack Henley, Albert Duffy	1943
Revenge of Frankenstein, The	Jimmy Sangster, Hurford Janes	1958
Revenge Rider, The	Ford Beebe	1935
Revenue Agent	William Sackheim, Arthur A. Ross	1950

415

TITLE	WRITER	YEAR OF RELEASE
Rustlers of the Badlands	Richard Hill Wilkinson, J. Benton Cheney	1945
Rusty Leads the Way	Al Martin, Nedrick Young, Arthur A. Ross	1948
Rusty Rides Alone	Walt Coburn, Robert Quigley	1933
Rusty Saves a Life	Al Martin, Brenda Weisberg	1948
Rusty's Birthday	Al Martin, Brenda Weisberg	1949
Sabotage Squad	Bernice Petkere, Wallace Sullivan, David Silverstein	1942
Saddle Leather Law	Elizabeth Beecher	1944
Saddles and Sagebrush	Ed Earl Repp	1943
Safari	Robert Buckner, Anthony Veiller	1956
Safe at Home!	Tom Naud, Steve Ritch, Robert Dillon	1962
Safe Place, A	Henry Jaglom	1971
Sagebrush Heroes	Luci Ward	1944
Saginaw Trail	Dorothy Yost, Dwight Cummins	1953
Sahara	Philips MacDonald, John Howard Lawson, Zolton Korda, James O'Hanlon	1944
Sail a Crooked Ship	Nathaniel Benchley, Ruth Brooks Flippen, Bruce Geller	1961
Sailor's Holiday	Manny Seff	1944
Sally in our Alley	Edward Clark, Dorothy Howell	1927
Salome	Jesse L. Lasky, Jr., Harry Kleiner	1953
Sandra	Suso Cecchi D'Amico, Enrico Medioli, Luchino Visconti	1966
Sante Fe	James Marshall, Louis Stevens Kenneth Gamet	1951
Saracen Blade, The	Frank Yerby, DeVallon Scott, George Worthing Yates	1954
Saturday Morning	(Unknown)	1971
Saturday's Hero	Millard Lampell, Sidney Buchman	1951
Savage Mutiny	Carroll Young, Sol Shor	1953
Say it with Sables	Frank Capra, Peter Milne, Dorothy Howell	1927
Scandal Sheet	Joseph Carole	1939
Scandal Sheet	Samuel Fuller, Ted Sherdeman, Eugene Ling, James Poe	1951
Scarlet Lady, The	Bess Meredith, John Goodrich	1928
Scream of Fear	Jimmy Sangster	1961
Screaming Mimi	Frederic Brown, Robert Blees	1958
Secret Command	John Hawkins, Ward Hawkins, Roy Chanslor	1944
Secret of St. Ives, The	Robert Louis Stevenson, Eric Taylor	1949
Secret of the Whistler, The	Richard H. Landau, Raymond L. Schrock	1946
Secret of Treasure Mountain	David Lang	1956
Secret Patrol	Peter B. Kyne, Robert Watson, J. P. McGowan	1936
Secret Seven, The	Dean Jennings, Robert Tasker	1940
Secret Witness, The	Samuel Spewack	1931
Secrets of the Lone Wolf	Louis Joseph Vance, Stuart Palmer	1941
See No Evil	Brian Clemens	1971
Seminole Uprising	Curt Brandon, Robert E. Kent	1955
Senior Prom	Hal Hackady	1959
Sergeant Mike	Robert Lee Johnson	1944

TITLE	WRITER	YEAR OF RELEASE
Serpent of the Nile	Robert E. Kent	1953
7 Guns for the McGregors	David Moreno, Fernand Lion, Vincent Eagle	1967
711 Ocean Drive	Richard English, Francis Swann	1950
1776	Sherman Edwards, Peter Stone	1972
7th Cavalry	Glendon F. Swarthout, Peter Packer	1956
7th Voyage of Sinbad, The	Kenneth Kolb	1958
Severed Head, A	Frederic Raphael	1971
Shadow, The	Milton Raison, Arthur T. Horman	1937
Shadow on the Window	John and Ward Hawkins, Leo Townsend, David P. Harmon	1956
Shadow Ranch	George M. Johnson, Clarke Silvernail, Frank Howard Clark	1930
Shadowed	Julian Harmon, Brenda Weisberg	1946
Shadows in the Night	Max Marcin, Eric Taylor	1944
Shadows of Sing Sing	Kathryn Scola, Doris Malloy, Albert DeMond	1934
Shakedown	Barry Shipman, Grace Neville	1936
Shampoo	Robert Towne	1975
Shamus	Barry Beckerman	1973
Shanghaied Love	Norman Springer, Roy Chanslor, Jack Cunningham	1931
She Couldn't Take It	Gene Towne, Graham Baker, Oliver H. P. Garrett	1935
She Has What It Takes	Robert Lee Johnson, Paul Yawitz	1943
She Knew all the Answers	Jane Allen (Jane Shore), Harry Segall, Kenneth Earl, Curtis Kenyon	1941
She Married an Artist	Avery Strakosch, Gladys Lehman, Delmar Daves	1937
She Married Her Boss	Thyra Samter Winslow, Sidney Buchman	1935
She Played with Fire	Winston Graham, Sidney Gilliat, Frank Launder, Val Valentine	1957
She Wouldn't Say Yes	Laslo Gorog, William Thiele, Virginia Van Upp, John Jacoby, Sarett Tobias	1945
She's a Soldier Too	Hal Smith, Melvin Levy	1944
She's a Sweetheart	Muriel Roy Bolton	1944
Ship of Fools	Katherine Anne Porter, Abby Mann	1965
Shockproof	Helen Deutsch, Samuel Fuller	1948
Shopworn	Sarah Y. Mason, Jo Swerling, Robert Riskin	1932
Shotgun Pass	Robert Quigley	1931
Shut My Big Mouth	Oliver Drake, Karen DeWolf, Francis Martin	1942
Siddhartha	Hermann Hesse, Conrad Rooks	1973
Sideshow, The	Howard J. Green	1929
Siege of the Saxons	John Kohn, Jud Kinberg	1963
Sierra Stranger	Richard J. Dorso	1957
Sign of the Ram, The	Margaret Ferguson, Charles Bennett	1948
Silencers, The	Donald Hamilton, Oscar Saal	1966
Silent Men	Walt Cobrun, Stuart Anthony,	1933
Silent World, The	Jacques-Yves Cousteau	1957
Silver Canyon	Alan James, Gerald Geraghty	1951
Silver City Raiders	Ed Earl Repp	1942

TITLE	WRITER	YEAR OF RELEASE
Sin, The	Iaia Fiastri, Antenio Guerra, Alberto Lattuada, Ruggero Maccari	1972
Sing for Your Supper	Harry Rebuas	1941
Sing Me a Song of Texas	J. Benton Cheney, Elizabeth Beecher	1944
Sing While You Dance	Lorraine Edwards, Robert Stephen Brode	1946
Singin' in the Corn	Richard Weil, Isabel Dawn, Monte Brice, Elwood Ullman	1946
Singin' Spurs	Barry Shipman	1948
Singing on the Trail	J. Benton Cheney	1946
Sinners' Parade	David Lewis, Beatrice Van	1928
Siren, The	Harold Shumate, Elmer B. Harris	1927
Siren of Bagdad	Robert E. Kent, Larry Rhine	1953
Sirocco	Joseph Kessel, A. I. Bezzerides, Hans Jacoby	1951
Sisters	Ralph Graves, Jo Swerling	1930
Sisters under the Skin	S. K. Lauren, Jo Swerling	1934
Six-Gun Law	Barry Shipman	1947
Sky Commando	Samuel Newman, William Sackheim, Arthur Orloff	1953
Sky Raiders, The	Harvey Gates	1931
Slaves of Babylon	DeVallon Scott	1953
Sleeping Beauty, The	Peter Ilych Tchaikovsky	1966
Slightly French	Herbert Fields, Karen DeWolf	1948
Smashing the Spy Ring	Dorrell and Stuart McGowan, Arthur T. Horman	1938
Smith of Minnesota	Robert D. Andrews	1942
Smoky Canyon	Barry Shipman	1951
Smoky Mountain Melody	Barry Shipman	1948
Smoky River Serenade	Barry Shipman	1947
Smuggler's Gold	Al Martin, Daniel Ullman	1951
Snafu	Louis Solomon, Harold Buchman	1945
Snake River Desperadoes	Barry Shipman	1951
Sniper, The	Edna and Edward Anhalt, Harry Brown	1952
Snorkel, The	Anthony Dawson, Peter Myers, Jimmy Sangster	1958
So Dark the Night	Aubrey Wisberg, Martin Berkeley, Dwight Babcock	1946
So This is Africa	Norman Krasna	1933
So This is Love	Norman Springer, Elmer Harris, Rex Taylor	1927
So You Won't Talk?	Harry Segall, Richard Flournoy	1940
Social Register	Anita Loos, John Emerson, James Creelman	1934
Soho Incident	Robert Westerby, Stuart Black	1956
Soldiers and Women	Paul Hervey Fox, George Tilton, Dorothy Howell	1930
Soldiers of the Storm	Thomson Burtis, Charles R. Condon	1933
Solid Gold Cadillac, The	George S. Kaufman, Howard Teichmann, Abe Burrows	1956
Something to Shout About	Fred Shiller, Lou Breslow, Edward Eliscu, George Owen	1942
Son of Davy Crockett, The	Lambert Hillyer	1941

TITLE	WRITER	YEAR OF RELEASE
Son of Dr. Jekyll, The	Mortimer Braus, Jack Pollexfen, Edward Huebsch	1951
Son of Rusty, The	Al Martin, Malcolm Stuart Boylan	1947
Song of Idaho	Barry Shipman	1948
Song of India	Jerome Odlum, Art Arthur, Kenneth Perkins	1949
Song of Love	Howard J. Green, Henry McCarty	1929
Song of the Prairie	J. Benton Cheney	1945
Song to Remember, A	Ernest Marischka, Sidney Buchman	1944
Song Without End	Oscar Millard	1960
Song You Gave Me, The	Clifford Grey	1934
Sons of New Mexico	Paul Gangelin	1949
Soul of the Monster, The	Edward Dein	1944
Sound Off	Blake Edwards, Richard Quine	1952
South of Arizona	Bennett R. Cohen	1938
South of Death Valley	James Gruen, Earle Snell	1949
South of the Chisholm Trail	Michael Simmons	1947
South of the Rio Grande	Harold Shumate, Milton Krim	1932
Southern Star, The	Jules Verne, David Pursall, Jack Sedden	1969
Special Delivery	Geza Radvanyi, Phil Reisman Jr., Dwight Taylor	1955
Speed Demon	Charles R. Condon	1932
Speed Mad	Dorothy Howell	1925
Speed to Spare	Bert Granet, Lambert Hillyer	1937
Speed Wings	Horace McCoy	1934
Spin a Dark Web	Robert Westerby, Ian Stuart Black	1956
Spirit of Stanford, The	William Brent, Nick Lukats, Howard J. Green	1942
Spoilers of the Range	Paul Franklin	1939
Sport of Kings	Gordon Grand, Edward Huebsch	1947
Sporting Age, The	Armand Kaliz, Elmer Harris, Peter Milne	1928
Squadron of Honor	Martin Mooney, Michael L. Simmons	1937
Square Shooter	Harold Shumate	1935
Squealer, The	Mark Linder, Dorothy Howell, Jo Swerling, Casey Robinson	1930
Stage Kisses	L. A. Brown, Dorothy Howell	1927
Stage to Tucson	Frank Bonham, Bob Williams, Frank Burt, Robert Libott	1950
Stagecoach Days	Nate Gatzert	1938
Stampede	Peter B. Kyne, Robert Watson	1936
Stand by all Networks	Maurice Tombragel, Doris Malloy, Robert Lee Johnson	1942
Stand Up and be Counted	Bernard Slade	1972
Stardust	Ray Connolly	1975
Stars on Parade	Monte Brice	1944
Start Cheering	Corey Ford, Eugene Solow, Richard Wormser, Philip Rapp	1938
State Penitentiary	Henry E. Helseth, Howard J. Green, Robert Libott, Frank Burt	1950
State Trooper	Lambert Hillyer, Stuart Anthony	1933

TITLE	WRITER	
Stepford Wives, The	Ira Levin, William Goldman	1975
Steppin' Out	George Verhouse	1925
Stolen Pleasures	Leah Baird	1927
Stone Killer, The	John Gardner, Gerald Wilson	1973
Stool Pigeon	Edward Meagher, Stuart Anthony	1928
Stop! Look! and Laugh!	Felix Adler, Edward Bernds, Clyde Bruckman, Monty Collins, Al Giebler, Thea Goodman, Searle Kramer, Zion Myers, Ellwood Ullman, Saul Ward. Jack White	1960
Stop Me Before I Kill	Ronald Scott Thorn, Val Guest	1961
Stork Pays Off, The	Fanya Foss, Aleen Leslie, Ned Dandy	1941
Storm Center	Daniel Taradash, Elick Moll	1956
Storm over the Nile	A. E. W. Mason, R. C. Sheriff, Lajos Biro, Arthur Wimperis	1956
Storm over Tibet	George Zukerman, Norman Corwin	1952
Story of Esther Costello, The	Nicholas Monsarrat, Charles Kaufman	1957
Straightaway	Lambert Hillyer	1934
Strait-Jacket	Robert Bloch	1963
Strange Affair	Oscar Saul, Eve Greene, Jerome Odlum, Jack Henley	1944
Strange Case of Dr. Meade, The	Gordon Rigby, Carlton Sand	1938
Strange Fascination	Hugo Haas	1952
Strange One	Calder Willingham	1957
Stranger from Arizona	Monroe Shaff	1938
Stranger from Ponca City	Ed Earl Repp	1947
Stranger from Texas, The	Ford Beebe, Paul Franklin	1939
Stranger Wore a Gun, The	John M. Cunningham, Kenneth Gamet	1953
Strangers When We Meet	Evan Hunter	1960
Stranglers of Bombay, The	David Z. Goodman	1960
Strawberry Roan, The	Julian Zimet, Dwight Cummins, Dorothy Yost	1948
Street of Illusion	Channing Pollock, Harvey Thew, Dorothy Howell	1928
Streets of Ghost Town	Barry Shipman	1950
Submarine	Norman Springer	1928
Submarine Raider	Aubrey Wisberg	1947
Subway Express	Eva Kay Flint, Martha Madison, Earle Snell, Dorothy Howell	1931
Such a Gorgeous Kid Like Me	Henry Farrell, Francois Truffaut, Jean-Loup Dabadie	1973
Sucker, The	Gerald Oury, Marcel Julien, Georges Andre Tabet	1966
Suddenly, Last Summer	Tennessee Williams, Gore Vidal	1960
Suicide Mission	David Howarth, Sydney Cole, Michael Forlong	1956
Summer Wishes, Winter Dreams	Stewart Stern	1973
Summertree	Ron Cowen, Edward Hume, Stephene Yafa	1971
Sundays and Cibele	Bernard Eschasseriaux, Serge Bourguignon, Antoine Tudal	1963
Sundown Rider	John T. Neville, Lambert Hillyer	1933

TITLE	WRITER	YEAR OF RELEASE
Sundown Valley	Luci Ward	1944
Sunny Side of the Street	Harold Conrad, Lee Loeb	1951
Superargo vs. Diabolicus	Mino Giardia, Jesus Balcazar	1968
Superspeed	Harold Shumate	1935
Surprise Package	Art Buchwald, Harry Kurnitz	1960
Swan Lake	Peter Illych Tschaikovsky, A. Messerer, Z. Tulubyeva	1960
Swedish Wedding Night	Lars Widding	1965
Sweet Genevieve	Jameson Brewer, Arthur Dreifuss	1947
Sweet Rosie O' Grady	Maude Nugent, Harry O. Hoyt Dorothy Howell	1926
Sweetheart of the Campus	Robert Andrews, Edmund Hartmann	1941
Sweetheart of the Fleet	Albert Duffy, Maurice Tombragel	1942
Sweethearts on Parade	Al Cohn, Jimmy Starr	1930
Swell Head, The	Robert Lord	1927
Swell-Head	Gerald Beaumont, William Jacobs	1935
Swimmer, The	John Cheever, Eleanor Perry	1968
Swing in the Saddle	Maurice Leo, Elizabeth Beecher, Morton Grant, Bradford Ropes	1944
Swing out the Blues	Doris Malloy, Dorcas Cochran, Rene Du Plessis	1943
Swing the Western Way	Bert Horswell, Barry Shipman	1947
Swingin' Maiden, The	Harold Brooke, Kay Bannerman, Vivian Cox, Leslie Bricusse	1964
Sword of Sherwood Forest	Alan Hackney	1961
Swordsman, The	Wilfrid Petitt	1947
Synanon	Barry Gringer, S. Lee Pogostin, Ian Bernard	1965
Tahiti Nights	Lillie Hayward	1945
Tainted Money	Stuart Payton	1924
Take, The	G. F. Newman, Del Reisman, Franklin Coen	1974
Take a Girl Like You	Kingsley Amis, George Melly	1970
Talk about a Lady	Robert D. Andrews, Barry Trivers, Richard Weil, Ted Thomas	1946
Talk of the Town, The	Sidney Harmon, Irwin Shaw, Dale Van Every, Sidney Buchman	1942
Tall T, The	Elmore Leonard, Burt Kennedy	1957
Taming of the Shrew, The	William Shakespeare, Paul Dehn, Suso Cecchi D'Amico, Franco Zeffirelli	1967
Taming of the West	Robert Lee Johnson, Charles Francis Royal	1939
Tank Force!	Richard Maibaum, Terence Young	1958
Tarawa Beachhead	Richard Alan Simmons	1958
Target Hong Kong	Herbert Purdum	1953
Tars and Spars	Barry Trivers, John Jacoby, Sarett Tobias, Decla Dunning	1946
Teen-Age Crime Wave	Ray Buffum, Harry Essex	1955
Tell it to The Judge	Devery Freeman, Nat Perrin, Roland Kibbee	1949
Temptation	Lenore Coffee, Edward J. Lesaint	1923
Temptation	Leonard Praskins	1930

TITLE	WRITER	YEAR OF RELEASE
Ten Cents a Dance	Lorenz Hart, Richard Rodgers, Jo Swerling, Dorothy Howell	1931
Ten Cents a Dance	Morton Grant	1945
10 Rillington Place	Clive Exton	1971
Ten Tall Men	James Warner Bellah, Willis Goldbeck, Roland Kibbee, Dorothy Howell	1951
Ten Wanted Men	Irving Ravetch, Harriet Frank, Jr., Kenneth Gamet	1955
Terrace, The	Beatriz Guido	1965
Terror of the Tongs, The	Jimmy Sangster	1961
Terror of Tuny Town, The	Fred Myton	1938
Terror Trail	Ed Earl Repp	1946
Texan Meets Calamity Jane, The	Ande Lamb	1950
Texans Never Cry	Norman S. Hall	1951
Texas	Michael Blankfort, Lewis Meltzer, Horace McCoy	1941
Texas Cyclone, The	William Colt MacDonald, Randall Faye	1932
Texas Dynamo	Barry Shipman	1950
Texas Panhandle	Ed Earl Repp	1945
Texas Ranger, The	Forest Sheldon	1931
Texas Rangers, The	Frank Gruber, Richard Schayer	1951
Texas Stagecoach	Fred Myton	1940
Texas Stampede	Charles F. Royal	1939
Thank You all Very Much	Margaret Drabble	1969
That Certain Thing	Elmer Harris	1927
That Man in Istanbul	George Simonelli, Nat Wachsberger	1966
That Texas Jamboree	Paul Gangelin, J. Benton Cheney	1946
That's Gratitude	Frank Craven	1934
That's My Boy	Francis Wallace, Norman Krasna	1932
Theodora Goes Wild	Mary McCarthy, Sidney Buchman	1936
There's a Girl in My Soup	Terence Frisby	1970
There's Always a Woman	Wilson Collison, Gladys Lehman	1938
There's Something About a Soldier	Horace McCoy, Barry Trivers	1944
There's that Woman Again	Wilson Collison, Gladys Lehman, Philip G. Epstein, James Edward Grant, Ken Englund	1939
These Are the Damned	H. L. Lawrence, Evan Jones	1965
They all Kissed the Bride	Gina Kaus, Andrew Solt, P. J. Wolfson, Henry Altimus	1942
They Came to Cordura	Glendon Swarthout, Ivan Moffat, Robert Rossen	1959
They Dare Not Love	James Edward Grant, Charles Bennett, Ernest Vajda	1941
They Live in Fear	Hilda Stone, Ruth Nussbaum, Wilfrid Pettitt, Michael Simmons, Sam Ornitz	1944
They Met in a Taxi	Octavus Roy Cohen, Howard J. Green	1936
They Rode West	Leo Katcher, DeVallon Scott, Frank Nugent	1955
Thief of Damascus, The	Robert E. Kent	1952
Things of Life, The	Paul Guimond, Jean-Loup Dabadie, Claude Sautet	1970

TITLE	WRITER	YEAR OF RELEASE
13 Frightened Girls	Otis L. Guernsey, Jr., Robert Dillon	1962
13 Ghosts	Robb White	1960
13 West Street	Leigh Brackett, Bernard C. Schoenfeld, Robert Presnell, Jr.	1962
Thirteenth Hour, The	Leslie Edgley, Edward Bock, Rayond L. Schrock	1947
30 Foot Bride of Candy Rock, The	Lawrence L. Goldman, Rowland Barber, Arthur Ross	1959
30 is a Dangerous Age, Cynthia	Dudley Moore, Joseph McGrath, John Wells	1968
This Angry Age	Marguerite Duras, Irwin Shaw, Rene Clement	1958
This Sporting Age	James K. McGuinness, Dudley Nichols	1932
This Thing Called Love	Edwin Burke, George Seaton, Ken Englund, P. J. Wolfson	1941
Thomasine and Bushrod	Max Julien	1974
Those High Grey Walls	William A. Ullman, Jr., Louis Meltzer, Gladys Lehman	1939
1001 Arabian Nights	Czenzi Ormondos, Dick Shaw, Dick Kinney, Leo Salkin, Pete Burness, Lew Keller, Ed Nofziger, Ted Allan, Margaret Schneider, Paul Schneider	1959
Thousand and One Nights, A	Wilfrid H. Pettit, Richard English, Jack Henley	1945
Three for the Show	W. Somerset Maugham, Edward Hope, Leonard Stern	1954
Three Girls about Town	Richard Carroll	1941
Three Hours to Kill	Alex Gottlieb, Richard Alan Simmons, Roy Huggins, Maxwell Shane	1954
Three on a Couch	Arne Sultan, Marvin Worth, Bob Ross, Samuel A. Taylor	1966
Three Stooges Go around the World in a Daze, The	Norman Maurer, Elwood Ullman	1964
Three Stooges in Orbit, The	Norman Maurer, Elwood Ullman	1962
Three Stooges Meet Hercules, The	Norman Maurer, Elwood Ullman	1962
Three Stripes in the Sun	E. J. Kahn, Jr., Richard Murphy, Albert Duffy	1955
3:10 to Yuma	Elmore Leonard, Halsted Welles	1957
Three Wise Girls	Wilson Collison, Robert Riskin, Agnes C. Johnston	1932
Three Worlds of Gulliver, The	Jonathan Swift, Arthur Ross, Jack Sher	1960
Thrill Hunter, The	Harry O. Hoyt	1933
Thrill of Brazil, The	Joseph Hoffman, Jack Henley, Allen Rivkin, Harry Clork, Devery Freeman	1946
Throw a Saddle on a Star	J. Benton Cheney	1946
Thunder at the Border	David De Reszke, C. B. Taylor	1967
Thunder over the Prairie	James L. Rubel, Betty Burbridge	1941
Thunderhoof	Hal Smith, Kenneth Gamet	1948
Thundering Frontier, The	Paul Franklin	1940
Thundering West, The	Bennett R. Cohen	1939
Tiger Makes Out, The	Murray Schisgal	1967
Tight Spot	Leonard Kantor, William Bowers	1955

TITLE	WRITER	YEAR OF RELEASE
Tigress, The	Harold Shumate	1927
Tijuana Story	Lou Morheim	1957
Tillie the Toiler	Russ Westover, Karen DeWolf, Francis J. Martin	1941
Time for Killing, A	Nelson and Shirley Wolford, Halstead Welles	1967
Time Out for Rhythm	Bert Granet, Edmund L. Hartmann, Bert Lawrence	1941
Tingler, The	Robb White	1959
To Find a Man	S. J. Wilson, Arnold Schulman	1972
To Sir, With Love	Edward Ricardo Braithwaite, James Clavell	1967
To the Ends of the Earth	Jay Richard Kennedy	1948
Together Again	Stanley Russell, Herbert Biberman, Virginia Van Upp, F. Hugh Herbert	1944
Together We Live	Willard Mack	1935
Tokyo Joe	Steve Fisher, Cyril Hume, Bertram Millhauser, Walter Doniger	1949
Tol' able David	Joseph Hergesheimer, Benjamin Glazer	1930
Tommy	The Who, Ken Russell	1975
Tonight and Every Night	Lesley Storm, Lesser Samuels, Abem Finkel	1945
Too Many Husbands	W. Somerset Maugham, Claude Binyon	1940
Too Tough to Kill	Robert D. Speers, Lester Cole, J. Griffin Jay	1935
Torero!	Hugo Mozo, Carlos Velo	1957
Tornado in a Saddle, A	Charles F. Royal	1942
Torture Garden	Robert Bloch	1967
Tougher They Come, The	George Bricker	1950
Town on Trial	Robert Westerby, Ken Hughes	1957
Traffic	Jacques Tati	1973
Traffic in Hearts	Dorothy Yost, Jack Sturmwasser	1924
Trail of Broken Hearts	(Unknown)	1924
Trail of the Rustlers	Victor Arthur	1950
Trail to Laredo	Barry Shipman	1948
Traitors' Gate	Edgar Wallace, John Sanson	1966
Tramp, Tramp, Tramp	Shannon Day, Hal Braham, Marian Grant, Harry Rebuas, Ned Dandy	1942
Trapped	Claude Rister, John B. Rathmell	1937
Trapped by Boston Blackie	Charles R. Marion, Edward Bock, Maurice Tombragel	1948
Trapped by G-Men	Bernard McConville, Tom Kilpatrick	1937
Trapped by Television	Sherman Lowe, Al Martin, Lee Loeb, Harold Buchman	1936
Trapped in the Sky	Eric Taylor, Gordon Rigby	1939
Traveling Saleswoman, The	Howard Dimsdale	1949
Treason	Gordon Battle	1933
Trial Marriage	Elizabeth Alexander, Sonya Levien	1929
Triple Threat	Joseph Carole, Don Martin	1948

TITLE	WRITER	YEAR OF RELEASE
Trouble in Morocco	J. D. Newsom, Paul Franklin	1937
Trouble with Angels, The	Jane Trahey, Blanche Hanalis	1966
True Glory, The	S/Sgt. Guy Trosper, Pvt. Harry Brown, Sgt. Saul Levitt (Army of the United States); Lt. Col. Eric Maschwitz, Pvt. Peter Ustinov, Capt. Frank Harvey (British Army); Flt./Lt. Arthur Macrae (R.A.F.)	1946
True Story of Lynn Stuart, The	Pat Michaels, John H. Kneubuhl	1958
Trunk, The	Edward and Valerie Abraham, Donovan Winter	1961
Truthful Sex, The	Albert Shelby LeVine	1926
Tugboat Princess	Dalton Trumbo, Isador Bernstein, Robert Watson	1936
12 to the Moon	Fred Gebhardt, Dewitt Bodeen	1960
Twentieth Century	Charles Bruce Millholland, Ben Hecht, Charles MacArthur	1934
20 Million Miles to Earth	Charlott Knight, Bob Williams, Christopher Knopf	1957
21 Days Together	John Galsworthy, Basil Dean, Graham Green	1940
27th Day	John Mantley	1957
Twist Around the Clock	James B. Gordon	1961
Two Blondes and a Redhead	Harry Rebuas, Victor McLeod, Jameson Brewer	1947
Two in a Taxi	Howard J. Green, Morton Thompson, Malvin Wald	1941
Two Latins from Manhattan	Albert Duffy	1941
Two of a Kind	James Edward Grant, Lawrence Kimble, James Gunn	1951
Two Rode Together	Will Cook, Frank Nugent	1961
Two Senoritas from Chicago	Steven Vas, Stanley Rubin, Maurice Tombragel	1943
Two Tickets to Paris	Hal Hackady	1962
Two Yanks in Trinidad	Sy Bartlett, Richard Carroll, Harry Segall	1942
Two-Fisted Gentleman	Tom Van Dycke	1936
Two-Fisted Law	William Colt MacDonald, Kurt Kempler	1932
Two-Fisted Rangers	Fred Myton	1939
Two-Fisted Sheriff	William Colt MacDonald, Paul Perez	1937
Two-Fisted Stranger	Paul Whitehead, Robert Lee Johnson	1946
Two-Gun Law	Norman Sheldon, John B. Rathmell	1937
Two-Headed Spy, The	J. Alvin Kugelmass, James O'Donnel!	1959
Two-Man Submarine	Bob Williams, Griffin Jay, Leslie T. White	1944
Tyrant of the Sea	Robert Libott, Frank Burt	1950
U-Boat Prisoner	Archie Gibbs, Aubrey Wisberg, Malcolm Stuart Boylan	1944
U-Boat 29	J. Storer Clouston, Emeric Pressburger, Roland Pertwee	1939
Under Age	Stanley Roberts, Robert D. Andrews	1941
Under Suspicion	Philip Wylie, Joseph Hoffman, Jefferson Parker	1937

Under the Yum Yum Tree	Lawrence Roman, David Swift	1963
Undercover Man, The	Frank J. Wilson, Jack Rubin, Sidney Boehm, Marvin Wald	1949
Underground Agent	J. Robert Bren, Gladys Atwater	1942
Underwater City, The	Owen Harris	1962
Underworld, U. S. A.	Samuel Fuller	1961
Unknown, The	Carleton E. Morse, Malcolm Stuart Boylan, Julian Harmon	1946
Unknown Ranger	Nate Gatzert	1936
Unknown Valley	Donald W. Lee, Lambert Hillyer	1933
Unknown Woman	W. Scott Darling, Albert DeMond, Fred Niblo, Jr.	1935
Untamed Breed, The	Eli Colter, Tom Reed	1948
Unwelcome Stranger, The	William Jacobs, Crane Wilbur	1935
Unwritten Code, The	Charles Kenyon, Robert Wilmot, Leslie T. White	1944
Up the McGregors	Fernand di Leo, Enzo Dell'Aquilo, Paola Levi, Jose Maria Rodriguez, Nina Baragli	1967
Uranium Boom	George F. Slavin, George W. George, Norman Retchin	1956
Utah Blaine	Louis L'Amour, Robert E. Kent, James B. Gordon	1956
Valachi Papers, The	Peter Maas, Stephen Geller	1973
Valentino	George Bruce	1951
Valley of Fire	Earle Snell, Gerald Geraghty	1951
Valley of Head Hunters	Samuel Newman	1953
Valley of the Dragons	Jules Verne, Edward Bernds	1961
Vanity Street	Frank Cavett, Edward Roberts, Gertrude Purcell	1932
Vengeance	Ralph Graves, F. Hugh Herbert	1930
Vengeance of the West	Jack Townley, Luci Ward	1942
Venus Makes Trouble	Michael L. Simmons	1937
Verboten!	Samuel Fuller	1959
Victors, The	Alexander Baron, Carl Foreman	1964
Vigilantes Ride, The	Ed Earl Repp	1934
Violent Men, The	Donald Hamilton, Harry Kleiner	1954
Virgin Lips	Charles Beahan, Harvey Thew, Dorothy Howell	1928
Virgin Soldiers, The	Leslie Thomas, John Hopkins	1970
Virtue	Ethel Hill, Robert Riskin	1932
Voice in the Night	Harold Shumate	1934
Voice of the Whistler	Allen Rader, Wilfrid Pettit, William Castle	1945
Voodoo Tiger	Samuel Newman	1952
Wackiest Ship in the Army, The	Herbert Carlson, Richard Murphy	1960
Wagon Team	Gerald Geraghty	1952
Walk a Crooked Mile	Bertram Millhauser, George Bruce	1948
Walk, Don't Run	Robert Russell, Frank Ross, Sol Saks	1966
Walk East on Beacon	J. Edgar Hoover, Leo Rosten	1952
Walk in the Spring Rain, A	Rachel Maddux, Stirling Silliphant	1970
Walk on the Wild Side	Nelson Algren, John Fante, Edmund Morris	1962
Walking Hills, The	Alan LeMay, Virginia Roddick	1949

TITLE	WRITER	YEAR OF RELEASE
Wall Street	Paul Gangelin, Jack Kirkland, Norman Houston	1929
Walls Came Tumbling Down, The	Jo Eisinger, Wilfrid H. Pettit	1946
Wandering Girls	Dorothy Howell	1927
War Correspondent	Keene Thompson, Jo Swerling	1932
War Lover, The	John Hersey, Howard Koch	1962
Warning, The	Lilian Ducey, H. Milnor Kitchin, George B. Seitz	1927
Warrior and the Slave Girl, The	Ennio de Concini, Francesco de Leo, Gian Paolo Callezari	1959
Warrior Empress, The	Pietro Francisci, Ennio De Concini, Luciano Martino	1961
Washington Merry Go Round	Maxwell Anderson, Jo Swerling, Eugene Thackray	1932
Watch it, Sailor	Philip King, Falkland Carey	1962
Watermelon Man	Herman Raucher	1970
Wattstax	(Unknown)	1973
Way of the Strong, The	William Counselman, Peter Milne	1927
Way We Were, The	Arthur Laurents	1973
We Were Strangers	Robert Sylvester, Peter Viertel, John Huston	1949
Weekend with Lulu, A	Ted Lloyd, Val Valentine	1927
Welcome to the Club	Clement Biddle Wood	1971
We'll Bury You	Jack Thomas	1962
Werewolf, The	Robert E. Kent, James B. Gordon	1956
West of Abilene	Paul Franklin	1940
West of Cheyenne	Ed Earl Repp	1938
West of Dodge City	Bert Horswell	1947
West of Sonora	Barry Shipman	1948
West of the Santa Fe	Bennett R. Cohen	1938
West of Tombstone	Maurice Geraghty	1942
Westbound Mail	James P. Hogan, Frances Guihan	1937
Western Caravans	Bennett R. Cohen	1939
Western Code, The	William Colt MacDonald, Milton Krims	1932
Western Courage	Charles Francis Royal, Nate Gatzert	1936
Western Frontier	Ken Maynard, Nate Gatzert	1935
Westerner, The	Walt Coburn, Harold Shumate	1935
What a Woman	Erik Charell, Therese Lewis, Barry Trivers	1943
What Price Innocence	Willard Mack	1933
What's Buzzin', Cousin?	Aben Kandel, Harry Sauber, John P. Medbury	1943
When a Girl's Beautiful	Henry K. Moritz, Brenda Weisberg	1947
When G-Men Step In	Arthur T. Horman, Robert Chalmers Bennett	1938
When Strangers Marry	Maximilian Foster, James Kevin McGuinness	1933
When the Redskins Rode	James Fenimore Cooper, Robert E. Kent	1951
When the Wife's Away	Douglas Bronston	1926
When You're in Love	Ethel Hill, Cedric Worth, Robert Riskin	1937
When You're Smiling	Karen DeWolf, John R. Roberts	1950
Where Angels Go—Trouble Follows!	Jane Trahey, Blanche Hanalis	1968

TITLE	WRITER	YEAR OF RELEASE
Whirlpool	Howard Emmett Rogers, Ethel Hill, Dorothy Howell	1934
Whirlwind, The	Walt Coburn, Stuart Anthony	1933
Whirlwind	Norman S. Hall	1951
Whirlwind Raiders	Norman S. Hall	1948
Whispering Enemies	John Rawlins, Harold Tarshis, Gordon Rigby, Tom Kilpatrick	1939
Whistle at Eaton Falls, The	J. Sterling Livingston, Lemist Esler, Virginia Shaler, Leo Rosten	1951
Whistler, The	J. Donald Wilson, Eric Taylor	1944
White Lies	Harold Shumate	1934
White Squaw, The	Larabie Sutter, Les Savage, Jr.	1956
Who Cares	Douglas Z. Doty	1925
Who Killed Gail Preston?	Fred Pederson, Henry Taylor, Robert E. Kent	1938
Who Was That Lady?	Norman Krasna	1960
Whole Town's Talking, The	W. R. Burnett, Jo Swerling, Robert Riskin	1935
Whole Truth, The	Philip Mackie, Jonathan Latimer	1958
Whom the Gods Destroy	Albert Payson Terhune, Sidney Buchman	1934
Who's Minding the Mint?	R. S. Allen, Harvey Bullock	1967
Why Women Remarry	Van A. James	1924
Wicked as They Come	Bill Ballinger, Ken Hughes	1956
Wide Open Faces	Richard Flournoy, Earle Snell, Clarence Marks, Joe Bigelow	1938
Wife Takes a Flyer, The	Gina Kaus, Jay Dratler, Harry Segall	1942
Wife's Relations, The	Adolph Unger, Stephen Cooper	1928
Wildcat of Tucson, The	Fred Myton	1941
Wild One, The	Frank Rooney, John Paxton	1953
Wild Westerner, The	Gerald Drayson Adams	1962
Winnebago	Karl May, H. C. Petersson	1965
Winning of the West	Norman S. Hall	1952
Winter A-Go-Go	Reno Carell, Bob Kanter	1965
Woman Against the World	Edgar Edwards	1938
Woman Eater, The	Brandon Fleming	1959
Woman from Tangier, The	Irwin Franklyn	1948
Woman I Stole	Joseph Hergesheimer, Jo Swerling	1933
Woman in Distress	Edwin Olmstead, Albert DeMond	1937
Woman in Question, The	John Presswell	1951
Woman is the Judge, A	Karl Brown	1939
Woman of Distinction, A	Ian McLellan Hunter, Hugo Butler, Charles Hoffman, Frank Tashlin	1950
Woman of the River	Alberto Moravia, Ennio Flaiano, Basillo Franchina, Giorgio Bassani, Pier Paolo Pasolini, Florestano Vancini, Antonio Altoviti, Mario Soldati	1957
Woman's Way, A	Izola Forrester, Elmer Harris, Will M. Ritchie	1928
Women First	Wilfrid Lucas	1924
Women in Prison	Mortimer Braus, Saul Elkins	1937
Women of Glamour	Milton Herbert Gropper, Lynn Starling, Mary C. McCall, Jr.	1937

TITLE	WRITER	YEAR OF RELEASE
Women's Prison	Jack DeWitt, Crane Wilbur	1955
World Was His Jury, The	Herbert Abbott Spiro	1958
World Without Sun	James Dugan	1964
Wreck, The	Dorothy Howell, Arthur Statter, Mary Alice Scully	1927
Wreck of the Hesperus, The	Henry W. Longfellow, Edward Huebsch, Aubrey Wisberg	1948
Wrecker, The	Albert Rogell, Jo Swerling	1933
Wrecking Crew, The	Donald Hamilton, William McGivern	1969
Wrong Box, The	Robert Louis Stevenson, Lloyd Osburne, Larry Gelbart, Bert Shevelove	1966
Wyoming Hurricane	Fred Myton	1943
Wyoming Renegades	David Lang	1955
X, Y & Zee	Edna O'Brien	1971
Yank in Indo-China	Samuel Newman	1952
Yank in Korea, A	Leo Lieberman, William Sackheim	1951
Yesterday's Enemy	Peter R. Newman	1959
Yesterday's Wife	Evelyn Campbell, Edward J. Le Saint	1924
You Belong to Me	Dalton Trumbo, Claude Binyon	1941
You Can't Run away from It	Samuel Hopkins Adams, Claude Binyon, Robert Riskin	1956
You Can't Take It with You	George Kaufman, Moss Hart, Robert Riskin	1938
You Can't Win 'Em All	Leo V. Gordon	1970
You May be Next	Henry Wales, Ferdinand Reyher, Fred Niblo, Jr.	1936
You Must Be Joking	Alan Hackney, Michael Winner	1965
You Were Never Lovelier	Carlos Olivari, Sixto Pondal Rios, Michael Fessier, Ernest Pagano, Delmer Daves	1942
You'll Never Get Rich	Bogart Rogers, Arthur Caesar, Michael Fessier, Ernest Pagano	1941
Young Americans	Alex Grasshoff	1967
Young Don't Cry, The	Richard Jessup	1957
Young Land, The	John Reese, Norman Shannon Hall	1959
Young One, The	Peter Matthiessen, H. B. Addis, Luis Bunuel	1960
Young Winston	Winston K. Churchill, Carl Foreman	1972
Younger Generation	Fannie Hurst, Sonya Levien	1929
Youth on Trial	Michael Jacoby	1945
Zarak	A. J. Bevan, Richard Maibaum	1956
Zex!	Charles Eric Maine	1959
Zombies of Mora-Tau	George Plympton, Raymond T. Marcus	1957
Zotz!	Walter Karig, Ray Russell	1962

Appendix B

JOE BRANDT

Co-founder (with Harry and Jack Cohn) of C.B.C., which was the forerunner of Columbia Pictures. President, Columbia Pictures, 1924-32. (d. 1939, aged 56)

HARRY COHN

Co-founder, with Joe Brandt and Jack Cohn. Vice-president in charge of production, Columbia Pictures, 1924-32. President, Columbia Pictures, 1932-58. (d. 1958, aged 66)

JACK COHN

Co-founder, with Harry Cohn, and Joe Brandt. Executive Vice-president, Columbia Pictures, 1924-56. (d. 1956, aged 67)

A. SCHNEIDER

Joined the Company in the 1920s. President, Columbia Pictures, 1958. Chairman of the Board and President, Columbia Pictures Industries, Inc.*, 1968. Honorary Chairman of the Board, 1973.

LEO JAFFE

Joined Columbia Pictures, 1930. President, Columbia Pictures, 1967. President Columbia Pictures Industries, Inc., 1969. Chairman of the Board, 1973.

---

*Note new corporate structure resulting from the merger of Columbia Pictures Corporation and its television production and distribution subsidiary, Screen Gems.

STANLEY SCHNEIDER

Joined Columbia Pictures, 1956. President, Columbia Pictures Division, 1968. Resigned to enter independent production, 1973. (d. 1974, aged 45)

ALAN J. HIRSCHFIELD

Former financial vice-president and director, Warner Bros.-Seven Arts, Inc., and Vice-president and Director, other companies. President and Chief Executive Officer, Columbia Pictures Industries, 1973.

DAVID BEGELMAN

Former vice-president, Music Corporation of America; former Vice-chairman, Creative Management Associates. Joined Columbia Pictures, Industries, Inc. in 1973 as President of the Columbia Pictures Division.

Bibliography

Cawkwell, Tim and Smith, John M., eds. *The World Encyclopedia of the Film.* New York: World, 1972.

Capra, Frank. *The Name Above the Title.* New York: Macmillan, 1971.

Casty, Alan. *The Films of Robert Rossen.* New York: The Museum of Modern Art, 1969.

Kanin, Garson. *Hollywood.* New York: Viking, 1974.

Michael, Paul, ed. *The American Movies Reference Book: The Sound Era.* New York: Prentice Hall, 1972.

Sennett, Ted. *Lunatics and Lovers.* New Rochelle, N.Y.: Arlington House, 1973.

Shipman, David. *The Great Movie Stars: The Golden Years.* New York: Crown, 1970.

Shipman, David. *The Great Movie Stars: The International Years.* New York: St. Martin's Press, 1973.

Thomas, Bob. *King Cohn.* London: Barrie and Rockliff, 1967.

Wright, Basil. *The Long View.* London: Martin Secker and Warburg, 1974.

Zinman, David. *Saturday Afternoon at the Bijou.* New Rochelle, N.Y.: Arlington House, 1973.

Index

(Page numbers in italics indicate photographs
of the listed subjects)

440

444